Fire-Rimmed Eden: Selected Poems ga[...] and varied collections. Lonidier published five poetry collections *Po Tree* (1967), *The Female Freeway* (1970), *A Lesbian Estate*(1977), *Woman Explorer* (1979), *Clitoris Lost: A Woman's Version of the Creation Myth* (1989), and a posthumous book, *The Rhyme of the Ag-ed Mariness* (2001). Her poetry links multiple poetic constellations of the 1970s and 1980s demonstrating linguistic innovations and radical reconfigurations sexuality and gender.

The poems of *Fire-Rimmed Eden* are in conversation with narrative impulses from the feminist and lesbian poetry movements of the 1970s and 1980s, including work by Judy Grahn, Audre Lorde, Adrienne Rich, and others, as well as experimental poetic impulses from the same period found in work by Robert Duncan (Duncan's partner Jess gave the cover art for *A Lesbian Estate*), Lyn Hejinian, Carla Harryman, and Etel Adnan. Some of Lonidier's work is concrete in the spirit of May Swenson's *Iconographs* while other poems are performative like Bay area poets Pat Parker and Jerome Rothenberg.

Previously completely out of print, Lonidier's poetry is ripe for a new generation of readers. *Fire-Rimmed Eden* assembles a robust selection of Lonidier's work introduced by *Sinister Wisdom* editor and publisher Julie R. Enszer. Rich and diverse, visually and aurally exciting, boldly experimental and intellectually provocative, Lonidier's poetry is imbued with wit, humor, originality, and play.

Strength, courage, humour and magical word weaving are long-time characteristics of Lynn Lonidier's poetry. This remarkable book brings together her last writings to keep the mystery of her genius with us.

—Pauline Oliveros

FIRE-RIMMED EDEN:
selected poems by lynn lonidier

FIRE-RIMMED EDEN:
selected poems by lynn lonidier

edited by julie r. enszer

A Sapphic Classic from
Sinister Wisdom

Contents

INTRODUCTION

Fire-Rimmed Eden:
The Poetic Vision of Lynn Lonidier

Encountering the polymorphous, poetic works of Lynn Lonidier for the first time is pleasureful, perplexing, powerful, and, at times, even preposterous. Lesbian-feminism, surrealism, dadaism, the Beats, the deconstruction and remaking of language, and fabulism all inform Lonidier's poetics. Her poetry engages with big questions about life, myth, the nature of the brain, sex, bodies, dogs, and play, among many other subjects and philosophical musings. Lonidier imagines new formulations of sexuality and gender through feminist and lesbian lenses informed by political analyses that, in recent years, have been deemphasized in feminist theory and history. As a result, Lonidier's work today has new valence and relevance. Rereading her work—or encountering it for the first time—reminds readers of the power of poetry, particularly when informed by feminism and lesbianism, to recreate, reformulate, deepen, challenge, and reimagine all aspects of life through language.

Lynn Lonidier wrote, edited, curated, and published five collections of poetry during her lifetime; Janine Canan, Lonidier's friend and poetry co-matriot, edited a posthumous collection of her work. *Fire-Rimmed Eden: Selected Poems of Lynn Lonidier* emphasizes her poetry published in these five collections. Lonidier was an artistic polymath, engaged not only in poetry but also music, performance art, and imaginative fiction. Lonidier left behind an extensive creative catalog, much of which is held by the San Francisco Public Library in her archival collection. Lonidier's creative oeuvre includes a variety of performance art pieces, many documented in her archive, sound projects created with the composer and musician Pauline Oliveros, and seven unpublished novels.

Discovering the poetry of Lynn Lonidier invites readers into the vibrant poetic world of the San Francisco Bay Area during the 1960s, 70s, and 80s.

A variety of poetic movements flourished there, overlapping, nurturing, and amplifying one another. From the Beat poets working out of City Lights bookstore; to feminist poets nurtured by Alta's Shameless Hussy Press and the Women's Press Collective among other feminist publishers; from Objectivist- and Black Mountain College-influenced poets to L=A=N=G=U=A=G=E poets; from radical gay male poets including those centered around Manroot Press (the publisher of two of Lonidier's books) to the ethnopoetics and performance poetry of Bay Area poets like Jerome Rothenberg and Pat Parker; Lynn Lonidier breathed it all in. A diversity of style, sensibilities, and poetics influenced her work.

♀   ♀   ♀

Born on April 22, 1937, in Lakeview, Oregon, Lynn Lonidier was the first child of Sampson Bill Lonidier, who was born in Louisiana in 1895 and moved to Oregon to work as a sawyer in sawmills, and Sigrid Francis Brodine, born in 1906 in Spokane, Washington. Sam and Sigrid married in September of 1934, three years before Lynn's birth. Five years after Lynn's birth, Sigrid and Sam had a second child, Lynn's brother, Fred. When Lynn was nine years old, the Lonidiers left Oregon and moved to Oroville, California. Lynn's earliest artistic expression was music. She played the clarinet in the school marching band and took piano lessons, but she pursued the cello most seriously. A gifted cellist, Lynn often performed with her mother who played both the violin and viola and taught music. Together, Sigrid and Lynn played in the Chico State College Community Symphony Orchestra. Lynn's teenage years included a variety of musical performances, solo and with her mother, in the Oroville area.

Upon high school graduation, Lynn went first to Chico State College then transferred to San Francisco State which had a renowned writing program. She continued to play cello but increased her pursuit of literary study as well. During her senior year of college, she informed her parents that she was dropping cello in favor of writing poetry; a decision that "broke her father's heart." Lonidier graduated with her Bachelor of Arts degree with a teaching credential in June 1960. After graduation, she secured a teaching job in Oroville and moved into "a cheap duplex across the Feather

River in the unincorporated area, Thermaleto." She taught there for three years then moved to San Francisco to immerse herself in the poetry, music, and art scene. During the early 1960s, Lonidier published her poetry in a variety of journals including *The Massachusetts Review*, *The Husk*, *Stolen Paper Review*, *Fiddlehead*, *Evergreen*, *San Francisco Review*, *Signet*, and *The Galley Sail Review*. In addition to publication, Lonidier also won a few literary awards.

While living in the Bay Area, Lonidier met Pauline Oliveros, a composer of electronic music and a professor at Mills College. The two became lovers and together performed Oliveros's music, often with Lonidier playing the cello or performing poetry and sound scapes in conjunction with Oliveros's original compositions. Oliveros bought Lonidier a Super 8 Beaulieu camera that she used frequently. During this period, Lonidier also created a multimedia film, video, and sound piece, *Owed to Oakland*. In 1967, Oliveros accepted a job at the University of California, San Diego and bought a house in Leucadia. Lonidier moved there with Oliveros. During this period, Lonidier and Oliveros performed music with the Wong sisters, Betty and Shirley, and the Wongs provided the illustrations for Lonidier's first poetry collection, *Po Tree*. While Oliveros was out as a lesbian later when Lonidier was corresponding with Barbara Grier in the 1960s, she did not want Grier to mention anything about the fact that the two lived together. Oliveros and Lonidier broke up in the early part of 1970; Oliveros fell in love with a student in the MA program, also a cellist, Lin Baron. Baron and Oliveros wed on July 4, 1970, in a seaside event orchestrated by Lonidier and covered by Jill Johnston for the *Village Voice*. Amid these activities, Lonidier performed as a "light-optics artist" at the Electric Circus in New York City, 1969, and the World's Fair in Japan in 1970. Shortly after the Oliveros-Baron wedding, Lonidier moved back to the Bay Area, then to Seattle, Washington, to pursue an audio-visual MA at the University of Washington.

After completing her master's degree, Lonidier returned to San Francisco. When her mother decided to move into a subsidized senior housing complex in Seattle and sold her home, she gave the proceeds of her house to Lynn and her brother Fred; Fred, in turn, gave his share of the proceeds to Lynn in thanks for the times that Lynn provided him with housing and food while he attended college. With that money, Lonidier bought a home at 76 Gladys Street in San Francisco. This move began a fertile period for her. She read and performed her poetry using slide, opaque, and overhead projections. Lonidier became involved with the founding of the San Francisco Women's Building; a project she worked on for two years. She performed with a group of women artists call "Avant Garden" and received a California Arts Council grant to teach performance at The Women's Building. She also began publishing her work actively with the feminist press. Barbara Grier accepted a selection of twelve poems from Lonidier for *The Ladder* in 1970; some of these poems were reprinted in the Diana Press anthologies. She published work in *Manroot* magazine in 1971 as well as *Women in Revolution* and *Tres Femmes*, two other independent journals. During the 1970s, she published two broadsided, "A Jellyfish Swim" with Tenth Muse in 1972 and "For Sale Girl Poet Cheap" in 1977 with Manroot. In the mid-1970s, Lonidier traveled to Mexico; that trip provided the foundation for her collection *Woman Explorer*. In total during the 1970s, Lonidier published three poetry collections, *The Female Freeway*, *A Lesbian Estate*, and *Woman Explorer*.

Lonidier also found reliable work in the California Poets in the Schools program visiting schools throughout the Bay Area. Eventually, she found a teaching job at an elementary school in San Francisco's multicultural Mission District, where she also was a member of the Mission Alliance for Popular Culture. Throughout the 1980s, Lonidier worked as an elementary school teacher. Her brother Fred noted her commitment to working with young children who "in her view, had not yet been squeezed into conformity by the adult world and still had the creativity with which she enjoyed working."

While conditions for lesbians and gay men teaching in elementary and secondary schools were better in the San Francisco area than in other parts of the United States, concerns about being out or being discovered to be queer were uppermost in people's minds. Although the Briggs Amendment failed in 1978, its effort to prevent lesbians and gay men from teaching in California public schools cast a pall on teachers and educators, especially combined with the rampant homophobia that characterized the 1980s as the community responded to the AIDS crisis and the homophobia of the Reagan and Bush administrations. Consequently, Lynn Lonidier, who was out as a lesbian, used the name Lynn Sommers as a teacher. In addition to this material reality, fiscal crises in the state of California and nation-wide effected California teachers. Lonidier writes about the material realities of teaching in some of her poems, particularly, "Teaching the 5 Sentences" and "Mountain Sickness" in *Clitoris Lost*. The extensive archives on teaching in her collection at the San Francisco Public Library demonstrate the seriousness with which Lonidier approached her job in education and her effectiveness as a teacher. In spite of her professionalism, she encountered problems at work; some issues are illuminated in poems from *Clitoris Lost* such as "Exercise for English Teachers," "Owed to Joy," and "Anarchist Working Dream." In 1990, Lynn received a pink slip from the San Francisco school district; the pink slip was a part of the theatrics of the school district in an effort to reverse funding cuts. Lynn was rehired, but the pink slip, in combination with Ilse Kornreich's rejection of her romantic advances, prompted despair for Lynn and her first suicide attempt. She drove to south to Santa Cruz and jumped off a cliff above the shore.

She was hospitalized after this suicide attempt and released, but her brother Fred notes that she "was a very changed person." She returned to teaching but had "a very stiff personality in contrast with the very outgoing and warm person [she had been] before." In addition, she "became less social and could not write at all for quite a while." Lynn never recovered from depression. In May of 1993, she attempted suicide again by taking sleeping pills while lying out on the beach. Bystanders noticed something was wrong and called 911; she was taken to the hospital. A day later, she discharged herself, took a taxi back to the beach, and jumped off a cliff in San Francisco to her death on May 18, 1993. She was fifty-six years old.

A memorial service was held on Sunday, September 12, 1993, at The Women's Building in San Francisco. It featured music performed by Astor Piazzolla, Peter Frantzel, Betty and Shirley Wong, and the Japanese Temple Gongs; Adelle and Jack Foley, Noni Howard, Allie Light, Judy Grahn, Beverly Dahlen, Mary Mackey, Mary Norbert Korte, Clive Matson, and Paul Mariah made remarks at the service celebrating the life of the poet and ancient mariness.

In the years since her death, Lonidier's work has slipped into obscurity. She published exclusively with alternative presses in the Bay Area which unfortunately meant that her work eventually fell out of print and out of circulation. Janine Canan edited a 2001 publication of her post-humous work, *The Rhyme of the Ag-ed Mariness: The Last Poems of Lynn Lonidier*, with a preface by Jerome Rothenberg, who Lonidier often credited as her poetic mentor along with Robert Duncan. *The Rhyme of the Ag-ed Mariness* returned Lonidier's work to print but did not include the important earlier iconic and defining work. This selection of Lonidier's work in *Fire-Rimmed Eden* highlights her full poetic oeuvre and invites new engagements with her work.

Fire-Rimmed Eden includes the full reproduction of two books which might be regarded as Lonidier's master works: *A Lesbian Estate* and *Clitoris Lost*. The other collections, *Po Tree*, Lonidier's first book, published in 1967; *The Female Freeway*, published in 1970; *Woman Explorer*, published in 1979; and the post-humous collection, *The Rhyme of the Ag-ed Mariness,* are represented with selections. The selected poems demonstrate the ways that Lonidier interrogated gender and sexuality as well as present the breadth of her work.

This selection of Lonidier's poetry for *Fire-Rimmed Eden* reflects a variety of goals. First, it profiles Lonidier's eclectic engagements. Lonidier as a figure invites new readings of a variety of poetic movements inflected by gender and sexuality. New engagements are particularly important where the histories of different poetic movements has been denuded of sex and gender analyses. Second, the volume is accessible and manageable for readers. While my desire is always for comprehensive collections of poet's work in order to trace their many paths of intellectual and poetic engagement, readers value a carefully curated selection enabling them to enter the work and guiding them through it. Third, *Fire-Rimmed Eden* highlights questions of sexuality and gender in Lonidier's work. Attention to gender and sexuality is one of the crucial foundations of Lonidier's work, and it informs new understandings of other poetic movements. At the same time, Lonidier's work also invites new readings of feminist and lesbian poets, particularly how their work engaged with other avant-garde movements of the 1960s, 1970s, and 1980s. Lonidier's poetry offers new depth and nuance to our reading and understanding of iconic lesbian poets such as Judy Grahn, Gertrude Stein, Gloria Anzaldúa, and Pat Parker.

One of the exciting things about Lonidier as a poet, writer, and artist is the protean nature of her creative achievements. In *A Lesbian Estate*, she listed her creative work at the end of the collection and included unpublished manuscripts. While most of Lonidier's poetry has been published, many unpublished manuscripts remain in her archive. Completely unattended to in this collection—and in the modest scholarship on Lonidier—are her novels, which are rich, Modernist texts very much in the spirit of Gertrude Stein. Her unpublished and published work is an exciting archive for readers and scholars to consider. In the next section, I provide an overview of the six collections of Lonidier's poetry to invite readers to explore some of the exciting themes that emerge through this work. In the final section of this Introduction, I offer some synthetic thematic engagements on Lonidier's work and questions for future research and explorations in the work of Lynn Lonidier.

17

♀   ♀   ♀

Lonidier's first book was *Po Tree*, published in 1967 by the Berkeley Free Press. This collection of poetry demonstrates both the influence of surrealism[1] and dadaism on poetry with its resistance to the logics of language as a method to refuse capitalism and other societal structures and the interest in breaking language, what Kathleen Fraser describes as "deliberate displacement of expected word orders and combinations . . . complete with lyric outbursts and covert strategies meant to dash any idea . . . of immediately understanding the writing" (64). For Lonidier, these influences converge in great combustion with her experiences as a musician and performer. The poems of *Po Tree* move in three general directions. First, in some poems, language piles on top of one another with a relentless and

---

1 While surrealism is an accurate description of some of this work, Lonidier chafed at this description in a review. In the poem "Making John Jacob Famous," she raged at a reviewer who described her work as surreal, describing surreal as "safe, easy to say, and an excuse for not look" (405). She preferred to be reviewed as a new Gertrude Stein, which is how Jana Harris described her in *Poetry Flash*.

cascading effect; this gesture can be seen in "Confetti Nipples" and "What Watt." Lonidier juxtaposes words in single lines and then piles the lines one upon another to explore the nature of language—and to explore the sonic resonances of language. Many of these poems appear first to the eye as list poems, lists of words strung together, sometimes arranged in a grid on the page, but sometimes just the string of words layered one upon the other. The visual experience of these poems is important, but the sonic experiences add an additional layer. Reading these poems aloud opens their sonorous qualities and creates new aural and oral discoveries. When composing *Po Tree*, Lonidier was performing as a cellist and collaborating with Pauline Ontiveros. Part of her artistic practice was always sound production—and her poetry expresses this investment. Her sonic engagements outside of poetry are evident throughout this collection. All the poems selected from *Po Tree* are enhanced by reading aloud, exploring the lingual tactility of the language assembled.

In a second gesture in *Po Tree*, Lonidier explores language in the spirit of Gertrude Stein: through accretion or through the creation and interrogation of nonsense words. Poems such as "I" and "Buttrex L" demonstrate this artistic move. Often these poems are a visual and lingual puzzle for readers to engage and unravel with new meanings emerging through each engagement.

The third poetic move that defines *Po Tree* is the interplay between language and the visual. Some of the poems are concrete poems in the tradition of May Swenson's *Iconographs*. Like many small press books during this period, the textuality is crucial to the poetry. In this collection, the cover, mimeographed on red cardstock, contains visual puns, including an image of Edgar Allen Poe, illustrations, and a few lines from a poem, "Peace." *Po Tree* is filled with hand-drawn illustrations by Betty and Shirley Wong as well as mimeographed and manipulated photographs that interact with the words in the poems. The text combines not only the poems and the words of the poem, but also images, writing, and other collaged visual elements to create a full tree of artistic expression.

Po Tree both teems with sexuality and is devoid of sexuality. On the first page, Lonidier renders the table of contents as though torn out from an art piece with poem titles emerging from within or underneath or inside a cavity below; the torn-out area is an opening like what feminist artists termed "central core imagery."[2] The language gathered in the early poem "Confetti Nipple" includes nipple from the title as well as gonads, heroot, female wedding, nomonorm—all words dripping with sexuality references. Yet, by the terms of current understanding of lesbian and feminist poetry, this first collection of Lonidier's lies outside of what we understand today as lesbian and feminist.[3] Partially, this may be because *Po Tree* was published in advance of the synthesis of lesbian and feminist identities through the movements' activism in the 1970s.[4] It's existence, however, demonstrates the vibrant engagements with gender and sexuality that were possible in the 1960s for lesbians and feminists, with inspiration from Gertrude Stein as well as other subversive and normative-challenging literary movements.

Lonidier's second book *The Female Freeway*, published by Tenth Muse (a reference to Sappho—the tenth muse from ancient Greece) in 1970, is a chapbook with thirty-two pages of poetry. The cover features a solarized photograph of Lonidier drinking from a cup. While *The Female Freeway* has some graphic elements in it, language is at the forefront. This collection of poems still plays with language as Lonidier did in *Po Tree* and still contains surrealist elements, but in *The Female Freeway,* gender and sexuality emerge prominently. Lonidier talks about menstruation, women's rights, and imagines herself as a man and talking with a male Virginia Woolf. She invokes women poets from history, including Ella Wheeler Wilcox and Anna Hempstead Branch, offering an expanded lineage for women writers. She also challenges sexism in her contemporary world, calling out Charles Bukowski at one point. Lonidier casts her critical eye to everyday sexism as well, observing "The Boys at the Beach" and presenting domestic violence in women's lives.

---

2 For an exploration of central core imagery in feminist art, see the work of Judy Chicago and Miriam Schapiro.

3 For an elaboration of feminist and lesbian poetry during this period, see the work of Adams, Bulkin, Clausen, Enszer, Garber, Grahn, Murray, Whitehead, and Vicinus.

4 For more on lesbian and feminist identities, see Collins, Echols, Gallo, Hogan, Rosen, Whitehead, and Whittier.

In the title poem, "The Female Freeway," Lonidier performs women's rage, identifiable as an important expression of feminism in 1970.[5] She writes:

> Imagine your penis skinned lying raw
> on a slaughterhouse floor   Don't   open car doors for me nor
> shift me to the insides of streets   We may murder each other
> now that I know where I'm going

She later notes, "We'd die unless I apologized for / mentioning Women's Rights," and then they head to Tijuana where Lonidier observes, "male shopkeepers bow and scrape and hate us." Rage about men's treatment of women enters this collection with Lonidier's unflinching eye—and that rage remains a theme as her work unfolds.

The Female Freeway contains the beginning of Lonidier's theorizing about the binary gender system. She imagines changing sex and conversing with Virginia Woolf when both are men. In the poem "Castle of Heterosexual," Lonidier introduces the hermaphrodite, a figure that plays an important role in much of her later work, but the imaginary of this book is dominated by crossing binary sex. In "Mona Lisa Was a Boy," Lonidier imagines the Mona Lisa as a boy "ogling / hitchhikers" and "letting his wild hairs loose in a circus of open cages." Similarly, in King Victoria, she plays with gender crossings imagining Victoria as King.

While political content from the burgeoning feminism enters *The Female Freeway*, Lonidier's characteristic word play, internal rhyme, sly changing of names and words, creation of compound words, and work with space as a part of how the poems breathe continues to be evident in this collection.

If *The Female Freeway* introduced Lonidier as a poetic voice in the incipient feminist and lesbian-feminist poetry movements, *A Lesbian Estate* established her as a significant voice. Paul Mariah of Manroot Books published *A Lesbian Estate: Poems* in 1977. Manroot, founded in 1969, published about a dozen issues of *Manroot* magazine and thirty books, primarily poetry, including works by Jack Spicer, James Broughton, Robert

---

5 For discussions of anger and rage in feminist poetry, see Lorde, Ostriker, and Rich.

Peters, and Thom Gunn, and translations of Jean Genet and Jean Cocteau. Before moving to the San Francisco Bay Area, Mariah served time in prison in Illinois, an experience that shaped his life and his work. Throughout his lifetime, he corresponded with many incarcerated men and advocated for gay men in prison.[6] *A Lesbian Estate* is gorgeous; printed with a black and white cover with a collage designed by the artist Jess and spot color in purple that matches the front and back pages of a deep purple, textured card stock, *A Lesbian Estate* is a large book measuring seven inches wide by ten inches high. To promote the book, Mariah also published the broadside "For Sale: Girl Poet Cheap."

On the first page of *A Lesbian Estate*, Lonidier establishes her linkage to Gertrude Stein, playing with and perverting her line. Lonidier writes:

a Rose is A
rOPe The   ROBe is A   sTONe.

The rose, which Stein both imbued with meaning and rendered meaningless, is transformed by Lonidier to a rope, to a robe, to a stone. Lonidier delighted in a lineage with Gertrude Stein; Stein, like Emily Dickinson, makes numerous appearances in her work. Part of the project of *A Lesbian Estate* is defining a physical space and intellectual lineage for lesbian poetry. Art is again important in this book, though not as integrated with the poems as it was in *Po Tree*. Graphics by Bonnie Bolster and Manroot in the book provide separator images for the different sections of the book. The author photograph at the end of the collection is an image of Lonidier with her dog on the beach. This image rejects the convention of a headshot and shows the poet active, not engaging the camera. As in the earlier collections, Lonidier works with language in *A Lesbian Estate* to energize it and fill it with new meanings that express her observations about the world and her lived experiences.

---

6 Mariah's papers and the papers of Manroot are in the archival and manuscript collections at the University of Buffalo. Little has been written assessing the influence of Mariah or Manroot.

In *A Lesbian Estate,* Lonidier questions and challenges to the systems of sex and gender emerge full-throated. She writes in the first poem about being a hermaphrodite and meeting another hermaphrodite. The idea of being sexless, of being an "it," appeals to Lonidier throughout *A Lesbian Estate* and the rest of her poetic work. In the opening poem, Lonidier stages a discussion between "my hermaphrodite" and "your hermaphrodite," exploring the expressions of hermaphrodism and contrasting it to W.I.T.C.H., a feminist formation of the early 1970s, the Women's International Terrorist Conspiracy from Hell. Lonidier explores rendering herself, the imagined poetic I, as a hermaphrodite and as a witch, comparing and contrasting the utility of each imagined response to the sex/gender system. It is a fertile dialogue even today. Like the outsider artist Henry Darger, Lonidier uses the hermaphrodite in her poems as a figure to work out multiple personal and cultural anxieties as well as to theorize gender and sex.[7] Lonidier's concept of a hermaphrodite challenging the system of sex is useful and interesting to revisit as new ideas about sexuality and sexual expression circulate. While Lonidier's embrace of hermaphrodism may be at times out of sync with conventional ways of thinking about bodies, genitalia, and sexuality now, in their time and even today they open new spaces and possibilities and imaginaries.

Two years later, Louise Simon's *Painted Bride Quarterly* Press published Lonidier's collection *Woman Explorer. Woman Explorer* combines two impulses in Lonidier's work: crafted poems, which explore her travel to Mexico and Mayan culture, and a narrative, impressionistic travelogue titled "Poet's Pilgrimage to the Pyramids of Mexico." The two parts of this collection speak to one another in significant ways. The narrated journal in the second half of the book lends texture and depth to the poems, while the poems animate a creative process of transforming experience into art. For *Fire-Rimmed Eden,* poems are selected from the first half of the book only. Readers are advised: the second half holds many poetic treasures. It is worth tracking down the full book.

Like earlier collections, visual elements play an important role in *Woman Explorer.* Lonidier and publisher Simon reproduced vibrant graphics, in-

---

7 For more on Darger, see Elledge.

cluding rubbings from Mayan and Aztec images, reflecting the influence of Mexico on these poems, and providing a vibrant visual language to accompany the poems. One of the striking things about *Woman Explorer* is its editing and curation. The divide between formally recognizable poems in the first half of the collection and the journal entries, which also include poems, in the second half is striking—and unusual for Lonidier. At the conclusion of *A Lesbian Estate*, Lonidier writes in a note that "the poems in this collection appear in the order in which they were written." *Clitoris Lost* is curated similarly. *Woman Explorer* is different. There is some temporal sequencing of these poems, but they do not unfold with the logic of the poet; rather the sequence pays attention to the sensibilities of a reader. I suspect this presentation is a result of an engagement between Lonidier as author and Simon as editor in the final production of the book. What emerges is a greater attention to craft in the poems in the first half of the book. These poems still have elements of concrete poetry as seen in earlier collections and similar textual engagements, but there is more attention to line and stanza in this work and fewer capacious engagements between and among the poems with dreamscapes or other flights of fancy. *Woman Explorer* engages deeply with the history of Mexico and the Aztec and Mayan people, exploring colonialism and its effects on Mexico and the United States, particularly San Francisco. Lonidier interrogates sexism in the production of culture and myth in this material with her characteristic challenges to convention.

The final book published during Lonidier's lifetime is the 1989 book *Clitoris Lost: A Woman's Version of the Creation Myth: a Take Off on John Milton's Ordering of a Heaven, Earth, and Hell*. Published by Mariah's Manroot Press, *Clitoris Lost* is Lonidier's most ambitious book of poetry and draws from a rich archive of Lonidier's concerns. While the title riffs on Milton's epic, that is only one part. Equally important to the rewriting of Milton is Lonidier's engagements in writing and imagining the life of Sappho for contemporary lesbians and engaging a broad imaginary of life in ancient Greece. She also documents her visit to Peru within the section called "Quipu Diary." In a letter to the *San Francisco Chronicle*'s Sunday Review section, Lonidier highlighted additional thematic elements of *Clitoris Lost* for consideration including, "women's lack of image of self in response to

[the] patriarch[y]'s perpetual negation of women," "the chicaneries of Sir Arthur Evans" about the Palace of Minos in Crete, and performance art "using poetry as a medium."[8] Still other poems in this collection present a more personal view of the poet showing readers the Lonidier who loved, lived, and enjoyed herself.

A number of poems in this book are transcribed dreams. While these poems are not among her strongest work, they provide insight into her mind as a poet and particularly into concerns and anxieties as a lesbian during the 1980s. In these poems, Lonidier reminds readers what is happening in the San Francisco Bay Area community with AIDS, the election of Ronald Reagan, and economic conditions, providing a contemporaneous account of these developments.

In *Clitoris Lost*, Lonidier provides her most extensive statement of and visions for a strand of feminism that she calls "Anarchafeminism." Lonidier considers anarchafeminism, also spelled in some instances anarchAfeminism, "a viable alternative to Marxist-Socialism." The maternal side of Lonidier's family had a tradition of socialism and communism, and her brother Fred was sympathetic to these formations; Lonidier's cousin Karen Brodine was an active leader in Radical Women and the Freedom Socialist Party. Lynn, however, during the 1980s increasingly became intolerant of these formations and hungry for alternatives. Anarchafeminism, as a feminist formation informed by reading and writing of her close friend Jean Lyons in Seattle, offered a different feminist vision for her. Lonidier said in that same letter to the *San Francisco Chronicle* that "Anarchafeminism embodies egalitarian, communal, cooperative, non-warring, non-hierarchical living evident in clan life portrayed in artwork and artifacts from pre-Greek Crete." A series of poems in *Clitoris Lost* articulate this strand of feminism with passion and zeal.

Clitoris Lost is both Lonidier's greatest artistic achievement as a poet and an enormously ambitious book publishing project. The 160-page book had, like *A Lesbian Estate*, a seven inch by ten-inch trim size, and the interior pages were all printed with colored paper creating a rainbow effect for the book. Lonidier said that the rainbow pages were a result of a dream she had in

8 Letter to Patricia Holt, March 5, 1989, Lynn Lonidier Archives, SFPL.

rainbow colors and that she believed that "a rainbow book is an alchemical book." The layout for the book was "a desktop publishing venture, and the cover, designed by Robert Berner, was a computer-generated graphic." New-fangled fonts appear on the section title pages of this book, and a centerfold spread features photographs of Lonidier's "family orchestra" as well as a lovely photograph of Lynn and her youngest cousin Karen Brodine. A large image of Lonidier holding her two pet garter snakes is in this center section of the book; snakes are a consistent thematic element of her work. Finally, a photograph manipulated by Berner transforms a photograph of female Lynn into male Lynn, titled "Multiple Personality (Or who really wrote this book)," demonstrates how new technologies engaged Lonidier's imaginary of hermaphrodism and crossing the gender binary.

One posthumous collection of previously unpublished poems was published in 2001, *The Rhyme of the Ag-ed Mariness*. This collection, edited by Janine Canaan, has as its center piece a "lesbian ecological opera." Dedicated to Ilse Kornreich, an Argentine lesbian-feminist activist based in Buenos Aires and with strong ties to the San Francisco Bay Area nurtured in part by Lonidier, "The Rhyme of the Ag-ed Mariness" is a play in three acts that engages myths and imaginaries foundational to Lonidier's work. This opera, absent music, is a vibrant synthesis of Lonidier's work. I made the difficult decision not to include it in this collection to emphasize work from *The Rhyme of the Ag-ed Mariness* that captures Lonidier's continuing thinking about gender and sexuality in the early 1990s.

♀   ♀   ♀

Performance is a vital element of Lonidier's work across all her collections. Lonidier considered her poetry as a type of performance art. Many of the poems of *Clitoris Lost* offer performance guidelines at the end, including, for example, "Exercise for English Teachers," "A Swedish Family Will Not Accept," "Running from AIDS," and "The Living Room." Lonidier's archive at the San Francisco Public Library contains remnants from some of her public performance pieces; material from "The Dolls" and "The Jar Piece" are particularly evocative. At the time of her death, the "lesbian ecological opera" was a large project. Might she have added a full musical score to the work? How might it have been performed? This attention on the page to how the poetry should be performed is significant because it imagines a broad audience engaged in her work. This imaginary of a broad audience for her open, frank, lesbian poetry is a bold and audacious act for a writer working in the 1970s and 1980s. Lonidier barely lived to see a presidential candidate speak to lesbians and gay men as a constituency, and she died in the middle of the uproar about military service after William Jefferson Clinton was elected President. Wide-spread public engagement with a lesbian poet, as we see today with the work of Mary Oliver or Kay Ryan as poet laureate, was more than two decades away. Yet, there she was, publishing instructions for performance in her final collection and laboring over a lesbian-ecological opera, hungering for an audience that she knew existed, that she might call into being from her desk and her word processor. Lonidier performed lesbian publicly with all the bravery and spunk she could muster. Eventually, that performance found a stage, though she did not live to see it. One legacy of her work is this performance, real and imagined, conjured and achieved.

Another legacy of her work is the context and lineage that she articulated with other lesbian and feminist poets. Emily Dickinson and Gertrude Stein are recurrent characters, but she mentions other poets like Faye Kicknosway, Diane di Prima, and Diane Wakoski in her poems. These poets suggest different types of lineages for lesbian and feminist poets than previously considered in scholarly or critical writing. This intervention by Lonidier is vital.

Part of Lonidier's lack of notoriety during her lifetime (she was never as popular as Judy Grahn and Pat Parker in the Bay Area, for example, nor any other poets known either regionally or nationally) is that her work fundamentally resists narrative. Much of the scholarship about lesbian poetry and feminist poetry has focused on poetry grounded in lyrical and narrative impulses. For example, Kim Whitehead's *The Feminist Poetry Movement* offers chapter-length readings of Judy Grahn, June Jordan, Gloria Anzaldúa and Irena Klepfisz, Joy Harjo, and Minnie Bruce Pratt; all these poets are important feminist poets, but Whitehead unwittingly offers a narrow vision of what constitutes feminist poetry through this selection.

All these poets work in a lyrical, narrative tradition. What if Whitehead had examined the works of Lorine Niedecker, Kathleen Fraser, Bernadette Mayer, and Barbara Guest? Or the work of Kicknosway, di Prima, and Wakoski, three poets that Lonidier mentions? While Whitehead's work—and the work of the poets she considers—is important, work in the narrative, lyrical tradition is not the only work that was happening in feminist and lesbian communities in the fecund 1970s and 1980s. Lynn Lonidier's work brings an important, previously overlooked perspective to conversations about feminist and lesbian poetry. 27

Lonidier's work reminds readers that feminist and lesbian-feminist poets had vibrant engagements in poetic traditions that are neither narrative nor lyrical. Despite this reality, the feminist and lesbian-feminist poetry heralded outside of these communities tends to be narrative and poetry that explores the conditions of women's—and lesbians—lives in political contexts. This poetry is important and vital, including to many feminist and lesbian-feminist readers, but it was not the only work. Lynn Lonidier exemplifies engagements by lesbian-feminist poets in outside-of-narrative traditions.

Lonidier's poetry engages what comes to be known as L=A=N=G=U=A=G=E poetry as well as traditions of concrete poetry, surrealism, and vibrant engagements between sound and printed language on the page. While Lonidier's work expands the ideas of what lesbian-feminist poetry was about, her work also brings to these other traditions important questions about sexuality and gender, which are often left out from those narratives. Ultimately, Lonidier's corpus of poetic work reflects an important recognition of the role of one lesbian poet in language poetry and the poetic avant garde.

While these exciting aspects of Lonidier's work—the performative elements and how her work invites new readings and understandings of lesbian-feminist and feminist histories and poetics—there are also vexing elements in Lonidier's body of work. Kathryn Flannery notes that Lonidier's poems "refuse to fit politely into a ready-made outline" (143). Some elements of Lonidier's work, which I have retained in *Fire-Rimmed Eden*, use language and images that contemporary readers may find stereotypical and harmful. Some of Lonidier's words and ideas are not politically correct, either in today's world or in many cases in the world in which Lonidier lived.

What do we do with work when a poet engages stereotypical language? When a poet uses imagery and tropes that are now regarded as racist or offensive in service to poetic vision? Lonidier offers opportunities to grapple with these questions. For example, she titled a poem in *The Female Freeway* "Slant Eyes." The poem itself is a moving meditation on a Japanese woman being physically abused by a former GI, yet Lonidier's internalization of racist stereotypes prevalent when she wrote the poem is present. The title certainly will unsettle contemporary readers who recognize this language as racist. Some may dismiss the poem—even Lonidier's work—because of this title. I considered excluding it from the book, but that seemed an inappropriate sanitization of her work. The poem stands in this collection, demeaning, disorienting, diminishing, yet reflecting a time and place and with other ideas that are meaningful—and inviting us to engage with the complexities of the lived experiences of Lonidier.

Similarly, in the poem "I Hear You Guarded Two-Sex Say My Name" from *A Lesbian Estate*, Lonidier falls into the familiar trap of associating goodness with whiteness. She writes:

Last week I was an hermaphrodite   this week I'm a witch   What
kind   of witch   A good one   What kind of witch   A white
one   What   kind of witch   A bad witch but never a wicked
one   Only as bad as
a bad boy

Each time I read the association of good with white, I pause. I recognize that my pause, my reading, my discomfort with this association is a result of years of feminist analysis and training. Lonidier did not have access to this work when she wrote the poem in advance of its 1977 publication. Yet, still, I pause and am sad about this one as well as the many other associations of whiteness with superiority. Collectively, I know this association and the thousands, even millions, of others in literature create and embolden white supremacy. I want my lesbian-feminist poets to be better; I know we are not.

As Lonidier internalized racist language and imagery, she also internalized anti-semitism, and it emerges at times obliquely and at times directly in her poems. In *A Lesbian Estate*, Lonidier's poem "Jewcat" draws on anti-semitic stereotypes about Jews and money and Jews and Hollywood. In "Sister Accused of Practicing Aloneness as Secret Art," she writes about *Men*tors and says of Jerry, "in a village he's not really a Jew he's a Woman," dismissing the religious and ethnic identity of Jerry. In "XL" in *Po Tree*, Lonidier includes the line "HELLEX SWATZIKI." Each time I read it I wonder, is she playing with the word swastika? To what end?

Finally, and perhaps most significantly, is the question about Lonidier's engagements with Mayan, Aztec, and Incan cultures. To what degree is her work inappropriate, even malicious, cultural appropriation?[9] She embodies the explorer model of feminism, to the point of tilting a book *Woman Explorer*, which Chandra Talpade Mohanty critiques powerfully, challenging white feminists to do better in their engagements with women of color and transnationality. This type of explorer feminism, where women turned away from their contemporary patriarchal cultures in the United States to other cultures around the world, either contemporary ones or historical ones, was common during the 1980s. This cultural appropriation turn, often by white women to cultures of people of color, accompanied repetition of racism, colonialism, and white supremacy both globally and in local communities. Again, Lonidier had neither access to these critiques about this work nor does she have opportunities to respond to these critiques today. In editing her work and promoting it to new generations of readers, I am mindful of the dynamics of Lonidier writing as a white woman about a culture that is not her own—and a culture that is occupied by women of color. Ultimately, I find value in the work and want to hold space for her engagements even as I recognize and honor the critiques and decisions by some to dismiss her work.

What do we do with a poet who is human and holds all the imperfections of humanity in her work? Lonidier grapples with this question in her work. I believe we struggle with the work and by highlighting a few of the passages

9 Paisley Rekdal's *Appropriate: A Provocation* is interesting to read in relationship to Lonidier's work.

in Lonidier's poetry with which I struggled, I hope others find value for their own grappling with meaning in the face of oppression, hostility, and indifference.

Not wanting to leave this introduction to rest on the difficulties of Lonidier in *Fire-Rimmed Eden*, though I believe they are important and fertile areas to consider and discover, I want to turn to a few other questions about Lonidier's work. I hope others reading *Fire-Rimmed Eden* will join me in responding to these questions—and more.

How is Lonidier making and remaking language in her work? How does lesbianism and feminism inform her work with language? Is she aligned with L=A=N=G=U=A=G=E poets? A neat narrative might posit her as a lost sister in this movement as a poet who situates gender and sexuality as central concerns for the movement. Yet as Flannery notes, Lonidier always resists neat narratives. Lonidier's poetry demonstrates how language is fundamentally concerned with gender and sexuality, but the nuances of how she challenges language in her work remain a puzzle. More explication, more reading and thinking is in order.

How does playing with gender and Lonidier's opposition to sexism play out in her poetry? Is there a sense of woman-centrism operating in the work of Lonidier? Or does she refuse the sex-gender binary system? How does the figure of the hermaphrodite operate as a response to the sex-gender binary in Lonidier's imaginary? Do the myths and imaginaries of Sappho and the lesbians of Crete offer a pragmatic response to sexism and homophobia or is it a flight of fancy? Is anarchafeminism a viable political solution? What would it mean to extend her theorizing in these poems into our world today?

Finally, how does Lynn Lonidier remake literary traditions with her work? What new conversations does she inspire? What new possibilities can be imagined through her poems? And what possibilities might the unpublished prose open for readers?

I first encountered Lynn Lonidier's work reading letters between Lonidier and Grier in the archives at the San Francisco Public Library. I was riveted. Returning home, I tracked down all of her out of print collections and read them with deep pleasure and joy. The idea of seeing her work in print and available to new readers became a passion of mine for over a decade. It brings me extraordinary satisfaction to see this volume available in the world. Ultimately, I hope that new and returning readers to Lynn Lonidier's work will leave *Fire-Rimmed Eden* with more questions than answers, sparking continuing dialogue about lesbian poetry and poetics so that in Lonidier's words from the final poem of *Fire-Rimmed Eden*, "Lesbian Heaven," "the gold of the painting shineth / on me and thee."

Julie R. Enszer, PhD
July 2023

Works Cited

Adams, Kate. "Built Out of Books: Lesbian Energy and Feminist Ideology in Alternative Publishing." *Journal of Homosexuality* 34, no. 3 (1998): 113-141.

Brodine, Karen. *Woman Sitting at the Machine, Thinking*. Seattle, WA: Red Letter Press, 1990.

Bulkin, Elly. "Kissing/Against the Light: A Look at Lesbian Poetry." *Radical Teacher* (1978): 7-17.

Chicago, Judy. *The Dinner Party* (New York: Penguin, 1996).

Chicago, Judy, and Miriam Schapiro. "Female Imagery." *Womanspace Journal* (1973), 14.

Clausen, Jan. *A Movement of Poets: Thoughts on Poetry and Feminism*. Brooklyn, NY: Long Haul Press, 1982.

Collins, Gail. *When Everything Changed: The Amazing Journey of American Women from 1960 to the Present*. Little, Brown and Company, 2009.

Echols, Alice. *Daring to Be Bad: Radical Feminism in America, 1967-1975*. Minneapolis: University of Minnesota Press, 1989.

Elledge, Jim. *Henry Darger, Throwaway Boy: The Tragic Life of an Outsider Artist*. New York: Harry N. Abrams, 2013.

Enszer, Julie R. "Lavender Press, Womanpress, and Metis Press: Lesbian-Feminist Writers and Publishers in Chicago during the 1970s." *Bibliologia: An International Journal of Bibliography, Library Science, History of Typography and the Book* 10 (2015): 71-83.

———. "Night Heron Press & Lesbian Print Culture in North Carolina, 1976–1983." *Southern Cultures* 21, no. 2 (Summer 2015): 43-56.

———. "Open the Book, Crack the Spine: Sixty-Nine Meditations on Lesbians in Popular Literature," *Queers in American Popular Culture*, Jim Elledge, editor. Santa Barbara, CA: Praeger Publishers, October 2010.

Flannery, Kathryn. "'Life's Disguise Doth Keep Flies Off': Teaching Lynn Lonidier's Poetry." *Feminist Teacher* 22, no. 2 (2012): 137-157.

Frasier, Kathleen. *Translating the Unspeakable Poetry and the Innovative Necessity.* Tuscaloosa: University of Alabama Press, 2000.

Gallo, Marcia M. *Different Daughters: A History of the Daughters of Bilitis and the Rights of the Lesbian Rights Movement.* New York: Carroll & Graf Publishers, 2006.

Garber, Linda. *Identity Poetics: Race, Class, and the Lesbian-Feminist Roots of Queer Theory.* New York: Columbia University Press, 2001.

Grahn, Judy. *The Highest Apple: Sappho and the Lesbian Poetic Tradition.* San Francisco, CA: Spinsters Ink, 1985.

Harris, Jana. "Review of *A Lesbian Estate.*" *Poetry Flash.* San Francisco, 1973.

Hogan, Kristen. *The Feminist Bookstore Movement: Lesbian Antiracism and Feminist Accountability.* Durham: Duke University Press, 2016.

Johnston, Jill. "The Wedding. Dance Journal." *Village Voice* (January 14, 1971): 33-34.

Lonidier, Fred. *PowerPoint Presentation of Lonidier Family Photos.* Author's personal collection.

Lorde, Audre. "Poetry Is Not a Luxury." In *Sister Outsider.* Freedom, CA: Crossing Press, 1984, 36-39.

Mohanty, Chandra Talpade. "Under Western Eyes Revisited." *Signs* 28, no. 2 (Winter 2003): 499-535

Murray, Heather. "Free for All Lesbians: Lesbian Cultural Production and Consumption in the United States during the 1970s." *Journal of the History of Sexuality* 16, no. 2 (2007): 251-275.

Ostriker, Alicia. *Stealing the Language: The Emergency of Women's Poetry in America.* Boston: Beacon Press, 1986.

Rekdal, Paisley. *Appropriate: A Provocation*. New York: W. W. Norton, 2021.

Rich, Adrienne. "Blood, Bread, and Poetry the Location of the poet" in *Blood, bread, and poetry: Selected Prose, 1979-1985*. New York: W. W. Norton, 1986.

Rosen, Ruth. *The World Split Open: How the Modern Women's Movement Changed America*. New York: Viking, 2000.

Swenson, May. *Iconographs: Poems*. New York: Scribner, 1970.

Whitehead, Kim. *The Feminist Poetry Movement*. Jackson: University of Mississippi Press, 1996.

Whittier, Nancy. *Feminist Generations: The Persistence of the Radical Women's Movement*. Philadelphia: Temple University Press, 1995.

Vicinus, Martha. "'They wonder to which sex I belong'; The historical roots of the modern lesbian identity." *Feminist Studies* 18, no. 3 (1992): 467.

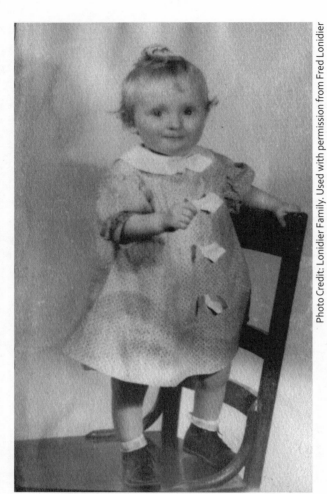

Baby Lynn on a chair, Lakeview, OR.

Introduction

Studio photograph of Lynn with her younger brother Fred in 1942, Portland, OR.

Photo Credit: Lonidier Family. Used with permission from Fred Lonidier

Lynn

Lynn walking on a log near the family home in Oregon.

Lynn, the oldest cousin in the family,
with the youngest cousin Karen Brodine outside Seattle.

Lynn with her brother Fred on a bike in Lakeview, late 1940s.

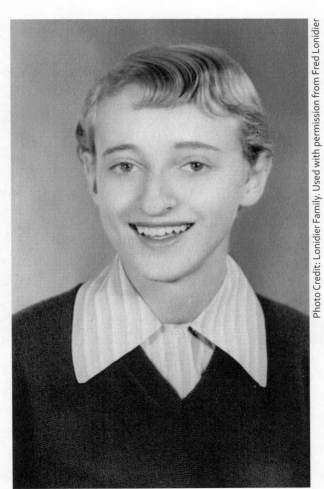

School photograph of Lynn
from Oroville Union High School
in the late 1950s.

Studio portrait of Lynn with her cello, taken during the early 1960s.

from *PO TREE*

The collection is dedicated to Fred [Lynn Lonidier's brother] and Pauline [Fred's wife and Lynn's friend].

The order of some of these poems has been modified from the original book.

I
I THINK
I THINK TAHH
I THINK THAT I
I THAT   THAT I SAHLL
I THANK THAT I SHALL   NEVER
I THINK THAT I SAALL   NEVER SEE
I THINK THAT I SHANN NEVER SEE A
I THINK THAT I SHALL   NEVER SEE A
I THINK THAT I SHALL   NEVER SEE A   AS
I THINK THAT I SHALL   NEVER SEE A   AS LOVELY
I THINK THQT I SHALL   NEVER SEE A   AS LOVELY AS
I THINK THAT I SHALL   NEVER SEE A   AS LOVELY AS A
I THINK THAT I SHALL   NEVER SEE A   AS LOVELY AS A

43

From *Po tree*

CONFETTI NIPPLE*

HISHERS

MIND BLINDER

VENETIAN TUBE ROOM

GONDOLA GONADS

AUTOBLOMB

POOM

MOM HARASS HEROOT

GERMAN VICTROLA HOAR CAUSE

CHARTREUSE COMB JUICE

---

* This poem includes two line drawings in the original printing. The first is of an antique sewing machine and it has the lines GONDOLA GONADS, AUTOBLOMB, and POOM printed over the drawing. The second is a line drawing of an old stove drawn between the lines SATIN MOUSTACHE TUCK and BUILDING BALL NOSTRIL. On the stove is the number 1939, possibly indicating the year of the stove and not included as a part of the poem.

RAIDER AIR RIDER

EYELID REGRIGERATOR RUST

HEART TRUTH FROSTING

SHAKE KNOBS

CUNT GOBS

SHUNT

MARRIED MORM

NOMONORM

HAVE ME TOOK

BROADSIDE BACK LESS FLOWERED PASTRIES

CHEST MEASURED FLIMSY

FEMALE WEDDING LOOK PHOTO

From *Po tree*

SHOULDER PAD STORE

TENDER TENEMENT TENNIS DENTIST

PATENT EYES

SATIN MOUSTACHE TUCK

ATTRACTION MASS

STOCKING MARBLE FRONT

BUILDING BALL NOSTRIL

CHECKERWIRE CHIC'N KITCHEN

PEEK PEAK PEEK PEAF

WORLD'S FAIR HAIRPIECE

NYLON PILEUP

SQUEAKY NUB

FIX EXHIBITION BUBBLE

TELEVISION SNOWSTONE VICTORY TEETH

FLOAT GUARD HYPE

NATURAL SNAZZLE CHAMBER

TRANQUIL POOF

SNAP

LAVENDER CANCER PASTE

TUMMY SNATCH

GONEDAD

From *Po tree*

EROSIONS IMPLOS)ONS
LUMP LUMP LUMP
STATIC CHARGER SAZZ
ELECTRIC CLIMBER ROTOR
SHIRT BLAZE TUBE
RORASS ROARASS RORASS
PORTABLE BOARD BOX
CRANIUM TEARS
VAPID AMBROSIA BAT
APHRODISIAC
VOMIT BIN
HOOROAR
HOROR

SATIN SCUM
SATIN NAST
SATIN SMIR
SATIN POPE
SATIN SMOKE
SATIN SAINT
SATIN SATAN
SATIN SATIN

DANGER STRANGER FOREST RAZOR
CUT
FLICKER LOVER GLIMMER HINT IT
CUT
OFF ENOUGH SURFACE CRETIN
CUT
EX FLAMATION
CUT
LIKABLE FORCE FLOAT GUARD
CUT
STUBBLE MOAT GRUMB
CUT
BLOOD COUNCIL
CUT
MAGAZINE PLAZ
CUT
THOUSAND LETTERS DEBRIS
CUT
CUT——————————————————————CUT
FLOAT
CTRRR
GEARS
CTTCTTCTT
LOCKSHEAD
CUTTUCUTTUCUT
PORES SMOLE
CURUTCURUTCURUTCUR
RUPT KLEEN
KUT

From *Po tree*

XL*
BREE XHELL BREEEEEEEEEEEE
WHUHUWWHUWHUHUWHU
HELLEX SWATZIKI
SKELLL
BELLY VELY FONEY BOOT GARMENTS
GIBBONGSO BONGSO BONGSOBONG
GANGAROO S
FAGITTYBAT LITBOYFATBATIGUE
SMITHEEREEEEEEEEEEEEEEEEEENIES
OWOW O SWUT

     SWT   SMT   SMUT
                        SMOTE.

    SOMOWOT   SOT

        SWHP SST
          ZT

        SSZZ

climb	Will	up	?	he	
will	ladder	He	up	.	the	go
!	apples	a	What	big	of	pile
?	here	apples	put	Who	the	

---

* A small handrawn saw is over the final SSZZ of this poem in the original printing.

BUTTREX L*

BUTREX FOLAVOR

BUTTRUCKS   FRAVOR

    BUTTROCKS   FULLAVER
        BUTTRUCKS

                  FULAVERTORIUM

BUTRUX
      BLAVERTOR

                FULAVATOR
                  EOMS

                FULAVOTER

PROPPED-UP TOSCANINI COFFIN
PUNCTUATION GREEN EXGLOMATION
PLEMGH CELEBRATION
HORMONE HOMECOMING
MASKSKSKSKSKS
PUTT PLOMP
GRANDFATHER WESTGRAVE
VOTEFORACIDITY

---

* This poem has a tic tac toe board set up over it with an x in the upper left hand corner and an o in the lower right hand corner.

INTHICURE	ANIMAL	TRUSION
BC	PLYWOOD	PEOPLE
ACH	SILENT	TV
SOMBULANT	MANI	ISSELF
PSYCHOMATIC	ELEPHANT	ISSINUE
ANNA	LIZBERT	BIRDS
DON'T	KISS	NORMAL
DR.	GODARD'S	GUTART
ROARCH	MANIFEAST	TECK
PAPEDGE	TESTA	A
NIMAL	BLOUSE	INIBADS
INGOUT	GLANDTAP	RAPGATE
LOCKHART	MESTER	MYOUMYOU
NATIONAL	MAGIC	HATCH
TIRMCRAFT	ANI	MALCRACKER
SOLID	STATE	SCARECROW
TALENTON	TTTHHOU	(X)WALL
CIATWISTS´	WAPS	WAIMS
WOBVECTIVES	STRAIT	MASTEER

WHAT WATT*

DIZZLE ZINGZANG

WATT LOP

MELLOW BALLS

CARDIAC HOP

FOG BAG

CLIMAX BENDER STRIPE

SOCKS SMAKE TIRE

DAZZLE CIRCLE SPOKE

LITE SATURDAY

From *Po tree*

---

* This poem is rendered all in bold in this printing, but in the original printing, the letters of the words are typed over one another, but off by a half a point so that they appear bold and blurry.

CYMBOL SUNDAY

EGGSHELL SERVICE MONDAY

EASTER CEILING

MOOD WINDOWBRICK

RAINDROP SNOT

ELEVATOR STACK STORE
COP CORPSE
SNARCH TRIUMPH
JETESCENT SKYSCRAP
LANDSCAPE HORROR CULTURE
    LESS LUMIN
    DOLLAR FOR A
    OUT GOWN DINNER 95.
REAL REALM
MALFORMATORY
LUMINOUS BABY BONES
PEACE BUTTON COAT

From *Po tree*

Pauline Oliveros, Lonidier's lover, reading *All Hallow's Eve* by Charles Williams.

Lynn Lonidier and Pauline Oliveros laughing in Fred and Paulette's
apartment, summer 1966.

Lynn Lonidier in front of a poster cleebrating the release
of her first collection, *Po Tree*
at Claus Von Wendal's metal shop, August 1969.

from
THE FEMALE FREEWAY

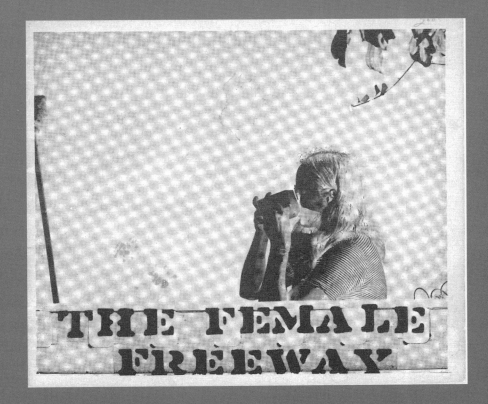

The order of some of these poems has been modified from the original book.

ODE TO MISTER MANN

Phaedra & Stepson

Her eyes wet so wonderful had love   been   Now   a hint of the return
While the other's head is turned as if it will continue there   Eyes move in
a atmosphere   disturbed

Sound of strata tearing

Sound of strata tearing   Rocks breaking apart   Phenomena moving upon
stones that lain about the hills make   dismantling music   Women draw close
their shawls   Birds   break open   the air   Unnatural that rocks would
open apart   To be dormant is to moan The rocks withdraw from their places
pummel the air   Son Orestes daughter Electra plot the thing vengeance
does to itself

All's a motioning

When woman holds the expression to speak   the overhead goes dowsing
It isn't inability that rubs a finger through her clayness until she's
slurry in the passages   Her voice   as not in her face
Her existence depends on your drumming   Something you know   but feel
restless   from   Neither love   nor the sound of the bed   But
the forever reiterating of the proof of the sticks   That tapping
louder than fear   Rapping on metal   is rapping on hand And   damage
Amongst the sound of hit   silence appears Silence taken for   Awe
Sight of you trying to remove that you dwell in the soft of hard
And Been   in tears as   well

LYNN SIGRID LONIDIER*

Women who include their middle names in the signing of their poems—
or a maiden name and husband's name separated by a dash and a
rose brigade   await   a young bard in the garden to demurely finger
with donut-coiled fifth finger   the conversation reminiscent of
Snow White and the chipmonks   SHE : the One-Who-Understands   her
teacup raised to the sun   Bluing toilet bowls while mouthing gods
Keeping genius from committing suicide by promising to publish
during her menopause a poetry magazine named Twigs Sparrows or Rocks
devoted to his work and   "any subject but Death and Obscenities"
I was seduced by a woman who didn't want anything but my beating
heart upon her sunrise   I the swan flapping forth from Leda 'til
Imagery mired in her running lipstick 'til   I swore I'd remain
a virgin with a headache

---

* In the original printing of this poem, the title is handwritten as a signature by the
author in both the presentation of the poem on the page and in the table of contents.

THE FLICKERING MOVIE SAID

Women are easy lovers there's so many of us

Wars have altered men to coffins   And so in this parched city   Woman
has to put up with a lot   Not with a lot of men   One   And she's lucky
to have him divided three ways w/three women   until   from lack of him
he begins to look pathetically more appealing   But not in such duress
as to lose place as the swift runner through the forest

Sightless of men

Sightless of men   Women waits in the dark of the door   Basking in the
pungency of an evaporated night   'til next man comes looking like   the sun

Reel

Woman Receive this Lot His cuff this slap   Anyone would if there were
less of them and more of Thee   I don't believe in fate   A woman is good
because she has to be   Times are Spartan   Women devoured of substance
can't cry nor peel their sight on the Klondike a hundred years ago
90 men to one woman   Or concoct nowadays statistics to ease awareness
that desirability is eligibility   That far-down list where one begins
to know the plight of the perennially hungry   The personal poem

61

MENSTRUAL

A week before the flow   houses continually adjust in my eyes
to the rain   Hills are light enough so I can see the   blood up me
Windows have lights on and are at yesterday   Two people in a room
One pushes up against a window   one whose eys* go ardent on
the wall   Actors act at me   In slowing notion of blood and body
I wearily know you   from my jargon of glands   your feet stuffed
into your socks

NEW DESCENDING

Do not celebrate the floating form Woman   Pliancy in the black waters'
wars   We don't belong We are the display thrown above the noise Meant for
stairs to descend beautifully   Anemonously   With breasts floating
the nipple end of ourselves extended toward   opening Unfurling   a July 4
Men fear us Our forms Keep us   subterrestrially   peeking out from houses
We lend ourselves to air Are   the silent part   of fireworks While
Death goes on over heads Men indulge   in each other   lie   Women survive
sorely Midst doors

---

* This error is in the original text.

EXORCISING THE SWEDISH

The relative

A man who puts decals of dead presidents on his 6 foot electric fence
replacing his teeth with 48 stars   nixing Hawaii and Alaska taking
redwhite&blue as primary colors   is an outcast relative of mine

Death/Oedipean pushed   out   away

We practice the 20th Century behind heartbeats within walls   War
tunes drown the reading of the War Dead   he most asking of
brotherhood   are quick   to form circles close doors   Acceptable
homosexual/Unacceptable homosexyouall   Orpheus still-locked to
Eurydice in destruct

By fire

One woman wore trousers the other woman circled into her side
Smoke climbed the hearth all evening   The disappearing snowman and
the marshmallow mother said they   didn't understand the relationship
Of the two women   I said they're not related they are not women
They are two Siberian shamans dipping their mirror poles into the Sea
of Unconscious   They are two scarabs   catching   light for heart
Iridescent-thickened twin suns brimming the blood damn of the Universe
Simply   sky covered over by bird outline of yourself   They are two rose
windows under Gothic arch   Two thumbs   on two organ stops
round which imagine   heady odor of rose water rising

Sensation of swallowing myself

When little   I lept into bed so the creature underneath wouldn't
grab my heels turn me   on my head for torture   This morning I
didn't allow the dream of the night on the sunlight bed

From *The Female Freeway*

Bam

When I say I can't forgive   you're not my friend I never want to
see you again   I am a modified version of that sentence passed by my
Swedish ancestors' Grandmother's tongue to Mother's Mouth To Mine
worse than resuscitating vampires beating in mine ears   on dearest
friends   shut

DUO CONCERTANTE

At the concert a woman

A woman sank down beside me asked Do you know who I am Added I remind her
of an old-time movie   Yes I told her You are an authority You live
in a three-tiered house and your husband is a dead doctor You are a
segregationist   and when you get up from me   your furs breathe

This woman told me she

She had blood on her   from her period or a smashed bottle   She said she
had a brother and had a drink   Would I take her to the depot would I
Transport her toward involvement   I let her out   Ripped dress
smear on her hand   She might   rob me

WOMEN'S RITES*

Who is ELLA WHEELER WILCOX Where is she-ee
Where's MAY RAPLEY MCNABB
Where's SISTER FIBROSIS the poetess
And ANNA HEMPSTEAD BRANCH authoress
Of "Ere the Golden Bowl Is Broken"
Will AMY CULPRIT BLANK stand up

65

*Poem is read except for first two questions sung to tune of Schubert's
"Who is Sylvia"+

CARRY ME BACK TO OLD VIRGINIA

When the sex changer comes
to visit you, are you ready?
Have you made your decision?
Have you given yourself to your maker?
If I wear castles I must be a queen   I folded out my silks from India
my Turkish dyes my threads of animal gut   The women in sewing class
nearly sewed their hands to their half-made dresses from looking at
my realization of a garment of indistinguishable sex   They wanted to
shape me   into the skins of their patterns: flaky brittle apparitions
fastened down with pins   I'm another era   I wish to call Virginia
Woolf back from the black sea trimmed in white   converse as two men

+   Lonidier included a handwritten musical score with the melody from Schubert
with the question, Who is Ella Wheeler Wilcox, Where is she? For this edition, I have
lineated the poem differently than it appears in the original.

From *The Female Freeway*

PLEASE DIANE WAKOSKI
DON'T SHOOT THE POET SHE'S
DOING HER BEST

May the fleas of a thousand camels infest your crotch   the points of
Your Miss Arabia eyes said over the fluorescent icing of the books in the
jockstrap store where the pink-shirted blond actor prefers instant boys
seated in blue on red at the Mongolian Barbecue Pit eyeing ladies in
high-heeled roses in Diamond Jim's bank promising Maps To the Stars'
homes FREE

I Guruless Girl In Hollywood come to town with sun-perverted skin sing
There's a frog upon L.A.   I am sick upon L.A.   Jets crunch upon L.A.
here's a singular perfume upon L.A.   There's something strange at the
bottom of my asthma vapinese ice cream cone   I'm at the end of my
poodle leash Miss Poland   if you don't give me back my Gold Ice Chest

In All Languages: GIVE ME BACK MY GOLDEN ICE CHEST Miss Germany
and Miss Denmark are hot dogs' pitiful fry on the pavement of my heart
All poems are about poetry I'm itchy to interrupt Robertcreeley Readings
Johnny Screech-Scratch is really the name of a piece of   a scrap of
Violin in the sunglint deathweapon Camus afternoon   Charles Bukowski's
shitty with women   and the moon shot never took place   May the freeze
of a thousand crotches infest your boudoir Miss Badlands   If You Don't
Give Me Back My Simulated Disenchantment Jayne Mansfield Kit TAKE IT!

THE BOYS AT THE BEACH

In drive-ins movie foyers men's magazines   they comment on my body
as though they owned me   are as familiar with my buttbreastthighs
as they are with   rings on their fingers   It's not rape that they
heighten their bodies by removing mind earsmindfeelings   tossing
away the body they've mass-raped Because   I'm their prerogative
to imagine their penises are   rolled-up dollar bills in my
penny vagina

SLANT EYES

A little Japanese lady who couldn't drive a car signed up for
a beginners' electronics course   Her husband was louddrunk
when he came to pick her up   She kept repeating she wouldn't
'sweep with him you won't get me to 'sweep with you tonight
They'd met in Okinawa He doesn't like Japanese food and they have
a months old baby   Her husband took her home from soldering
the mini-parts of space-age candy and   they had a fight
The little Japanese lady tried to phone her sister but her
husband ripped the phone off the wall   Whether he was drunk from
her being away an evening   or whether he's an out n'out alcoholic
isn't the question

From *The Female Freeway*

OVER TWENTY, UNDER THIRTY

Over twenty and under thirty,
how they clutch at infirmity.
Imagine that great majority
walking canes into middle age.

Peter

Before love   you showed me the tube taking waste products out the side
of   your stomach because your internal system was too fouled
tight from mother love too long

You dreamed you grabbed me and kissed me   You tried it on a
teenager   then didn't want her   Kissing you was kissing the taste
of all those tablets and grasses you dropped   half clouded by
mouth purifiers and rye   When I looked into your eyes your eyes were
coming into the horizon or going out   The pupils siesmographing
a high   instead of delineating entry into a secret arabesque soul

When I said the tube in your side didn't matter   you still couldn't
get your penis into me   I imagined you later   red-faced   telling
your psychiatrist you couldn't help that you were mush

Barbara

From nun to schoolgirl to filmmaker to topless dancer whatever
You do   is rumor   I heard you slipped away from the nunnery
slipped back in   You held hands with another nun in the nunnery
You never learned in school   You never looked at the movie
You made   You got kicked out of a gay bar for baring your breasts
climbing onto the GoGo boys' platform showing all those queers
a thing or two

Why'd you do that then confess to me   you're gay and afraid you'll
be made fun of you'll be alone you won't have any friends   Then
You're off   disappear for six months in a noise thick of avoiding
what you are   Wearing the mod wide pants shouting Age of Aquarius
for bravery   while your breath comes to you in a frightened
puppydog pants   saying shit repeating everything is groovy man
Next confession I'm going to say   Go ahead   be the one thing
you haven't tried

From *The Female Freeway*

SATIN PUFF, VELVET HANDBAG

I faint on the curves of your limbs   trembling giantess   straw
in a room inside   Will you put me in your side   to sand shovel
satin puff and climb and climb   Will you put me in your garden Lioness
I am trees at the heights   and cherub gazing idyl   I am raw
appeal to jaw   I am ginger in your stomach   and all the roots
and all the toppings and all the wind to pull to make you have gardens
Don't be frightened

WAVES DO ME THIS, WRITE THIS

No night like last night and no one in the waters but your Fish Born

There were two of us in bed   By morning there were three   And slower
And though the light made your bodies   milk   I couldn't feel you so clear
as the ocean surface as   before   You "Barely kissed her" said   A New
Island raised between yours and mine's sandforms   Now there are four For
I want to learn to turn the edges of a dance   A man has to take me
It's not proper for women to go sea voyages alone   Or   together
Always has to be plenty more

Toe

Play around with the tow   To me the ocean is serious undertaking   Has   span
to take under   Though the waves yet give   throes   Ten-In-The-Bed   is
more like   taunts   The shape of a flaunt   I'm not amicable to more than
one at once   I will show you   before for me 'Twas love that Rolled the sea

Crab walk side wise

Remember the reason the prisms were not exhibited   There for everybody the
lighthouse less beautiful   because it could not be gone through   I would've
given you tour But you'd have addressed me Keeper   Twasn't me to prison you
in the first place Mate   So go the way the shape of your lady of wood
Lady What-Was-Her-Name   Bessie   Hester   Carressa   takes the front of your
boat   The Bow   Multi-sided sanddancing   set me dancing   with a man

CASTLE OF HETEROSEXUAL

The boyfriend

When he refused to read Summerhill and said   he'd put our six
unhappened children   through boarding school   I felt   my fingers
to my hairends   come loose from   his emerald estate

Out of Adam

He opened his mouth   Salt came out   He turned on his loudspeaker
Out of the salt came a grass blade across bugles' lips   A rabbit
rotated between bushes of red pearls and ivory trumpets   Out of
the rabbit came rabbits   Out of the rabbits came a lady's sunlit
sewing basket   Out of the lady came an escaping sound   Out of the
the loudspeaker   came a cat of a thousand answers   Out of the cat came
marble thimbles   In every thimble was a finger drummingdrumming

An help meat

The lady folds herself in in sewing class Her classmates compete
in pregnancies   their asthma souls   pricked   flamingo   The lady
sits spidering gold from her mouth her belly her nostrils   a wrinkle
full of children pulled tight   plotting chesspiece movements over
bone carpets in a glazed mansion of unseen little people   mincing
Midas' fantasies of female   'til   the lady   is   shookwrungswept
out by the witch of no-such-thing on Man Street

Back   and   forth   of the Oz   Saw   Horse

Two artichoke diamonds rubbing frictionlessly together on a satin
presentation pillow making announcements about dinner in Siamese

Crossing over

The house of the hermaphrodite is higher and bigger and richer
with a devil doing shits atop the chimney   slibbering his tongue
giving the four winds the finger   North East West South of History
You Are Invited to squeeze In as a frog between Lions   Come in
comes the lambs come in Comes the twins   Welcome to the seven
wagon wheels   One fell off   One ox dropped   The sides of my ship
creaks up as a pipe I walk of the morning lightning on my dreams
under a unicorn bedspread   Open   One side of the house is sudden
lights   and then the other

House of Hermaphrodite

In this jeweled house the bird's throat rubs rubies together and
dogs spend their days upsidedown   Bluejays make imitation dog squeals
: wind's luxuriant chipping away at rubies   Out of chipings come
Teacups   Out of teacups comes thinning mirrors   Out of thinning
mirrors comes a pendant   CLANK   on the dresser top with ice on top

Malemeet

There are reports   Southern California's slipping off   I'm on the
edge going backward in a passage with things crossed over   I'm face to
face with a beautiful cracked wooden maiden in front but a man behind

Galley-Ho

A galley supports The Good Life   In the bowels of the equally-evil
ship of a good old earthen fuck are more than two women hungry To Be
Men in a time of things kept   A galley invisible to all but those
in it   swarms with hordes of legions of female suppressants   their
bodies battened down by appetite   waiting to strike at His "Sir"
Presence's slightly spoiled fly-covered meatballs   getsome

ROBERT & JESS*

The Gift of Gods belong to the gods   When I think of Robert & Jess
I hear angel whirr   bodies constant in mid-air   a daguerreotype
of Mercury in flight   a hummingbird entering a keyhole   a cloud
opening out a Bach trumpet   The opening at once of all the leather
bindings of the 1911 edition of the Encyclopedia Britannica
Knowledge cross-eyed coming out a cellar bursting through the first
floor to the ceiling of the third flight   of Apollo   Robert's voices'
tremolo spreading a three-inch layer thick of glow over old books
keeping them warm   And Jess fixing tea and fixing tea and fixing
tea 'til it's known   the darkling darling of Victorian territories
is very high   <u>So</u> <u>much</u> <u>made</u> <u>necessary</u>

Lonely in recording love   I think of pack-rat rabbit-startled gun-shy-
ess & owl-of-an-appetite Robert-Poo-Bear   Robert seated at the head
of the round table   cutting pomegranates in half   saying "Seeds"
saying "Cross-section of stars" saying "Red rain"   Saying (said
from experience)   "Don't give a love poem to someone who doesn't know
your love"   No matter how much I read Robert's poems I only begin them
I only begin to think of Jess magnifying glass-eyed over paintings'
packed layers of the last earth century beds of baroque doors hanging
eyes shades on bone leaf lamps surrounded by key-surrounded carpenters'
horns buried midway in unicorn carvings Haley's Comet crowning the sky
entering the tree of duality of   the heart of a single signature
The Embodiment/R&J   <u>Because there are so few   makes necessary</u>
<u>the possibility</u>

From *The Female Freeway*

73

---

* Robert Duncan and his long time partner Jess.

I WAS A TEENAGE POET
AGE THIRTY-TWO

If Emily Dickinson comes to town

If Emily Dickinson comes to town tell me   Town where Sappho
jumped into the sea and Princess Anunca followed my muscular
camera around until   she (dissolved) Body slowly going backwards

Swathing

What was to be a super suburb eroded into the perfect place for
the stumbling fellow: Penis wrapped in bandages: worth recording
I even learned to walk like a mummy   my eye sealed to camera's eye
cadmium batteries' mini-motors whirring images up like froth
The men in my lives   the time it took to lift an eyelid   gaze
                        sideways in old 30s movies   reveal
                        sharp incisors
Emily   I am saving myself for you Hurry   before my body's X'd
by men   I keep your longings in my closet   I haven't read a poem since
you   I haven't written a poem since I ran out of poets
A preserved blonde

When Emily

If Emily comes to town tell her   I'll run footage through her system
like an endless snake   focus the constricting dream spots of her eyes
Men flailing their absence inside their spiral spacesuits'
airless plains : Emily's   hunched   shuffling toward the beloved

MONA LISA WAS A BOY

Handsome as the Medici family   when are you available   At 2 AM
cruising   San Diego for your favorite fleet   or letting a stranger
come in your mouth midday on a couch in a strange town   I'd take you
myself   telling me   encounters   through   invisible veils   touching
me with photos of   your family in Florida
Awkward flattened-down father   75
                  mother's scrutiny through glasses & wired hair
                  brother   the devil's version of yourself   &
sister you are not close to
Medieval Americana family of which   Mona Lisa was a boy ogling
hitchhikers   letting the out without putting a hand to their
surfboards   Mona Lisa glows   because   Da Vinci   leaves him feeling
like a Saturday night masterpiece   He dreams his body crucified
fixed gazing from the wall as armies   pass   His mysteriousness
launching a thousand bush-tangled men abandoned   to dropped   pants
letting his wild hairs loose in a circus of open cages   Promiscuousness
is subdued wisdom a nerve Knowledge   of urge of little boys to paint
moustaches on Mona Lisa's 2 o'clock shadow

From *The Female Freeway*

THE FEMALE FREEWAY

There are no markets for women's feelings   They asked was she
a good lay   laughed before she could answer   To get her to
cry strength   was an entertainment an amusement   They knew
she never would

Someone in the room mentioned Women's Rights and if it weren't that
cobwebs were holding the cupboard china would've shattered and
Father Clock Face broke and quaint furniture creaked with the stir
of men's throat-clearings

Someone mentioned Women's Rights but her dress was short her hair
long and up on her head like two swollen lakes   The ultimate
female impersonators are women their faces mirrored in the
middle of their blackening   their wooden bodies' mystic coals
fetching and fingering the boldest offering to rub them into ash

Take the breast and thigh of a "chick" and chomp   In turn   offer
foreskins to her   Sir: Imagine your penis skinned lying raw
on a slaughterhouse floor   Don't   open car doors for me nor
shift me to the insides of streets   We may murder each other
now that I know where I'm going

Women's Rights were mentioned in a car driven by a man so incensed
he didn't see the freeway   We'd die unless I apologized for
mentioning Women's Rights and   turn my talk to baby talk heed
his fantasies of The Cave   We were on our way to Tijuana where
male shopkeepers bow and scrape and hate us

YES WE HAVE PETS

We have a nodding dragon outside our window between ourselves and
next door neighbors and   the Telephone Company   It's facing us It's
looking in Sometimes it nods Sometimes it shakes furiously Sometimes
it looks like a man   It's something you referred to in the garden once

KING VICTORIA

I live with Queen Victoria and she doesn't like it her title that is
<u>King</u> Victoria then   The Victorian said you couldn't possibly live
with her   If I don't live with Queen Victoria   where do you think
the name "Victorian" came from   Remember her mighty voices piping out
of her speakers like out of plaid animal stomachs overhanging the sea
We live in the highlands with the moral sovereignty of nine children:
Two dogs (public honor) four cats (private virtue) and ten pigeons
(devoted to art music and literature)   I dote on the marbleization of
a woman surnamed Empress of India's eggs each morning   not too soft/
not too hard   An Era is This Woman overextending Emily Dickinson
on either side   Victorians asked how come Gertrude Stein lived with
Queen Elizabeth how could I live with Queen Victoria   I decidedly
live with King Victoria

FIREWORKS AND WATER MUSIC
IMPERVIOUS TO EARS, LIVES,
AND MINDS

Mouth on hand on Mouth

I put my mouth on my hand   Hand was your mouth   Words came in starts
Our bodies kept rocking in their tether   Continual did we move along bed
center   'til Bed went To the Top and House made Sound of The Coming Together

Noah new

I never knew before how many animals are stored in moistures   Your wet eyes
on your wet face   Your body's urges off on me

Dove

You are the dove in my hand The dove   not held

Don't love off

Don't love off touching me to the hemispheres of your tender   Days my body
lies between you and the sea   Masters to my willing   Assuage   then roll me
into uttermost delicious lip

Swiggle

I saw/was black curling things I   never saw/was before

Lit/Sizzling/There

Sweet on my face are the moments that run out of my lips Of the weaving Of
Your Firmament Over Me   Whole days downpull into this Magnitudinal
                                                    Raising

Richness Rushing Off The   edge   High heaviness Then
                    lightness   lightness   lightness

Night which on the roof reigned dear   79

Which on Myself am Edge Which On   Comet Gabriel slid profuse   the
                                            fledgling on
the swedge Which   am Eager Edging   quaffing eaglet am   me On
                                            Dancer   Which

won't Let Sleep On

Let's sleep On Jupiter while the sun throws red sand In Love's Steaming Rep-
tilian Repetitiveness   Sleep Prolific Sleep   While In eyes' lives lives Olive
Dream of Dromedary

All day I want to keep on the smell   of   you   on me

lean to-ward the po-lite   Emily Dickinson   's   Dolly "K" tea
pol-len ex-plo-sions   'the powdery residue of a substance that has been burnt:
    usually in the plural'
light-ness-es' Legend   ledge which On The Wine Stood

Miltonic extract

The morning over I take time to house once more The   Indian   The Medusa
The Trumpeter   The Mother   My SELF am Found in the morning In an
                                            eagle's roost
Celebrating the Complete Person   The Multitude Of Your Person

A LESBIAN ESTATE

Cover of *A Lesbian Estate* by Lynn Lonidier. The cover is a collage mural designed by Jess that wraps around the front and back of the book.

The order of some of these poems has been modified from the original book.

opening dream*

I HEAR YOU GUARDED TWO-SEX
SAY MY NAME

A-frame

It is a mistake   these varicose veins and fat   tempting to
pinch off the backs of the legs   fat/as on a chicken cooking
The same legs that fit like a wishbone over the pinto pony the man
led around to take children's pictures   TinT job of The War years:
Hair yellow eyes hazel lips red complexion pink Say "CHEESE"
Summers's and winters's lost count held by Kodak Company's XX border
with fold-back tab   A   triangle   the mother placed on the mauve
buffet   A   30 years' body of exposure to hair and skin and emotions
unknown to itself   The cardboard learning of the alphabet The feeling
of a great hulk of pointed head   Legs set at weird angles to the
earth   Sex   obliterated by a straight line
            The little girl   who got a gold star
            for letting   the red-haired Sunday School
            teacher   with pince-nez look   pave
            the flames   of Hell in her   three Sundays
            in a row   is the same little angel face reading about
hermaphrodites Sunday morning January 18 1970

---

* In the original printing of the book, this page contains the dedication "For Merrille"
and a line drawing representative of flowers and snail shells.

There is god   there is man   and there are monsters

When my hermaphrodite meets your hermaphrodite   the 3rd hermaphrodite
the one with two arms two legs and two heads   erupting salamanders out
its sex   lets all creatures under earth   and a kettle of fish
up under hags' skirts

When my hermaphrodite meets your hermaphrodite   the sun and moon
play tricks on a toad: A roCK iS a cONe A DOve is A bONE
A tHORN   is   A POPe   bLOod   Is   tHE roAD   a Rose is A
rOPe The ROBe is A   sTONe

Where witches walk   beasts and bad smells arc let out the shadows
of their centipede rags   Hoop snakes tails in mouths   jump out
of their skirts   roll uphill scarin' the slithers out of villagers
The villagers scatter like stars

When my hermaphrodite meets your hermaphrodite hermaphrodite will
turn from hermaphrodite (body kiss of body)   Heaven turn around
and   song stand still   when Hermaphrodite   Your meets Hermaphrodite
My

Uroboros*

Your hermaphrodite is a breastplate with nine big tits down the side
of Zeus   Carl Jung in armor   The shining might of the Myth of the
ani-Ma and ani-Moose

My hermaphrodite is a young boy   initiated into manhood by taking
a woman's dress Off   him
Your hermaphrodite is the same boyhood finalized by putting on male
attire never before touched   by woman
My hermaphrodite was a disease   lowered by umbilicus into

----

* This word, an ancient symbol depicting a serpent eating its own tail, is surrounded
by a hand-drawn serpent eating its own tail.

the sea   the boat maneuvered to deep waters where the cord was cut
so the blood of   a   hermaphrodite wouldn't pollute shore
Your hermaphrodite is the head removed from   an Greek hermaphrodite
the sex of whose head is impossible to tell   as were thousands of
such heads of statues

My hermaphrodite was an abandoned baby found by a shepherd and raised
as a boy until   he started menstruating and his chest   grew moons
The shepherd took the boy to the village   Ropes were slipped over
the confused youth   Wood and leaves were heaped upon him   And set
afire
Your hermaphrodite   women bring flowers to   men erect temples for
Men and women exchanging clothing   in the shadow   of the phallic
altar   erected by men   brought flowers to by women

My hermaphrodite will bleed to death in a ward full of tangled organs
if (an half)a man(half a) woman   isn't/separated/by/the/sterile/
implements of Man
Your hermaphrodite has a woman's breasts and   a man's penis covered
by The Lady Museum's Restoration League and uncovered by The Museum
Friends' Society That the school teacher in quest of Art   hurries
her tittering charges out of the room of

My hermaphrodite is half Don Quixote half windmill   I a woman
attending a Women's Liberation meeting wearing a man's mask flying
a witches' flag over my crotch The women wouldn't let me in
the door I a member of W.I.T.C.H.   The Women's International
Terrorist Conspiracy from Hell*

---

* W.I.T.C.H was a name adopted by a variety of independent, feminist, direct action
groups in the late 1960s and early 1970s. Many of these groups made public dem-
onstrations to raise awareness about sexism. As was the tradition for many feminist
formations at that time, membership was by declaration and affiliation. For more in-
formation about W.I.T.C.H., see Jo Freeman's article, photographs, and graphics about
W.I.T.C.H. (available at JoFreeman.com) and Alice Echols's book, *Daring to Be Bad Rad-
ical Feminism in America 1967-1975*, (Minneapolis University of Minnesota Press, 1989).

A case

Leave the hermaphrodite   where one of the few authentic maidenheads
left on reserve   won't let you at the hermaphrodites in l. c. meaning
"locked case"   unless you are an doctor an psychologist or charmed to
pass through glass and wood How I got in

Leave the snakeous unction of organs vulgarized in an surgical   diagram
like an stomach speaking in an dream   Leave the sacred sack all of
nature   folded and tucked like His/Her lingerie   into so little
space   compounded in an suitcase   bobbing along an terminal conveyor
of lost revolving and unclaimed tenderness

Leave the hermaphrodite to suffer   severe abdominal pains from a
undescended testicle   Probe the one gonad   which on microscopic
examination   proves to be   an testis   Dissect labial folds fused
posteriously concealing between them anteriorly an phallus five
centimeters long   Apply scalpel   and scribble in   the unknown:
Urethra complete patient married coitus normal

Leave the hermaphrodite without clothes on   her shoulder blades
hooked over the height chart   Tell her   to look straight
into an camera so large it is an room full of negative pronouncements:
An female with   receding hairline increase of muscle   deepening
voice   and no breast development I say female because prior to
operation   she stole lowcut sweaters from I. Magnin's*

The wish to be both sexes

The mythological figure Tiresias came upon two snakes   copulating
 He hence turned into   Joan of Arc who wore men's clothing against
judges   When ordered burned Tiresias again saw   two snakes

---

* I. Magnin & Company was a west-coast luxury department store.

copulating   and turned back in
              to a man abandoning Joan to the
                    psychiatrists
                    Looking at herm-
aphrodites under lock and key at the nearest medical library   I felt
a lowering in my throat a   Highness   in my head The descent   of
the conquering fang of the vampire   Wolfman's hairs   take hold the
crackling power of this old skin of the female that flowed over these
ladybones   The Laser lady   87
                    e

                    vap

                    or
                    a

                    ting

                    at the

                    rain
                    bows
                    ben
                      ding
                          The Myth of Penis Envy evaporates
from women's quarters situated at the outskirts of The Sun   I too
had seen   two snakes   ringing halos through the grass The Physique
of Mixed Form Light   LIGHT

A little dream of me

Last week I was an hermaphrodite   this week I'm a witch   What kind
of witch   A good one   What kind of witch   A white one   What
kind of witch A bad witch but never a wicked one   Only as bad as

a bad boy

How do you spend your days   In suspension   How do you spend your
nights Waving my broom to Hades   What do you do there   Greet each
witch on the fly with a snif f to the side of the nostril   What
do you do there   Drop live frogs in a pot of hot water   Why do you
do that   The devil told me to   Why do you do that To help
the Revolution   What revolution   My own

So you are guilty   Unwind her from the rack Prepare the boiling fat
By her confession she is proven deserving of such end   I knew
all the time she was a witch   What kind of witch A frightened one
What frightened her   A nursery rhyme   "There
        was a little girl, and she had a little curl
        Right in the middle of her forehead
        When she was good she was very, very good,
        But when she's bad she should be salted,
        Peppered, and cooked alive."   That's
how the nursery rhyme ended No   That's what the good little girl
was afraid of when she was horrible

ECLIPSE

My face is neither a man's   nor   a woman's   And   if you lay
beside me my body   would feel   good
      if you knew me
      before you lay
      beside me and
      began to love me
      and I too   found
      I   desired you
      Then would shape of my parts matter
My hair is long   So were centuries of men's Hair grow on my legs
So do generations of women's If you touched my body   you would
have knowledge of hard places and of soft   I admit both
      I wear pants   So do women
      I wear a shirt   So do women
      And boots   So do women
      Tall heels   So do men
      And an earring   So do men
      And no bra   African women now do
I am without soot eyebrows
      grease lips
      oil skin   unless   I have worked and sweated
                  laughed and loved

                  I love
      without make-up   Some women go without   If I want   I can
find make-up at men's counters   But I want neither or either I want
both And none

I am more interesting than either sex   I am hard soft cold warm
I can touch you   knowing response   I was born male or female
It feels as good to put my penis in the front as in the back of
whom I love My mouth feels as good to receive as my vagina

And my finger can know the throb of a vagina   or rub its way into
a swoon as a penis
            If I am on top
                        that is God working Life into Water
            If I am below
                        that is Water worked into God by Life
            If I am everywhere
                        that is Water lifed into work by God
                                    God
                  is a
hermaphrodite Hermaphrodite Supreme

The hermaphrodite Tiresias   was the wisest figure in all mythology
There is no reason why Water can't lie on top of a mountain peak
            Pool of it to receive   Or stem of it to erupt
            All that there is   is hard and soft
            and every person   embodies both
            Look at my face   and see bones
                                       My cheek ridges
            are penetrating   My lips   are penetrable
The skin stretched   between my edges forms   dunes
                  You will find
               of every person
            all the variations of all
          the hardnesses   and softnesses
there is   Capacity for gentleness   Potential for strength

There are so many myths you have been taught to think   It does not
matter   which clothes you choose   to put on the limbs of your
            beliefs   When beliefs
         be clothes   you miss half
            of life half of all reactions half
         of feelings

There are
people going about now looking like saints
You cannot tell whether they are man or woman
And   after half a life of denying I am attracted to
saints: I am attracted to saints   The SELF exists
extraneous to clothing
Yourself sitting in the dark
with all your beliefs on
while closest and most intimate
parts of you   cry out for light   fresh
air

FOR WHOM RICHARD BRAUTIGAN
CAN DO NOTHING

The poet in the sunlight said he would do twice as much for a woman
with only 15% more beauty   Richard Brautigan is not 1% more handsome
than I am beautiful In addition   he has curvature of the spine
and is pushing me to the point of reminding him of that delicate matter
If I kept up the digs at the hump as Richard Brautigan reads off women
light airy nothings   the lump of listening men and women   would
grow   into a din overpowering my crude attempt at rhyming likenesses
To think in the beginning   I too thought a poet in sunlight beautiful

A MOTHER IS A BROKEN MUSTARD JAR

Have you ever seen a mother with three children in a supermarket who
has just passed the mustard rack   a giant-sized mustard jar
oozing chartreuse like a rupture in the sun left out too long or
a two-year old left alone with an ice cream cone   The little girl
saying Mother there's mustard on the wheel of the grocery cart
and it's on my fingers and on your coat   And the mother says
consistency of a diarrheic diaper on the loose between the third
shelf in the third aisle between the iron pills and the pickle
jars

A JELLYFISH SWIM

The Atlantic is woman   The Pacific is man   On coral beds
they meet and breed two-headed serpents   called dreams*

The sea out there all the time we talked

You headed for the sea but only got as far as a hanging fogbank and
said what a beautiful bloom gravity is O   the sea the sea the
serious sea where even that old vulture Frank Sinatra hangs his head
over: Frank Sinatra   bald as a baby bird stretching his nearsighted
throat toward sea

>   Witch way does it flow,
>   Witch way does it go—
>   What's out there for me?

Sirens Marlene Dietrich and Greta Garbo answer from opposite shore:

>   Nuzzing, Bay-Bee.

Greta Garbo wore the skin of a lamprey to her favorite discotheque
while in accompaniment of a female companion   You could spend
your life   wondering

A figure in a fake gorilla suit in a 1930s night club setting
took off   one of its hairy hands   revealing a delicate hand which
removed   the other hand   And that the two delicate hands then
pulled the gorilla mask off   revealing (Behold) Marlene Dietrich
about to break into song   And she did

---

* These first lines are the only ones that appear on the broadside of the same title.

Subconscious submarine

That you swore off a fishing pole is very significant   like giving
away a rainbow   To give up fishing you say   is to save the fish
but crave the yacht   The sea is a vessel of fish   a great vat of
semen in which all the creatures of fertility through history slide
Is it paradox the ultimate sunfish was Jesus and sunfish are easy
to catch   like giving away a rainbow or a bent pole to your friend
And what of your friend

You aiming a carved ship into water is very important   Our lives are
full of flattened fish   all their features pushed to one side   much
resembling bankers   all of Middle America and a person who's made up
his mind   or been stepped   on more commonly called "floundering"

On Jellyfish Row

There are creatures in the sea called jelly in the shape of combs
The larger variety called "Venus Girdle" a girdle exactly the length
of a penis (A floating penis is a boat)   Now do these combs
run their fingers through the sea creating electricity that Stands
atop Water like Ecstatic Realization

Did you know the Man-of-War jellyfish is Portuguese and can blow
itself up like   General MacArthur or a machismo   meaning "A South-
of-the-Border stud"   Why go south

Out of the sea   you slipped on board in barren night Clear of Stars
shook off the unconscious   put on a peacoat   and cut your hair
No one but a few sailors   noticed the spitting image of a cabin boy
assigned to watch instant potatoes and eggs swell in a frying pan
had been given rank: GENERAL Deckhand

You fought a 175 lb. marlin for 4 hours Or was it a 4 lb. marlin for
175 hours Which gave you such a good fight you let him go Why say
"he"   That great fish might have been a woman   or just your

imagination   It could be big or little   As little as a pussy cat
or as big as the abyss   What do you do with a whale you've hounded
across seven continents   Whale you've pounded after with your
peg heart until your hair turns grey and everyone calls you The Old
Woman and The Sea that you suddenly face

The sea is where you fish out yourSELF macaroni-bit-by-macaroni-bit
The sea is a spelling bee: O Z PDQC   I had an aunt who came across
a package of alphabet soup   She boiled it and served it   The family
bit in   It was like eating jewelry   The letters wouldn't break up
but her son did   saying Mother have you seen my package of computer
lettering lying around the house

Heart swims by

Women think their centers are jellyfish   A man thinks a woman is an
upsidedown triangle: Two breasts and a cunt call-ed Trinity   A
Trinity of Jellyfish call-ed Mary call-ed Mother call-ed evil

A jellyfish is sexless   A jellyfish in water looks like a dead leaf
All you see is red brown or purple veins resembling bones   A skeleta
arrangement in a forest of fallen rain   But touch a jellyfish and it
exudes the most sexual quiver on earth   Some jellyfish are so sexual
they think of nothing but   hurting you

Look at a jellyfish called the moon a moonjelly fish is invisible
If you run your fingers through water you might catch one   It won't
hurt   It is like holding your heart in your hand   or a breast   A
handful of milk   shirking and winking like a giant teardrop that
any minute might harden   in a kleenex

Your own heart beating outside you   What to do but put it back in
before the almost baked nictating muscle glistening like a jellyfish
stops   answering the sun   Jellyfish of a poetic carcass lifted
out of water: Feeding fucking and sensitivity awesome as a cut-off
Medusa's head held   at arm's bay   in moonlight

EXPRESS

I do not see a bridge   I just saw a pig   A cloud hump a hill
Dogs in Osaka have curled tails   The weather today is many impure
dogs   An half-breed atmosphere   What are you Kabuki of the moment
in a country of an eternity of opposites of a thousand painted
dolls' constantly altering faces   I put a wet finger out to
polyethylene fish flying helter-skelter in rain

Blue tile red tile grey tile red green green red grey grey grey green
grey red grey grey grey grey red red red blue green grey tile blue
tile red tile grey grey grey

The white-maned lion was once   The Empress of The Marmalade Tree
The Marmalade Tree looks like the repair job on the face of
a Hiroshima Maiden   I said marmalade

Tiger Man   has air inside   With a tiger's face and a body and
sound like a lung   A dishtowel tied on for flying   Not to be
confused with Soft Man on a bicycle wearing a surgical mask
out of courtesy for having a cold   On his way to the plastic
ice cream cone factory

How many miles to old times old smiles   When my reflection was
gold fleck in the black pearls of your ancient eyes   Where names of
cigarettes were Hope and Peace

Rage of the taxicab youth   driving toward death   Missing life an
inch   honking endlessly at every   stone   garden   narrowing
At the slow layout of affairs   Our single affair   No longer love
but deep love   No longer an ancient city but full of slow toilets
a Venice of sewers above which poetry is written of cherry blossoms
and escape

Past pillars past water-immersed eyes past the slow drag of
the heartbeat modernizing me   This morning you told me through
bitter eye drinking   I'd have to wait   I wanted to make love
You wanted to pack for Tokyo

A great Japanese actress down spiral glitter stairs followed by
a long train of smooth-flowing tresses   masses of Japanese
breathing steamily move rope-handled bags and different feet
some wrapped in cloth   wooden clomp-clomps   shiny rain leather
black & white 1940 oxfords shuffling over trowel-smoothed land
As though the Japanese were Detroit in the grip of an electro-
magnetic crush   Bodies feelings pressing in on all sides A race
of people reduced to cubicle one-foot-by-one-foot American
livingroom conversation-piece coffeetables   The kindling features
of old men and women snapped in front of Kodak Camera's Pavilion
the souls of their gold teeth showing through chocolate   People
from the provinces wearing distinct straw bonnets or silk ribbons
at the 1970 World's Fair   to keep from getting lost   Men
standing like children in the women's bathroom so as not to lose
track of the female half of the province

Japan   glimpsed from a night train   *O Awkward dream of a maiden
bidden under sequins*

You wear 10 gallon stud hat   Men want to feel my blond hair apart
omen hug you   They've never felt such big earth   You are my
manager   moonlighting as a genuine Tokyo Texas salesmanwoman of
cowboy boots   worth a million   I am the Japanese blond dream
Hankyu department store dummies are blondes   I'm going to paint
my face   shock white geisha   wear shimmering spangles under a
pagoda of gold hair   have surgery on my eye corners   get rich
appearing on stage as an American impersonator   The clincher:
I sing the latest hit with the voice of Japanese wrestler

The drunk lady went into the men's toilet to find out if the American
had a big one or a little one   He had a little one

You were not drunk   You were you I was not me   We fought
Two godzilla monsters wending their way at nineteen o'clock night
their feet on roofs   Webbed rage raising itself through a thousand
prisms of spiny fly bodies   You   Waving   Saw-Toothed-Back at me
Me my mouth Full Of pins   Miniaturizing Joy

You sent five monkeys home to respond to you   Do you hear their
cymbals clapping across the ocean   a mechanical band of approval
flying goldenly into the sun   :   The beginnings of the first Monkey
Empire in America

I've lost weight   nibbling   all that sushimi affection served in
inch-by-inch cakes   slurping up all those noodles for approval
going into the future with consuming hunger for the past

Nanji desu ka kudasai   :   What time is it please
 Time I rubbed your soles and calves   Time I talked   Time I cut
through squid   or Time I was silent   An impeccably arranged
unpained cottage   The particles of our affair swept into a corner
Cornered   I sit and watch for hours   What is the Japanese   word
for "dustpan"   How do the Japanese rid themselves of panicles
Where do feelings go   :   The reduced footstep   Hush   Hello Hush
Rush on train   in a tunnel   out   I force fast-moving evasions
to the surface   They boil   You ruv me   You don't ruv me
Define please   Sank you

The strength of the Bunraku puppeteer drawn into the puppet until
the puppet drags the man behind it

Who occupies your compartments now And all your births   I'm in
the one with plush yellow that goes swoosh over the bridge
rumbles past tiny manufactured cities   clangs back into sprigs
of pink permanence   thrusts out to hillsides of silk exposure
I like and I don't like that your new girlfriend's emotions were
my emotions dripping down to you from peppermint-edged envelopes
(Envelopment)   (My new girlfriend is too new to ask for a postcard
She still has an old girlfriend)   (If this is too geographic I will
make it more pictorial)   (Your new girlfriend plays pool with her
old girlfriend while Oldyu travels with Newmi to Tokyo)

You and I not say Sayonara   Sayonara is like Jade   like chipped
crystal   It is easy but expensive   Rather two steaming dragons
breathe on each other as in a bad play   The sun rising red of
hunger   at outskirts of sliding screens and tatami mat breath

EMULSION

Picture a lesbian estate on the cliffs of California where doors
open green and bodies open blue   Where dye is let down on the
rooms each day and Amazons wearing tiger rags come out of trees
for lunch served by monkeys stained purple   Amazons eat monkeys
A most satisfying experience alive in the digestive tract as the
rooms water and color and wait for the night

Picture female figures pregnant with purple monkeys carrying bows
and arrows   netting more monkeys albino monkeys with warning light
eyes chattering pink on the cliffs of California   their snarls
frozen purple   Night uninterrupted but by a monkey's scream
Picture   fuchsias in the dark   under pressure of animal skin
Amazons in rooms

GIRL AT THE END OF THE WHARF

Hurtling her thoughts about with an aura of polished sea cabins
cigarette stuck out her mouth   Merrille tosses nylon into the sea
fishes side by side with a fat man with a laugh like the assistant
to the Phantom of the Opera

Fatman with classic cigar   lands two fish at once up the channel
of each cheek   Overture full of holes   pouring things in   until
Merrille who lived next to Bela Lugosi   remembers peering through
red velvet curtains   at a cape   a chair   with lion's feet
and a photo   of a morphine addict

Bela Lugosi lived alone with a cat   Fatman leaves a two-inch hook
in his arm   muttering more   Fat man A great actor   And Merrille

HERO

Age range 26 to 30   Strums guitar   can box   Likes everyone to light
their cigarettes on his flaming chest hairs   Future   falls into
imitation Early American furniture leather   Righthand beer-in-hand

Ambidextrous doublefeatured flipping 'twixt Abbott n'Costello bootcamp
hernia and once-a-year Army/Navy rawhide hypochondria Wakes to fend
off dreams   with the haircut of a shaved murderer

GRAVESIGHT

A forest holding a match in its hand The burned-out side of a hill
An ice prince stealing into a sleeping bag   Fog pushing its way
onto cracker flavor   A. R. T. carved on a wood table   Stone stove
No wood available   Super camper freaks throwing sugar cubes to a
raccoon   its eyes instimatic flash-glazed   My lover centering
glass beads on a fishline in dark glasses by firelight   If I speak
midst her coloration   will her eye   slip a bead   Will last
century's lover bring me flower monuments from next morning's hill

ESCAPE

Where a school is not a school   I saw you little   your eyes'
smears of sadness your parents' pain to visit baked buildings
You sat on the edge   Youth in rain in moccasins   slipping from
the soft place   sinking into fields of highways: Grecian girl
in loose garments running from   salt to sea-air in   rose-petaled
sunsets

A cabin cruiser reserved for young girls and one thirty-four-
ear-old curly mons veneris* resembling Ingrid Bergman's
You told the priest you   were having a relationship with a
woman

        "An unnatural one"

        "Yes Father"

            Only a vision of a priest   but baits
and sinkers dropping from the woman's teeth   were real

VISION THROUGH THE TREES: A thirteen-year-old   frantic
in levis waving in rain at the highway patrol   because another
inmate had told you the mental institution was surrounded by
quicksand   *Secondary kind of seduction*

Fire-Rimmed Eden

---

* The mons pubis, literally "mount of Venus."

PILLOW: NOTE

JaneJane   If and If I ever was published and never was again I'd
dwell in a corny posthumous belief in a fine old house for turning out
fictions touring The Garden of Helen indulging my mood of big
blooddrop fuchsias and bleeding fingers of pyracantha

Helen Regalia   Last night you removed the hooks today you wash
the curtains I'd like to send you something ethereal like bottled
rainbows you could hold For Jane: A hundred-year-old unopened
midafternoon aperitif called Deerantler Velvet of Melancholy

Helen Jane   Thank you for room for my proclivities toward recluse
my seeing things in circumspect to time-lapse photography of daisies
pushing against a window shuddering like glimpses of a golden dream
(Sometimes I find myself dancing when I'm stopped————————)

You allowed that I love a woman called Wormwood that I wear red shoes
to protect to assure earthlings I am Good-Witch-Patchwork-Girl
in Time of a Visit to Oz   *Remember me as the blonde boy standing
staring out a Andrew Wyeth canvas field of wheat*

ARMADILLO ON ICE

The hockey goalie is my kind of man   a veritable bastion of security
caught in mad genius grimace   strategying the mint   the plate the
brick   intimating a dull glint   surrounding it with O instant
electrical storm   A sting in the brain   A Frankenstein revival of
aurora spreading purple through a shin   Overprotecting

Fire-Rimmed Eden

                                        eye-rolling
                                    cold feet
                                    fending
                                    and wending
                                    imagination
                                    of assault
                                    of injury
                                        over an ice
                                        precipice
                                        in a blood
                                        arena of matador-
                                    ripped groins
Gargantuan the mask that hides the face that hides the slight gesture
of ice skate swagger (heel turn in)   The blade / In Error Eternal
Affirmation of imperfection emphasized and exaggerated in all its ram-
fications in all its grotesqueries   Click : to : click   men in their
eyes being batted   All for keepsake of dark clippings and bullgore
reward   overHope   I go for you goalie   My kind of man

DORA

Mother has a girl friend   a Russian   !Help)Help)I)am)running(from
(the(Russians!   The woman speaks bell-like and with an accent
of a sign in a park not far from Kiev on which is written   NO DOGS
OR JEWS   And her little nose and eyes are troika bells hanging on
a rack in a row on her leather-red face   She is gracious intelligent
unpainted soft-of-voice and fixes blood-red borsch running both cold
and hot for lunch   On holidays: A heavy little rumcake representing
one great snowfall-laden Kremlin   I love a lovable old cupcake of
Socialist Order   Of Mother's choosing   Whether they do or whether
they don't   (whether she's trueblood Russian)   doesn't matter to an
only erotic daughter of a mother

THE WHITE INSIDE A PINE SEED

Ingmar Bergman and I agree   the Norwegian fish run shall not outlast
a Swede's loyalty   Ingmar and I()Bosom buddies   Thru aquavitae
treachery and plague   the towhead   remains   yours true   True
in Sweden to one order   of farm folk who do not speak   They with
complexion of snowflakes   converse thru song   Loyalties intoned
back and forth until feelings passing between them grow swift thick
and higher than a logjam   Great hand of a collective of people
squinting in their beer   takes my head and steadies it toward the
burning light

A VOICE ROSE LIMPING

Marilyn Monroe is Janis Joplin is Jimi Hendrix   All died for our sins
for tipping the sweet core of life into an ever-scaling fuck   Two
whose bodies boiled down to junk   and the one you'd least guess
never had a climax

Witness Jimi with big looming apache guitar   pouring kerosene on it
lit it (Ssspt)   Buddhist monk amplifying his war sentiments by
immolation

Witness Janis bigger than the sloe-eyed hashburied daughters of the
rich   Janis afraid of her voice ghosting at age thirty   shunted
through backdoor ballrooms in soul neighborhoods O-O-O Yaaa-ahhhhhh
(She had a woman lover)

Not sex but sadness and still I wanted her Instant Unobtainable Avail-
bility   I wanted that they all became commodities at an audience's
taking   Audiences need an orgasm of agreement(don't we)over who to
worship in order to survive-In/Mass

Trio Most Wanted Murdered by imagined rapings everybody gave them:
How could they live in big mocking lavender stagecenter sunlight
bathing them in afterglow of loneliness

Marilyn Mind made to sing a body put through the shuck of flesh in
the dud of an evening dress   Witness Marilyn make the third member
of the trio (Even that sounds of sex)   *Thy voice is like a rose-
bush lilting*

Turn on the record run the movie climb any rock fence to hear the
latest glued conked body sing Venus Adonis to death
Itself out

Jimi Marilyn Janis never had a physical audience climax   (Lord they
tried)   Everyone Wanted it   glOWNINg bIGTIme COMEon HIT   Later in
pieces   The Needle Stuck on Janice   Even To the last: A Piece ex-
horting   Aw come On

In a meetingplace midway to the headstone in Peace Bessie
will you sing the last set—

IT IS WRITTEN ON THE WALLS OF THE WORLD'S BATHROOM: A RUTABAGA* IS THE WARTHOG OF THE VEGETABLE KINGDOM

I am a lesbian   I am a gay queer Christian queen   a homosexual
faggot fairy   a transexual bisexual unisex bivalve hermaphrodite
I am an albino biggot   a tripod sodomite   a Catholic Martian negro
masher heterosexual Doppelganger   Jew-Potato Alien-Pervert Commie-
Convict   I am an American-Hell's-Legion-Angel-Irish-Junkie
        The Top O' the Mornin' do you, Mrs. Calibash,
        wherever you are, do you, do you do?

*A Swedish turnip

the lynn lonidier airlift*

QUARTET OF CELLOS

A British woman asked what car I drive British I said Year 1959
Sure is an attractive little sports car she said   her lips   bent
into a beaming jewel atop a silk cravat atop a plaid riding jacket
atop a Year 1939 renovated rare roadster   Sporting I roared

A woman kissed me   She put her lips softly to mine and pressed
while her lover looked on   I let her kiss and kiss me   entrails
of ivy lips' single perfect milk-to-wine morning glory's spreading
tendrils: The finger ends of her suspended lover looking on

A girl told me I felt like a cello player   What does a cello player
feel like   She didn't answer almost gone   She hangs about the beach
and never heard of Pablo Casals   I didn't give her my phone number
She couldn't know to here to touch

A woman I thought I recognized thought she knew me We didn't speak
I liked her I love her I dwell on the stars the moon The Blonde Archer
of the Night   stringing blue without a bow   /HER) I thump out on
a mourning fingerboard

---

* In the original printing, the page contains a black and white drawing of a cyclone
with a bird emerging out of the top and the dedication "for Verrill."

HANNAH
OF THE NORTHERN LIGHTS

Admission

If I'd seen your relationship as the aurora borealis I wouldn't have
touched your lover with a ten-foot poem   Canadian-born For you   the
orthern Lights were a vague thing hanging there I would give a
pint of poet's blood to see

Astigma of a Jewish Mother

Knifing through her lover's clothing insisting something was faded
a hem not straight   Labeling everything Butch or Fem   I won't go
with you to the Female Impersonator show in that stomping dike jacket
Nor would she put a foot in any German restaurant in La Jolla while
telling her daughter You have a plain face your clothes look schlocky
Interrogating the eighteen-year-old (Half hoping for the hint of
curtain glow before the First Act of A Daughter-Saving Mother finds
the trashier pocketbooks from her collection on THAT subject in one
of her daughter's drawers):   You're not a lesbian are you

Hannah in overhead light

She asked a question only to interrupt the answer   As if the role
Querant of Queers   was flattering to a maturing figure   How could
you how could you   the She-Husky of the North howled   whose ears
were jaded to the break in the ice   whose eyes were jazzed-up day-
light in the middle of the night   I heard her coming through the
front door and scrambled into a closet   She opened a second door
to find her sleeping lover nude in a double-sleeping bag   She tested
the other half: Warm   I slipped on a robe   entered the scene

nonchalant   my mouth full of cigarettes Not to have to speak   Lynn
not *you* how *could* you   And to her sweetheart's scarce stirring
perfumes In love: Get *up*   *You're* going *home* with *me*   You *BELONG*
to *ME*

Last time I saw Hannah

Last time I saw Hannah she was between two white-haired social worker
lesbians with motherly expressions doing 70 miles an hour in a black
16 cylinder cadillac   Trio resembling Cerberus the three-headed dog
Guardian of the gangster world   Missing props were cigars to be
bitten down on   Hannah watching out for Hannah on either side The
left head fulfilling all her urgencies   The right head listening to
her every chirping   (as well as wolfhounds can be expected to obey a
 she-bitch with big dugs playing one against the other)   Both up
swatting flies over gaily-laid Sunday brunch table setting

Lover-leaving

Hannah doesn't love who she throws a bone   She pats them dusts them
like bookends after holding intercourse every Saturday night in heat
with all those art books on the coffee table made by her former lover
It's *OURS* you made it *FOR US* she proclaims Koffee-Klatch-Like
refusing to let go of a coffee table in the middle of a sky-collapsing
migraine

OF GAMING HENS
AND FALCON CHAINS

Hymn

My other half being Vintage Nun Not *London* but *Loudon*: 1634   Sister
Hysteria tears her habit open   Her breasts peer out in long gravity
noon   causing novitiates' faces to bloom and bloom inside (Luxuries!) a
wall inside a wall

Mother! Mother!   Sister Hysteria's ill   Mother Superior runs folded
to her charges instructing them to think of curds and plain desserts
Too late! Too late!   They've turned to crows pecking in a pie plate

Tarantella

Mother Superior and Sister Hysteria are under a lunch table grappling
with their souls   Mother Superior covers the soap breasts with
her hands brandishing Sister Hysteria with remonstrances

Nuns line up vulnerable as a lone row of candles   do the jerk the frug
the Watusi   without music   their brains reeling rumors of bodies
caught in monkey harems   Mother Superior falls onto nuns' knees
stirring higher on the claviers   Parchments of undergarments give
off shudder of golden-crusted hymnals   Nunnery covoluting to doves
blinded by wimples and the tears of angels floating like fires tinkling
through darkened jewel boxes

Ours it was Ours

A sundial marking the moment marking it marking it striking it   The
Armored Iron Maiden Fellow called Invincible   sliding along a steel
track   his arm Holding Scythe Toward Sun

Fingers into the chapel   playing miniature churchgoers' music
shattering ecstasy onto the little town   down—down *(Try to buy
a house from people who abhor the sound of two women / or else become
aroused / in a way that is not nice) (said Alice*

Last to Leave

Little blonde half chicks scuttling from under Mother Superior's
skirts: Flee Fly Flo Fl-u-ng   Alluded to: As Flown the Coop   In
her visitations to solid cells of habitation she scoops up one EX-
claiming THE MOST SACRED   while The Last Loved Sister Does Penance
For Mother-Baiting

Thank you for that most furious and satisfyingly curious last fuck
The Matriarchal Eye Arches   My body competing with My soul to equal
SMoKing hoLy penumBRAS   Nearsighted Sister Hysteria's star-anointed
pie-slanted vision more commonly called rain   She—She—She—/ the
French/the Swede   possessed stroBING BeHoIDING tHe
                                   CHrLSTIaNING of
HER Initiate Flesh by Mother Superior's HIM : *My Joy Is Like
the   Falling of-the-Rain*   Lite-Crosst Sun!— — —(Sundial My Oldtime
Tongue!)   *Blessed: Is: The: French: Kiss From In My-Father's-Hermitage*

I LIVES INNA GARBIJ CAN

Corso Kerouac Cassidy McClure Orlovsky Ginsberg Burroughs I came
'cross your old school pictures   From row kneeling like angels
lifted outa pickpocket files   down onto finegrain photographic
sands dissolving in hypo tears   Mistygustyyouths   in fascination
 of your own wonder there wasn't semen smears on your pants' pleats

In this only Writer's School of its kind   I'm not sure where
Ferlinghetti fits in Call him Handbill   The only girl in class
Denise Levertov   was told: Stay home   the   Day the Picture Took

CorsoKerouacCassidy   BIGFRAMING   rlovskyGinsbergBurroughs
                                                          Lil'uns
sidlin' up to Big'uns Mouthing Hiya   Gunslinger McClure with arrows
coming out his chin   chips coming out his shoulders like Gillette
dispensers   gets to be Blueblade Badboy   )Bad boys only get
to wear boot roar of the skin of the transvestite of the lion(

                    Hart . . . . . .
                    . . . .!. . . . . .
                    . . .Crane. . .
pinned-pining in lockers of lockshorn hicksalior Ginsberg   The
Poet-Aboard-Boat   Of wild-spinach expression toot-tooting hooks
to Algiers   A one-stuntman band leapfrogging in handspringing
love to Peter Frau-licking another firm-bodied author upon Freak
Beach   (Peter Orlovsky authored Allen

                    In Tangier
                        the Bluemen
                    Parade Blackmen paint themselves)   blue
Aunty Burrough's Blue-blooded Finishing School of   limping Voices
Growing Vaulted over back row of mirrored boys immune to girls
segregated from locker room stances of saints' blowjobs on Clark-

Gable-Beatuful   with-an-earthquake-going-on   workout
Work-It-On-Out Coruac CasslureOrlovbergough   You never let me be
in the school picture   Ferlintov   you never put my poetry
in yourYearlyYearbooks   You sent my poems home with coffee blood
ass stains on them   I'll have my turn at the top o' 1970 I'll be
QUEEN O' THE CLASS IyamIyamIyam While youse dead or turned into
old men peeing in your cinched-up rant pants Sheiks in your pockets
holds in your Trojans So ancient you'll turn into OliveOil Crones
I'll be yr wust w'mun English teacher's favorite pet in an EXclusive
ALL GIRLS'   School for Writers   IcanIcanIcan

OTHER TWIN OTHER SHORE

Frying bananas a Chinese twin frying bananas confessed she dreamed she's

two homosexuals   making love

6 ft. religious cowboy hymn-singing Sunday morning Him-sidling horse
upta nearest preachermobile   singlehandedly sprinkling tobacco outa
pouch onta skywriting wisps of prairie guitar-plucker's finger uvuh
woman turning thread in   rolling horizons inta thunderEnd TITAN'HIGH
Spit: licking ends   lassoing constellations along the creamy steerhorn
all the zigzagnight holds match to finger   Sptt:fireforth expertise

Hornrimmed silver homosexual stage designer drowning British stages
in roles of chintz wallpaper as if it was women in purple-wound fevers
unraveling in elevators on-top-of coffee interior sounds   halfmilkhalf
tea   Twin stage designers whose accidental oriental preference for
cowboys at banana fries becomes evident the third accidental oxidental
waltz 'round the Virginia Woolf cast party punch bowl   Virginia Woolf's

        two women   with men's voices

(When Virginia Woolf changed sexes she didn't   change voices)   Some
enchanted stranger evening Virginia Woolf's oxidental oriental other
shore: George Sand:Singlewoman:Twin of Two sitting puffing wallpaper
crossing stiff denim legs like tied-up tumbleweeds identifiable as next
morning's society page pantsuit man:Sand's other twin frying bananas
offering stogies to Theboys

GOING AWAY PRESENT

We walked thru imaginary furnishings   You bought me an ancient iron
shirt   with cornflowers the color of my hair coming out the top

Walk thru fine things   Womanvase   absent like a pale clattering Glass
spilled Wood splitting   I cried you cried over dead white bear rug

Earth
earth   talcum powder
earth
Earthroom surfaces

Cameo clear woman   not just one all of you your upper half lowing   your
lower half shuddering in your mushroom surfaces

Walk through imaginary gardens When you moved your precision shadowed
mottled thoughts across china   light dropped out of bone plates

    Mother-of-Swirl
    Earthquake Lace
    Blackpearlblue jonquil   berry   lotus
    I want to buy you

All the fine things I want to buy you all the fine things You bought me
a wrought iron shirt (the color of your eyes)'s In   Ocean Orbit

I shall never take off   shirt of the antique earth   nor part from
Early Period of A Last Day House

    Practicalities of Iron
    Pressed aged flowers
    Shirt of faded lovers
    all the fine things

WHY I ORANGE LOVE THEE

Quiet a case

Yellow turned to Orange and said, "I love you." Orange said, "What?"

    Orange lady who I orange love I gave an orange violin case having sold orange violin to orange market where purple rug merchants arriving hugging up scarlet emotions in orange scrolls of heavy red stomach gestures roll back their black embarrassments and slice and quarter orange violins for green children to suck out blue harmonica juice until amber evening is pink fragrant with Tasmanian devil variations on wall-to-wall Bach hoedowns and the naughtypine freckled orange house trembles with my orangeblossom heart tremulous of the pain of green love coming out the gold violin I wish I'd not sold

Orange I love her   horsehairbow crossovers   softening

Elongated daydreamer

I am not a very goodhumored man   In a Time of Orange pine needles falling from my head of tree   down to my twin orange popsicle legs' melted blonde bamboo panpipes (t-weet t-woo) I orange sensation Plaint of Woe of sleeping with stuffed orange pandas given me of former lovers

    I love the widow of sunsets the   Dipper of Orange
    paddles in rivers backwards

Twin orange trees

Arch of Orange Kind of Triumph   The persimmony other party longing panting standing guarding possessing   looking out a kitchen at two Bird-of-Paradise   nimbus-gazing women in red apple orange garden

Orange honest orange warbonnet   sonnet   upon it

When Mona smiled at Lisa   music hardened into marmalade drops   clouds
curdled rinds   curled   The burnt orangepeel bone x-ray showed useless
(I can't stop you if the game is orange charades)   I'll smoke sixty
cigarettes simultaneously in defiance of the three-alarm fire within
"dem bones" connected to medulla oblongata's bodycrown connected to
sacroiliacal embraces connected to the wine-eyed serpent at the base
of the spine unsprung

I looked at you looking at another's yellow while we played basement-
flooded music   Chest ex-raid crushed   sunlight turned the shade of
paper bags   duller than dollars harder   than dog collars   When you
looked at another's yellow

          the orange dog howled
          Knives fell on China

Cook of India's Out To Lunch

'Twixt oregano and turmeric   Stands Orange   'Tween the slowest moving
color: Passion red   and Himalayan monks in cayenne robes   'Tis Orange

        At a moment's notice I'll give away everything orange

Nina sings wind's smoky Simones

Cougar is gentle to its own but ruthless to shades of yellow other than
its own

High Camping trip list:
Ribs (point toward blood)
Haunches (draw sight)
Claws (tighten on territory)
Jaws (let out sound of devourment)

I will eat alive all tawny young pretty empty huntresses of Orange

Virile V. Vs. The Encounter Grope

An older woman has a warmer sense of apple pie   When The Group
accused her of being craftier in her coldest apple heart at seeming so
the Orange Ice Lady With the Popsicle Sideburns   cried throughout
Through and through   threw out

Orange Popsicle Dream

I was driving a car   You were seated next to me   A small orange dog
(Dudley) was curled in my lap   and a small black dog (Pierre) was
curled between us (Lap dog of Infinity-In-Rest(mouth-to-tail-to-mouth))
We were having trouble going anywhere   The car was full of belongings
The car rolled against the side of house eaves   You got out to look
We managed to get the car away from there There continued to be many
obstacles on the road   It was difficult to steer   We weren't taking
a trip   We were transporting belongings   I wanted to and did suddenly
put my hand on yours   You removed my hand   I felt disappointment
But soon you began touching me   We began reaching out to each other
making contact with our hands   I was no longer holding the steering
wheel   The car was coasting smoothly and evenly over the road as if
guided by outside forces   There were no more obstacles

Orange Popsicle Dream Too

We were with my friends   I wanted you but didn't want them to know
because you were with another woman   You approached me laughing
bent down   and kissed my forehead then stood back amused studying
reaction   I sat as if I had melted into the yellow hardwood floor
You kept approaching me embracing me in different ways   My friends
had stopped everything to watch   I felt embarrassed and helpless
yet wanted you very much   I could not move   You were enjoying my
embarrassment and my arousal

Never metal with a poet

You showed me light gone out of your hope chest
                              I display mine garden
full of rosebud chest medals   Triumphs marching in miniature over the
curve of my back so you see MY VERY HAIR ENDS BEND
                                          TOWARD YOU
(The potential of genius is to be the orange half of tiger and the
blonde half of monarch)   Will it matter to you I am a tigerswallowtail
way up there and a multiplied rabbit way down there and An Authority On
LOVE   with a degree in Swedish   papers in French-Cajun   and head
of the Lynn Lonidier Airlift STRAIGHT TO THE POPPY FIELDS OF
                                          FEMALE

You know I know   poppies are rare   When I find one I no knot to
accost it: WANTED - REWARD $50 Bounty On Orange Poppy Pickers - But
I can elicit pollen   trading   glances with orange butterfly   catch
her glances

Do I have an Orange problem

Do I qualify Is Gold good enough Did you know gold is the most durable
medal but fake gold is Jealousy-In-Eternity turned green

        the orange dog limed under table legs
        and lines fell onto china

Orange bedtime story: The Persimmon Gingerbread Woman

You climbed a persimmon tree in sunlight and pulled off orange
earrings from leaf lobes letting the persimmon breasts into another's
hands   It grew dark   You wouldn't come down   The tree grew higher
The other person piled persimmons against you   and left   You stayed
with your feet planted on bark   The fruit turned black Halloweeny
orange-by-orange splash-on-the-ground   The tree trembled from your
struggle to get down and from wind lifting everything off but you

Frost   lined you and the tree like sister and brother in flannels
Then it melted turning you to damp jewels   People passed and
admired   You stood still an entire season   did not try to get down The
sky cried and cried   You liked tears playing over yours and
the tree's forms   By spring your white flour arms were joined with
he tree's   You felt nearer the sun   Your red hair blending with
changes in the air

Summer a yellow bird sat beside your heart and out warbled its life
You found you could touch the bird without moving   You watched Fall
fruit filling with adolescence   A strange hand shook the tree
Bird went invisible   I picked you and pulled you off   You were in
gingerbread form   I lifted you to earth   Thinking I wanted to eat
you   you ran from the tree which had become your familiar place

You sank into a river struggling as you had in the tree   Current
carried you to the other side   You resumed running   Watching you
was watching sailboat's   disappearing crescent on the horizon
I worry whether I should've taken you out of the tree   Tree misses
you   You miss the bird   The bird thinks of you as in the tree
unafraid as you grasp the yellow orb of daylight daily from branches
in the form of a Persimmon Gingerbread Woman   *aware* the pounding
is not her feet running but   heart back inside

Orange segments of my past   pulled off sucked out

1. Broad subject of a mother I will not go into

2. Sunnyschool teacher's red hair curled tight as coils of electric
heaters   intimated Hell was fireeaters eating kerosene cones of desire
(Orange Julius devils lurking on Southern California streetcorners)

3. Grammyschool principal polished apple I brought her 'til crystal
glands dripped thru hourglass hips

4. Your eyes are the wise eyes of my cello teacher   Lead Trout Cellist
of Forsaken Cities for   smiling fishing garden arias

5. Dream concertmistress   Professor of One Sundown Student seduced
only with eyes so searingly I nearly disintegrated into the Emily Dickinson
summer without me

6. To recover   I requested a woman psychiatrist who convinced me of
The Superiority of Going Straight on her couch   I did and I didn't

7. My Orange best friend with children husband and diverse boy friends
insisted she was gay and why didn't we   I didn't   My best friend

8. Your oinkgirl friend was my oinkgirl friend all grease-pigged up
for last lap of the Catch-A-Pig-And-Win-A-Prize-Contest

Count the ways

> *Tree Spiritual: How long has it been since you've had*
> *an Earth Physical*   I orange count the days

Orange Alice

I loved Thee the orange instant I new You   New when Gertrude Stein
left Oakland California For THE NEW WORLD and twin flat worlds GREW
INTO ONE settling once Love For All of A-rose-Is-an-Orange-sliced-thru-
sunlight   (You I)knew she'd find Alicebee alighting sweetness of
That Orange Journey

A Lesbian Estate

ORANGE FEAR

I dreamed I sat on the edge of the bed of the woman I love she was
reclining   She propped up on an elbow to talk   She told me she'd
decided not to be further involved with me because of her entangle-
ment with two other women (Joan Who-Died-In-a-Dream & The Dropped
Kidney Kid)   While she was relating this I was holding and petting
her siamese cat   The cat scratched me   I kept petting it   It
snagged my hands and arms until they were bleeding   Injury from
the wounds and the woman's words were very painful   I suddenly
noticed why the cat had attacked me it had blood dripping from
wounds of its own   I wondered why I kept petting it why I hadn't
let it alone in the first place

PEGASUS BOUND

Lady has a hobbyhorse

The keys are complete   The four-eyed lady who has everything spends
all her time looking for it   She hires a thousand grovel worms to
lover her   None could turn up The Third Eye   The keys are complete

The four-eyed lady hires flies' tongues to scour her eyelids of in-
isible keys   She hires lizards to tongue arousal on her arms
She commands ants to march to the edge of the bed they are on falling
Insect Kingdoms flamingo at the edges of her negligee   She holds
back wisdom bunched between her eyes 'til her eyes cross

She holds the third mortgage over unliberated needlework girls to
upholster her lover   so key-chucked from catching her losses that
the dumb animal once flesh and blood and poet i   s hung up over her
fireplace: A fifteen-foot wingspread head of horse that once flew
greatly

Where are M'Lady's keys to unlock her from her taxidermy world   Keys
I let down gently onto the North East West South table of the
Venetianblindlady   create thunderous clattering hoofbeat

Keys to THE MAGIC THEATER

KEY 1: Mentioning me and Me Dropped Kidney Kid in the same sentence
is like sentencing Beethoven and a P. E. teacher to the same breath

KEY 2: The Sleeping Bag

"What do I want with an old bag like you." (Your words.)

A Lesbian Estate

You tire yourself out to sleep rather than make out with me
to sleep   I get even I get drunk and vomit all over your sleeping
bag all over your lilywhite couch:Ouch

> Who do you care for more: Your Couch
> > Me
> > Mr. Clean
> > or Ajax the Greek Hatchetman

KEY 3: You exited excited girlfriends until there was you and me
and the night and the YEK badge awarded you for satisfactorily
completing a three-month course in HOW TO REVIVE JOAN FROM
THE DEAD
WHILE KEEPING LYNN DANGLING

KEY 4: It hurt to find the record entitled I MOAN OVER JOAN back on
the record player it *HURT*

KEY 5:   The Moon In June is a beginning middle end B-Grade Movie:
You violate sacred burial ground of dreams
You beckon the corpse back of the love you dreamed dead
You love the lion on the card that says *Remember*

KEY 6: That I broke breasts in the sink in the form of two oranges
cannot equal Joan squashing Orange down until Aura of all-of-you-
inside-out lies snug in the trash bag under the sink

KEY 7:   King Arthur hurled one of a set of four chairs across the
room of the completed form of friends seated at round oak table
What does it mean to have knights sitting in your chairs empty of
friends around around table

7 of Cups

Tarot card of a deck figure beholding apparitions within cups coming
out of clouds: Snake castle jewels wreath demon   cloaked penumbrous

triple-decker threat:Head of Femme fatale/Eurydice/Witch   Alas   Atlas
holding hopes of a beneficent female form

I spent my soul searching dimestores for a kite from a dream that
didn't have a war picture on it   I finally found figurehead of
PEGASUS THE FLYING HORSE OF POETRY emblazing a big red
white and blue
kite that she and I could fly

March 19th the birds of Capistrano came back   The kite remains curled
in a corner   She said she had a reoccurring dream as a child of
falling   I fear her fear of falling holds   I have to fasten the
four corners of the world together alone

January February March string goes up into the sky   Shazammm   The
sky divides into 7 kites   Each kite has a key   Each cup has a life
Things and rings attached to KINGS move across the sky   SKYWRITING
BIGGER THAN LIFE

keys are kites connected to giants*

Carpet flowery flying

I am High Heaven from which you Mighty-With-Tears will be let down
easy   The salt mined out   It is Springtime for forgiving   Keys
float on The River   None sink   The keyholes float also   A slab of
door passes up into the sky   I will help you enter thru   You dived
in The River as if the watchband on your wrist were Siren Joan bound
to your side   pulling Tomboy down   Say forgive and all hurt falls
away   old loves fall into place   I will be your friend   I will touch
you at the point where your mind and heart cross to form a kite a bird
Superman

A Lesbian Estate

---

* In the original printing, this line is handwritten in cursive with all of the words con-
nected and cascading down the page at a ninety-degree angle.

I will write poetry to you   You will be Superwoman   Joan and you will
be lovers again Ring ring   And you will be gold light to me Ring
And I will find another's breastcymbal to meet mine   All will come
round   You will help me arrive at safe crossing with an older woman
You will fly high and I will not be dragged down   I will turn into the
wise woman I so sought And   you shall pass thru a thousand dreams'
surmises   All will come true thru talking seeing distance flowers
forgiving learning Delight O   *Ring the circular ring from which all*
128 *glory goes*

A FUCKING POEM

You need to find the woman I look for   We need the same woman
Feel into me : she is Seed   Look over your hill   She looms huge
tonguing desert sands so satisfyingly   winds at her breath push up to
mounds   I see her in paintings   She looks like you   You are
grain she is holes in   wind-caves in Arizona or half-eaten pepper-
cliffs in New Mexico   Great Clay chipped into cities by dark figures   129
She beckons like the gold tips of Tibet empty without us   She is
lost worries   Space   of Joy to be in   We are on our way to her
Silver-Her/She is whole She: Sheen of Illusion   We are half   Form:
Forebirth: To enter deep bodyroom   be that

HALF-FORMED KEYS IN FLIGHT

Know sunrise makes a sound Glorious in Stereo of beating of
BIGBIRDS' WINGS   That the sun is the breast of an ever redberry
forever   And   crows in Tokyo crow backward to midwest morality
of your Gothic Crow forerunners of invisible crows' nest-hoard of
guilt

I watched small birds   go far   for long   come onto your lawn
You watched birds under eaves putting mud between you and the sun
You asked what I thought of birds feeding on your bedroom walls
I'm moved that they are you: Paper on paper as though they feared
movement   Forgo

Not long you touched me   offered berries of your body and asked
what I thought of birds feeding on the walls of the night   In dark
you feared I'd be everberry hungry I'd put the Fall of the horse
with the long orange mane and the hoofbeaten Spring   ridden
not far   not long   on paper

Formed light I received from you from the hills: You do not want to
make love in the house of so much news in the night of a day without
sun   You'd gone South in the Spring/North in the Fall   In a day
without sun   birds turn their earholes to the whisper in the grass
that you love me   Forlong

keys in flight

∞

A bed will fly at night   I take your arms You take my side
Gowns breezy we shall ride   *Haveanotherdream   Doanotherjig*
Bedposts lift from their stays   Back-back—windowcurtains
Ledge Ledge make way for Great Gulping Relief   Shadow of
women shattering shadows   *Doanotherjig   Haveanotherdream*
All Earth thinks the underside of a magic carpet is dark manned
by demons demons manned by dark   You I   Feel   The   OPENING
DREAM

LITE FOOT OF FAIRIES

An Indian named STRAIGHT FRUIT I found myself falling in love with
a woman in welfare line with red hair named SECONDHAND
                                                        SWEETHEART
There was your body / Here   is your giving   "Your body should be
giving" suffers the word *should*   "Should" is a circuitous deformity
of "Soul"   a deviate called "unfeeling"   You claim to be a rock
The rock complains of gas Hardup Inher   Beans Macaroni peanutbutter
donated by The Department of Wind: NOT TO BE SOLD OR
                                                        EXCHANGED

Not to be sold or exchanged is my concern   Clouds marbleize Earth
(Pain being everywhere)   This chipping-away is not unhappiness   I
shall find fragments of you oft bits and pieces of women anywhere
You I:Big Commune: Spiritualanimal world in one room   Ark did exist
They found fossils of one man's dream LIVE IN SIBERIA   (Terrible
isolate vastness of going away)   Prisoner has nothing more than
Sweetheart to memorize him in photograph of her (he thinks)

I go to snowcountry with heavy shoes Sad heart   not unhappy   The
Tarotcard is of a cripple and MYSELF AS SLIVER passing in snow outside
a churchwindow   O'er Southland I laugh: The Handicapped and The
Lesbians of Los Angeles share social quarters to save rent   That's
a propitious union I could enjoy   if it weren't Gold presented me on
my birthday by my sweetheart in place of her body in place of   The
Sun   In Igloo sing: "You Are My Sunshine and I Am Rich"

Wonderful things happen in Siberia   Shamans are allowed to be homo-
exuals and snowflakes cluster in microscopes in universal revelation
Archeologists unearth the first drycell battery: Proof of electricity
before History   Proving there is never loss   The last card turning
up THE LOVERS   I CHING in Form of The Flying Bird I   EXIT *Flying*
not fleeing   Indians understand barking and mewing at The Moon
Menagerie everywhere I Found Myself Home

coming thru the locks*

THE SUN IN REVERSE

The poet loves   The poet loves and loves and loves and loves   The
poet loves while the woman points the flowers out   The poet whispers
wanna fuck   Flowers stay little sequins on wires attached to foreheads
of rocks   Sunsets nod no while the poet leaps over glintless sticker-
prisms imagining YES jamming the air

Cold coming in the poet hot insight involve with a woman pointing to
the dark   All comes to a burning point   The poet loves and loves
Poet loves the sun down   The poet folds into a cot   The woman sleeps
All night   stars hang a great grape garden with strange eyes in it
grow azure for the poet   in needle work garden   knot side out[+]

---

* The original printing includes a black and white illustration in a square shape evok-
ing flowers with the dedication "for Jean"—presumably, Jean Lyons, a close friend of
Lonidier.

+ In the original printing this second stanza is printed upside down.

FACTARTIFACT

Damn you for The Age you are damn   me The Age I am damn damn damn
slam damn   I feel so bad I want on all fours   In a vase there is an
orange and a yellow I can smell them in motion from the bed   Purity
in magic of reason   Sense in defilement of need   Lizards build great
bodyheat in cold systems   could not keep your finger out of me

South America breaks off from Africa   moves seven feet apart a Woman's
Lifetime   DamnDamnDamnDamnDamnSlamdamn   Dams flood
                                                           SYSTEMS'
ARTIFICES   finger sticks his peter in the dike   could not stop
splitting of broomsticks in this sorceress' den All-for-the-age-we
                                                           are—*

I'd sew up your curtains embroider GOODBYE if I weren't the timberwolf
damned to move in circles at the zoo   The Night Before Liberation
the seam stresses Apprentice In Love With splitting hairs: For every
one there's two   I believe in love animated in an old fantasy movie on
ice skates called FOLLY'S COME TO TOWN AND MIXEY MOUSE'S
                                                        NOT GONE

A comix character called Clear A. Bell Cow on her hindlegs gravitated
while a moth's rocketship grabbed a candleflame   burned!against!the
!sun And witches in weird circles' ellipses let loose wind from hems o'
fear Longevity: Grab a lollipop Hey Daisy: HAY   Behold MIRACLES
in This plain-as-a-dog-named-Dog Age we are in

*All-for-the-love-of-you—"from "Bicycle Built for Two" (the original printing in-
cludes music to the tune.

DROPPED KIDNEY KIDS

Kidney broke   It dropped off the highboy at the edge of epicanthus
and fell up to the ankles below   It was no ordinary kidney   Highboy
is not a hautboy   Highboy is a chest o' drawers under one's lover's
low brow   Whoever heard of goats' knees filled with concrete so that
kidney dips n' tickles her testes'   nest Suppose I put a finger in the
kidney and tickle   Would kidney come up her throat Would it feel like a   135
heart full of humanitarian spigots that flap open and shut on their worth
Or like panties around ankles

A Lesbian Estate

TWO SILLIES CRYING BECAUSE THE
MOON FELL IN

Everyone has an image of what they are that they aren't   Wherever
eyes travel is carried plaster bust instead of real Venus   Venus
acquired the paper-look of someone who invested money by the rise
and fall of her blood   and won   Twenty years ago I had a crush
on a mirror in a woman I hardly remember

Reality is flowered wallpaper plastered over my eyeballs in sunless
flat picture called View From An Aged House Of Warped Glass Window
Ten years ago a friend asked Lynn why put others' words over yours—
I'd rather hear what you say   I say the moon in the river's been
had

SISTER ACCUSED OF PRACTICING
ALONENESS AS SECRET ART

Sister accused of practicing aloneness as sacred

She wanted to lift the fringe of an eclipse off hierophants' vestments
with a fork   and chuck it in her cheeks She wanted an apocalypse
in human form made of bone ivory with a hole thru it she could hang
She wanted Saints with paraffin complexions in candle flicker to
whisper:

136

> Nothing ever happens by chance.
> Here only the right guests meet.
> This is the Hermetic Circle . . .
>   Hermann Hesse

Hermits

The Hermetic Circle is in a heaven like bees darkening the sun in
golden hovering   When the top of her head brushed it Emily Dickinson
went off   IT IS NOT A HALO IT IS NOT THE FOOL'S FOOT
                                        TRIPTRIPPING
It is a fairy convention   Litefeet leave tracks in a July 4th of
people who never forgot the pollen of parting fireworks   Hermes
do you hear me Hermine: The hermitic circle HER*

---

* In the original printing, there is a woman symbol hand-drawn around HER.

Wisemen from your High Chairs start

St. Lucy toreout her eyes   St. Eusebia cutoff her nose   Sheepherder
Margaret said, "Tremble proud enemy, thou liest under the feet of a
woman"   The Devil answered Beheaded her   Paula prayed Disfigurement
Heaven answered   The man pursuing her passed her   LucyEusebiaPaula-
Margaret in men's clothes   THAT way they travelled

*Men*tors   137

Jess I visited your second story window from outside
Jerry* your beard is balm on the chest of a man who kept it hidden
in a village he's not really a Jew he's a Woman
Paulean Robert
                    Double in Unutterable Tongue
Robert Paulean
Carl held til HE held HERMAPHRODITE   IT HELD
David gathers saffron with a solder sucker

The Hermetic Circle

The Hermetic Circle is saffron factory employees touching fingertips
in Heaven   Saffron is the upper tip of pistil off 4,000 crocuses to
make 1 ounce crimson threads resembling the veins of the fragment
of a nod   the simpleton gives the sun

---

* Presumably Jerome Rothenberg.

THE MOVIE STAR DREAM

I was in a sleazy subterranean one-room apartment I had all my ex-pensive light projectors locked in a closet my brother was in the room I was in bed it was late at night the windows were at street level the sidewalks were wide it was within the metropolis the well-lit streets
shone light in the room

Suddenly a group of young men in white sailor suits were fiddling with the windows I was relieved the windows were locked and that my brother was there but I didn't know how he was going to protect me against the men then I realized one of the men—a dark-skinned foreign student—was already standing in the room he'd slipped through the window screen to show me how easy it was to enter

Then the men were gone my brother said it's a good thing we weren't in a city in Vietnam over there the sailors would've broken into my room and I would've been raped

Later the room was as large as an entire floor of a house—one room extending into another without doors—and my friends were arriving to stay with me wondered if there would be enough beds another friend was arriving that day I looked around a corner and saw a dou-ble bed I forgot was there I would put my friend up in that bed

I went on a small errand upstairs in the same building where my apartment was I was let into a posh apartment by a white-haired man in his late fifties or early sixties he was dressed in a suit he was heavy-set with heavy-jowled face and his eyes reeked of the red look of an alcoholic his daughter in her teens was with him

I was let into a spacious airy living room with antiques Bette Davis was standing with her cane in the living room she looked to be in

her late sixties I knew somehow that the man at the door was her husband
and the girl her daughter the man had a reputation of run-
ning around with women I was in awe of Bette Davis because I had
I was in the same room with her her husband and daughter wander-
ed into the kitchen I debated whether to tell Bette Davis before I left
how much I admired her I imagined most actresses were tired of
hearing that I almost didn't tell her then decided why not—I hadn't
seen her smile she had the look of someone resigned to dreariness I
told her how attractive she was and that I thought she was the most
wonderful actress in the world—that I loved her

Bette Davis' face lit up she smiled and slowly put her arms around
my waist I put my arms around hers in this loose embrace we looked
at each other with growing recognition we didn't say a word we mov-
ed slowly together out away from the furniture we were so aware of
each other by then we drew close until the lengths of our bodies were
against each other we held ourselves together with our arms around
each other held tight like we could never let go we were one being
delighting in fully experiencing what the other person was experienc-
ing Bette Davis didn't have her cane now and she didn't have trou-
ble maneuvering our legs slowly lifted in an unearthly slow dance
cheek-to-cheek she was lithe as I we were a bird sitting in one posi-
tion playfully challenging its gravity on a fence or on a telephone
wire not conscious of balancing itself in a breeze yet correcting its
balance when we began to lose the poise of the bird—coordinating
with the elements without being rigid and laughing together know-
ing exactly what the bird was experiencing

Next we were the bird flying—still pressed to each other and without
effort—banking an air current—swooping in and out of the wind

Drink-in-hand Bette Davis' alcoholic husband returned from the
itchen the daughter following behind him they watched us from the
edge of the living room we went right on being a bird flying though

aware of the two spectators so astounded by our embrace and our
motions they couldn't speak or interrupt

As Bette Davis and I finished being a bird we moved away from each other
with such elation I woke smiling feeling ecstatic—in such re-
lease a tear rolled down my cheek I cried some

LOVE OF YOU I LINED THE HOOK

You taught me to line the hook: Take it right on out the eye   I
wanted to impress you   I'd handled the oars so floppily—more on
the left more on the right—I'd never heard you yell   You took
the oars   stroked straight   I heard fishflop in boat's belly
Gills like bent popbottle caps   A form in an other boat said Throw
them back

Fish-colored water   feet on ground   you showed me how to cut off
head tail fins run knife up belly take guts out scrape off the
rainbow   Some people don't like eating eggs of female fish but
leave them in   they're edible you said as you came upon the unborn
massed   Throw innards to the fish   I stood around thinking hook in
a fish's eye

WHEN THE SPOUTING GATES
OPEN AT ASWAN

When the spouting gates are open at Aswan near the First Cataract
370 ton obelisks of Queen Hatshepsut float-down-the-Nile   100,000 men
in 20 years don't complete The Pyramid   The Tower of Babel stands a
rotten tooth   Statues emit sounds at dawn as their pores expand and
air rushes in   Harps hammer   Avenues of Sphinxes hint magnificence
100,000 men crumble at the whip   Time wind and sand beat A KING

I let A San Diego QUEEN dream I was a Great traveler camper seashore
guide   I with Californias of Hair prove by my dog's tag I belong to The
State of Washington *What in Germany are Tibetans doing with
German uniforms on   What in Switzerland are German soldiers with
chariots and Roman Legion uniforms on at the bottom of a lake   doing*
Nothing doing but wait for a fairy and read of Egypt in woods north

FOR SALE: GIRL POET CHEAP

Dept. of unemployment

Pincering lips over teeth into a bowtie the man showed me how to
smile   told me the way I dressed wouldn't sell   Spruce up   What
do you do for a living   I make movies of girl friends in my present
life   What did you do in the past   I was Devi covered with
snake-intaglio tattoos who rode in a parade locked in a room of
things to do forbidden

When I grow up

O to be an Egyptologist with a child coming out my head with snakes
inching my biceps and a beetle in my belly   Beetle holds the sun
up Arms raise up Praise Ra   When I get big I want to carve female
impersonators' and candlestick makers' fruits 'n' labors on my tomb

These stares were not the hard stares I found to climb

I carried a dead armadillo thru the city like a sling I carried a
dead armadillo thru the city like a sin and everyone looked headon
at it   I carried a dead purse full of prizes   I climbed to my
crawl-away place   like a protected being   like a hulk like a hull
like armor   and clattered away   waiting for the sun to roll
out under the rug   My pet my weapon I carried a dead armadillo into
armed camp   Windows rattled drums: Should this half-rotted spoiled
girl-child be allowed to carry the soul of the forest as a departing
armadillo on the wing as Tibetans wear necklaces of human bone
*"Reach into the dead armadillo cut out the mysticism and pull out
the winning ticket"*

OVERGROAN

Theodore Roethke said people of Seattle do not appreciate me   Added:
Seattle's nothing but an overgrown logging camp   (He was in San
Francisco)   Wasn't he a little mad   Men: Notice women turning
female-professed-air-to-the Roethke-thrown

I am Theodore Roethke reincarnated   Of course I like women   Didn't
Theodore Roethke   Wasn't he a little mad   Can't a woman be her
favorite poet   Doesn't Seattle suffer provincialism unequalled but
by A Great Stake In Our Vampire

Montana outlawed drag shows because a logger in the audience threw
liquor in a boa constrictor's (drugged for one of "The girl's" acts)
face and the snake came alive began to squeeze the queen (Honest-m'-
gosh)   Thus Montana gentlemen cannot dress as California women

I am a female pretender to Theodore Roethke's throne   Didn't he
write a poem about the green shoot turning up at the surface like
a worm   or A Snake uncoiling like thousand-year women who swallowed
their worth and stretched foreverout in sleep

A coffin was put around the Female Spirit stretched around the earth
Snake ♀♀* a double snake an either-good-or-bad snake   Depends how
Theodore Roethke's treated by descendents of lumber camps in Her
NEW LIFE

A Lesbian Estate

---

* In the original printing, a double woman symbol is hand drawn, interlocked, repre-
senting lesbianism and snake eyes.

I, TARZAN

Dear Jane

Letters I received from you are like letters from Emily   Snowflakes
held by paperclip to dry***The kind children cut***forever ticking
pizzicato in the sky

In a Tokyo wooden house that fit together like old matchbox (not
clock) I met the world expert's widow on snowflakes   Huge ENLARGED
SNOWFLAKES looming universe   The violin voice of the widow saying
lonely shock-oo-haut-chi* on the mountaintop

Stars' eversides reminding Crystal of pentacles of tunes played in
perfect orient on my mother's ear   She was a fiddler
                                        fell from the sky

                                        snowpoint

                                        snowpoint

                                        's no point
                                              going south
if you can't see for the snow   Love forms
                            snow forms on ski sweater
                                                            Girl+

*Bamboo flute

+ Handwritten in the original printing.

JEWCAT

Wanda Landowski has balls and Jew has pendulums   Jewclaw collects
around it collection plates to pass around for more   denies
onslaught of cobweb collection of veils holds her in Hollywood
Capillaries worn her largesse flesh in makeup of Death exclaiming
I want away

Rumming thru lox Look of the beefsteak alcoholic lines you her face
Deadly raps on harpsichords Aztecs rip heart of the person in
offering out   Roman banquet climax lascivious lingering   Blood
coming out the Lion(Giant spelled with a J)   Pieces of meat prizes
of You(Yowl spelled with a U) are passed around the Jewcast

FALCONESS

She has made on her wrist   a falcon   of papier-mâché   named Desire
Between legs   handpainted it gathering fruit   It picks   berry out
but does not lift it   It is for us to elucidate overafterunder break-
breakfastfast (polish polish)   Desire gathers grapes to modest places
We can take   care   of our falcon upclose named Thunder   Put wee
hood over it   or   repeat "Land on meat repeat"

ON THE SWEETHEART OF MY MORNING
LOOK THRU GLASS

With the rivers on our fingers and listening to Sphincter Man singing
soprano we continue to feel up the amber bottle   Jean's* hands shaking
rainbow showers from the sea   Jean Jean
                    wet dream

                    JeanJean
                    sticky key

                    Liongiant

                    Jewelfall

                    Jean Jean
                    dieting. Her dinner rings. Kissing
she said "Two hours of fuck and a bottle of beer and keep my breath"
Garlic oregano rubbed into wooden bowl in early hour of sweetheart
Part odor   part arousal   in a dark bed of salad

---

* Jean Lyons, a friend of Lynn Lonidier in Seattle, Washington.

FOLLYBEASTS

My name is Lion-Deep-In-Den   In the winter of women I go bounding
after paw-Deep-In-Snow One who is dashing after a genuine Hollywood
furpiece you can't distinguish from snow

Furpiece   Paw-Deep-In-Snow One   and Lion-Deep-In-Den   scurry
over Ancient Forest with rickety legs like scurvy   panting love
and lack of want   and don't stop for meat

Raw raw winter knife cleaves down into red pieces (red and warm and
dead) Streetmice hurry for little handouts   keep Follybeasts
company

I am off after Gone One   Love is off with Soft One   Lovelove curls
into nests under snow into hollows into lures' carves   curves of
landscape soul

Glass of fire you go trembling to your lair where Nightshade (moon
pupils) and Scimitar (spiked eyes) peel like gumwads off walls rub
against you   purr operas to your wounds

TV on all night   shapes and patterns of pursuit throw zeroes on
your bedspread so you won't dream on an Animalclaw Couch For Lovers
where you draw fur collars   around you

I can't breathe (seizure of snakes while you go foamy   dogging the
Jew) You bought a dogsled in your sleep   and a whip   tailend
reaches clear around to you

In winters of women I go   bound   Roller-Skate-Owner-On-Ice-Out-Of-
our-Element skids over   and under Furpiece bounds on beyond you
overhilloverdale

A Lesbian Estate

Clumsy-Bump-Into-Things I tromp after you   tennis rackets strapped
to my feet   Dumbo on snow crying I want Hotwaterbottle Woman
I want to fuck a lion

With hot hard breath Follybeasts land bottonnsideup in snowbank
awaiting wallowing arrival of the mistyeyed beast with the canteen
of (rahrah) hot release

THE HARD RIDE DOWN

One summer one winter

Your former lover vibrant instead of the corpse in the picture   Her
face vital thru forest firewatch   instead of   flesh taking on   fat
of her latter lover hoarding in Christmas tree turkey presents

Winter roan

To think   To be going in reverse   To learn something   Japanese
Everest team with dayglo paraphernalia and aluminum ladders had
harder time going down than up   As a friend you mistreated your horse
As a lover   you didn't

O SOJOURNER

Call a sailor a cake with candles   Peacoat anchors embedded in buttons
and swell of dark wool at the pockets   Call a sailor Sentinel

Gates are locked   Locks are closed   Sailor speaks little   Sailor
full of knots   I hold in my mouth starting eggs fragile as flood-
dried maps   Sailor will not perform appendectomy in belly of Japanese
Gaa-Gaa monster   Sailor is learning what sinks   what sails

Sailor will reach into her stomach   reveal   kidney liver and sunlight
so baby birds born out her mouth where first tailfeathers of dawn
smack saltwater flutter   like   spit primitives spit on their hands
raise toward the sunrise

Call a sailor a cake with candles   Peacoat anchors embedded in buttons
and swell of dark wool at the pockets   Sailor-full-of-chains floats-on-

heights

A Lesbian Estate

THE COOKIE MONSTER

Cookie Monster said Set the albino child out in the sun to fry   But
Child was not albino But intelligent   There was no sun   Cookie
Monster entered in out of the storm   with snowshoes on   Every step
melts sweet   Offered her limbs   Child bit off mind first   then
the decoration   Cookie Monster   broke   into   pieces running thru
the bloodstream   and multiplied   Amoebas   with sand-castle coatings
that say EAT ME   Ever-edging spines and whips and cilia

Albino Child mined big black valentines from Cookie Monster's interior
turned them on end   so big black teardrops hung from colors of hurt
that mounted her pink   punished   eyes   Cookie Monster devoured
Child's dark movie star glasses and moved Milky Way away Why haven't
you eaten me I am so small Albino Child cried eat me until I turn
into crystals of feelings passing in and out the very taffy froth heart
of your sweetened stiffened system

      Beauty of pain tastes like the sunrise,
      the sunrise pains your beaty, My Sweet,
       the beauty of pain tastes like saltwater horses, Cookie
Momstir lulled petting her child's white mane   and slipped her sugar
Child whinnied pranced and peeled her clothes and paraded virgin
before dark Mother Surrogate   and blushed And the Cookie Monster lay
on top of her and took her   Heh-heh-heh

PIERRE IN THE AIR

Little dog by my side   getting light on his winter body   barks at
guns   and oppression   and men   unless they are gentle men   My
dog the Hollywood movie star   comes over the hill onto western
setting and the cowboy says Must be a French Prairie dog

Carl Jung said little animals are on this earth to tell us about
ourselves   I carry a dead armadillo   as a reminder   Superiority
once said But Lynn you only care for a dog   And what is wrong   is
wrong

151

My dog talks to me he walks with me he arranges himself like a dodge-
ball among long legs of women   Motionless dreams thru fourposter
motion   He is a hypocrite a retired army colonel homosexual an
Egyptian on hind legs who keeps The Dead company

Love once dreamed a three-dog dream: Raggedy was a Gypsy   a ring
in his ear   Dudley had a dress on   Pierre was a tap-dance man with
cap and cane that went W. C. Fields Ho-Ho-Ho-Ho   What kind of dog is
that   Pyramid head balancing on point

He has the voice of an intellectual   and the profile of a couch
His name: Colonel Rogues Pierre Gump   In the Land of Oz a gump has
broomstick legs and   body of a couch   that flies   Raggedy's gone
with the gypsies   Dudley was killed by a car

Pierre*   body splashed by sun   survives   All species are vanishing
I don't tell him   He has seen enough   Someday—though I don't tell
him (I might disappoint him)—I'm going to save money   and take my
dog to see The Sphinx

A Lesbian Estate

---

* Pierre was Lonidier's dog and included in a photo at the back of the original printing
of _A Lesbian Estate_. That photo is included at the end of this book.

AN ORCHID IS A PARASITE

An orchid is a butterfly lying in a forest   slow and hard to hold
Give it room
                An orchid's in a box
                           An orchid growing   on   An
orchid   performs   Bach is tropical A tropical orchid given
velvet   will produce
                An orchid is a Paradise   an air plant
with out-of-reach roots   looping thru
                            Orchid lovers   climb
recipes   wade thru decay   brave headhunters   to get at   a
vagina   ruffled by royalty
                         An orchid is a parasite Of The First
Order   Proud of it

PUNCH & JUDY

She left her shoes you left your belt her shoes strike you your belt
stuns me my throat is what she wants   I took my voice you wear my
throat I love your belt you kiss her sole she wants her shoes you
need your belt you've heard my voice the belt fits me the shoes hold
you*

*Sing from here to the end

O bring back, bring back, O bring her ba-ack to me, to you,
Bring back, bring back, O bring back her teethmarks to you, you're hurt—*

---

* Original printing includes music.

DIRTY LAUNDRY

The History Of The World consists of one-thousand-one-hundred-ninety-eight pages of one paragraph with a crack in it:

> *There was another meeting of these two potentates*
> *at Erfurt, in which the Tsar was manifestly less amenable*
> *to the dazzling tactics of Napoleon than he had been.*
> *Followed four years of unstable "ascendancy" for France,*
> *while the outlines on the map of Europe waved about like*
> *garments on a clothesline on a windy day. Napoleon's*
> *personal empire grew by frank annexations to include*
> *Holland, much of Western German, much of Italy, and much*
> *of the eastern Adriatic coast. But one by one [crack]*
> *the French colonies were falling to the British, and the*
> *British armies in the Spanish peninsula, with the Spanish*
> *auxiliaries, slowly pressed the French northwards*

A Lesbian Estate

Thirty-five years of my time in this life pressed northwards I
changed   into an apple with an arrow in my heart   sitting examining
science-fiction writer H. G. Wells' *History of the World*'s cracked
paragraph pressed under glass mounted to my turning eye   No mention
of Emily buried in alabaster   coming out the crack she never left
Emily Dickinson winning ribbons canning fruit for the county fair
Emily: Prize preserve-maker   pronouncing butterflies on the wind
on a clothesline day

Emily Dickinson—This Is Your Life

She wore continual white   An albino newt sitting rooting for the
beast in Japanese TV horror flick   Beast does not know what it is
doing or who it's for   (It is hunting butterflies for its baby)
It does not know its Self this parent fierceness this innocence

(about five feet high)   Emily Godzilla Dickinson pressed northwards about to step on six-inch-high Empire State Building in a cardboard country   Emily never left the county she was born in   Can an army leave a lizard called "Lesbian" alone

154

HERMIT CRAB

Shell A-Beauty Crab once dreamed a woman was in half

In moonshell curled

House Beautiful you keep assuring Purity it's just her body
that's missing

Oversized red

The day we snail-walked sideways from the dark hole of
your shell to the ship's canal   sun   salting your skin
to pepper   tasted burned as autumn leaves of freckles—
galaxies of freckles on the solar limbs of your shifting
system's universe jeweled in salt: Painted cracked lips'
hull of a sailboat   and its mascara sail

Sluggirl*

Logs being floated to a mill   a spike-footed Swede jumped
back and forth   kept logs straight in the locks with his
pitchfork   The water lowered   Strain O'Swede I emerged
Half Pure Light   You hold Purity's stretched-out body
with your jewel-claw   Identification is made on the body
by a gold ring: Ring three times   hang up and dial again
My ring distinguishes me from Electric Junky Dildo Girl
who incessantly mainlines your carapace and sucks the meat
'til you scream

* "These carnivores feed on other shellfish, which they engulf and smother with the
aid of an unusually large foot"

REAL ESTATE

You are POSSESSED   Sex gets you   Call The Spiked Iron Vise:
"She"   She ls Skull   uninvited as claque gnarled in your side
whispering *Come!*   She is covent   You are owned   She is Hell's
Bell Telephone Company's sliding tongue disguises

156   You are Real Estate   I am The Angel Of Creation Announce QUEEN
OF CATS CAN LOVE   The Battle For Heaven's begun: Hurling Bricks
Vs. The Rainbow Shirt   I weaken but hold   You unfold shirt's
Blazing Room   try THE PROPERTY OF LIONS   on

FAIRY TALE

Hairdressers would say she's the centerpiece   Big black fluffy
evening gown of a cat in her chocolate coach   Bella Donna
going to the heterosexual banquet with poison rings on her toes
With the grace of a poised Venetian goblet of scarlet on her
Medici head   Bella Donna mounts the banquet table   tiptoes
along rows of gleaming table settings   petite hinged doors of
her rings hanging open.

JEAN LYONS

If you'd told me your goldfish names were *Peninsula* and *Pathos*
nothing would have come of our acquaintance   Peninsula died
and was replaced by Ethereal   Pathos lived five years

Ethereal and Pathos lay on a leopard skin sharing the latest
hunchback whalehit song   exchanging underscored passages
espousing Libertarianism   and arguing virtues implicit in the
respective names Pathos and Ethereal

You assumed the name of a living dead goldfish: Peninsula
Pathos Krigbaum   PP for short   I asked again   You said you
were Beverly Diaphanous Desiderata   And again: Marianna Falcon

If you'd told me your names for fish when our acquaintance struck
 would've thought you odd   As it was   you only mentioned your
two cats *Lysistrata* and *Belladonna*   Such discretion sparked a
most rarefied relationship called Meat

FALCONBANE

Female fencing expert with a heart on   tosses her cat falconbane
Lysistrata plays with falconbane like hay   Rolls in it sniffs it in
gets drunk   lies motionless   Frozen companion Of The Patroness Of
Save Our Little Feathered Creatures From Feline Reach League
save for her eyes

ADDENDUM

—And you tell me you're going to name your next two cats *Good* and *Evil*—and raise them together!! . . . ?

MINNIE MOUSE IN LEVI'S

Jill Johnston told me she wanted a harem of women in the woods
Pictures of it are in her latest book entitled How to Manipulate Others
for Fun and Profit   I quit every movement and join the ocean   when

we are the chosen   gets voted in   Moral: Don't hold your harem up to
Lynn Lonnie Dear, Jill John Stone cause under my Lois Lane clothes I'm
Amazon Mouse   I'll rat on you   When *we are the chosen*   gets in

　　　　sailor goes to sea again.*

---

* Lonidier reworks this poem in *Clitoris Lost* and retitles it "Mayamouse"; it is on page 335 in this book.

SAILORJIG TO SEAPATCHWOMAN

Down the briny paths of rime,
I join hands with an encrustated lion.

Transpose a lion on a whale and have upheaval to the last
tumescence of seadrop (water-holding speck of life) I am

Mid-Forty Woman   Deep tonnage tensor of wisdom   Weedpatch woman
with brio-bulge crop   mat   carpet island   Thicket   fishhooks
monster bites   Slew of parasites hang loose in the gold lion's
mane   Hoar nest   Primeval catch   SeaROAR cRest sWell Woefroth
/PROMISE: Green land grows on your bullback   wending invisible
harpoons R   uddy mantle of rush in Green Sea Contest

Supernova

We burn our elements at such a terrible rate,
I am afraid we will implode, fall into our cores
and become dead black stars.

Jean

The whale ambles   Accordion bilges willow garbled years' poundage of
speech in me   Fossils knot in the catch of ages desert whale
wears   Geyser monolith elicits tailspinning-freckled-ribbon-kelp-
coral-blotched language vaulting from dreams I edge blue vision
/PROPHECY: The dandelion leviathan drink you offered me at Admir-
able Rainbow's Inn   *Nor Will You Have Rest*

Lynn

FEBRUARY SHOWERS

Marrymarry how doth your garden blow   with windy kiss and maidens'
trillings ALLROLL   All over my rosegarden sweater you came warm rain
only heaven could make and angels flame   Merrymerry hairs of my cock-
L-bells and silvershells   need your legs gently stream ALLROW
Springbee Be not contrary   quiet fairy   Marymary am wed to thee all
wet in thy bower Tolltoll   the bell's dewbowl cloth brim double R A   I
N   B   O   W   S

FAMOUS WORDS
OF THE MORNINGFUL JOY

I just read my beauty-eyed daughter's   first written greatness
(42-year-old Emily Cranky Dickinson* crawls from cover   closeyed-ear
perked toward immortality   cigarette-poked words altoing out a
slouched petunia: "I'm in trouble I think It is really that late")

*According to Jack Spicer, E. D. started writing poetry at about 40.

"eadie"

Grammy said throw grass at people who mistake your three-year-old voice
for Bette Davis   A grownup head on a babyframe is an improbability
the look-alike scouts   didn't consider   They say you look more like
Bette Davis than Bette Davis but Bette Davis always played Bette Davis
You're Bette Davis' daughter you say as you slip into an I

People made her you-her   She played a part   in twin   Your line would
burst   if two   Another movie's end Bette Davis went blind   then dead
Bette Davis' aura amassing from pinhole   onto you   Bette Davis
in a blonde wig in public insists she's ordinarily   in life   You say
you're going blind Wondereyes   Bette Davis never felt Emily Dickinson's

hand   tug   B.D. and E.D.   Wouldn't   people saying "Did anyone ever
tell you you look like B.D." turn you into a compulsive handwasher
clothescollector pastewaster cigarette-puterouter light leave-her on
I do not hesitate to tell the blind girl in the Mary we share   you're
Emily Dickinson and I invented the projector obscura

Life's disguise
doth keep
flies
off.

Gone from the bathroom we leave   a light   for Her

Lynn Lonidier at her typewriter, June 1969, Leucadia, CA.
In addition to her poetry, Lonidier wrote a number of experimental novels.

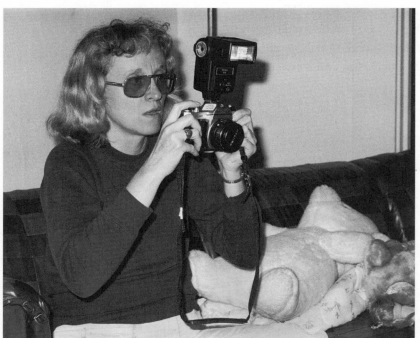

Lynn Lonidier with her camera at home in San Francisco, December 1981.

Lynn Lonidier with a doll's head on a silver tray, early 1970s, Seattle. Lonidier titled one of her multimedia/theater performance pieces, "The Dolls' Piece." The props from that performance are available in Lonidier's archives at the San Francisco Public Library.

Woman Explorer

by Lynn Lonidier

Woman Explorer is dedicated "For B. A. and all who spirit the sun. . . ." and contains this epigraph

In the early cold part of this century, Edith Södergran, the "Emily Dickinson of Sweden," wrote:

> *You will show me a wonderful land*
> *where the palm trees stand high,*
> *and there between the pillars*
> *longing's waves go.**

*From *We Women: Selected Poems of Edith Södergran*, translated by Samuel Charters, Oyez Press, 1977.

THE WALLED CITY

If a wall
is built around San Francisco
as it was at Mayapán,
it will keep out the ocean longer,
Providing the wall does not succumb
to the earthquake
prior to the tidal waves.
The Mayans
have an incredible sense of time.
Scientists say
one's entire life
Parades before the myopic eyes
of a drowning person.
Learning about life
instant before death
is a distraction from pain.

Of course,
not everyone will be able to live
inside the wall.
You will be weeded out
according to nobility
and knowledge
of the occult Zuyua language.
All others
are misfits. Of course,
through heredity,
you may stay—who would want?
The court that judges *who*
occurs once every twenty years.
Apply in 1995.

The Mayans'
timing
is marvelous.

Mayapán
Thrived as long as the U.S.A.:
two hundred years.
Then the COCOMs
went to Xicalango
and brought in Mexicans.
The COCOMs took over.
From then on, the city
went downhill.
One day
when all the ruling COCOMs
were in the walled city,
they were caught within
and slaughtered,
and the walls
pulled down
on this,
the only known capital
of the Maya. This,
the pronouncement
of seven times 7,200 days
or twenty years of 360 days
to the minute.
Take yr pick.

The Mayans
were brilliant
at filling space.
San Franciscans
Are not bad at it either,
and an earthquake

is a little like a jungle.
Take your pick
and pack your sack.

In the spilling face
of a red rising morning skyline,
the Fool is starting out—
the rosy countenance

of the Fool
with the Hourglass Face.
An earthquake, you say,
thick as a jungle beat?
Hoombah* hoombah hoombah hoombah—
rest of the way
is downhill, Baby—
HOOMBAH!

*Beat with fist on table, floor—
whatever your reading surface is—
making it shake with each "hoombah."

COSMOPOLITAN

There is evidence they were here.
Beneath the triangular hill—a shinbone clean of flesh.
Beneath that naked hill—a suit of flayed skin.
Houses stacked up until they lean together
in corbelled arches at the top.
Suburbs devastating as ever.
Freeways agonizing at our backs.
An accident on the road to the ruins.
Man with a cross of blood on his face.
People stand around, jolly—
fastened to the holy configuration. People everywhere
attracted to such places. People of all races
take their fingers to the maps to these places.
X marks the cross on which Spaniards put the Savior;
Aztecs, the sun. Floating city of San Francisco
and Mexico City founded on a floating garden:
blue-artery trees, sanguine-veined flowers
Montezuma oversaw on banks of human salt.
Diego Rivera moved in both cities.
Where he moved, gigantic promise sprang.
Around this floating man, fingertips of the living
made inanimates move. He saw two cities together,
two countries—the North and South American continents,
one. Around him, tongues slithered
sinister utterances: "Do not let him paint this picture
in our city." Nelson Rockefeller told Diego
to remove a bloom from Creation.
Picasso knew better, Matisse knew better:
did not let pigment from their fingers for the man.
Diego weakened to trust but refused
to remove Lenin's face from life.
Rockefeller paid Diego off, ordered the finished tropic

smashed.* This, the vice president of this country;
and in the other country, the president allows people
shot in the streets who are unhappy they cannot belong
to the living. The poor. There is evidence
they are everywhere. In Diego's murals, beside
Rockefeller's face painted in in the mural Diego
repainted in his own country-the mural Rockefeller
"murdered" by remote control in this country.

172 The poor. Rockefeller, there is evidence—.

"Holocaust in Rockefeller Center," an account of
Rockefeller's destruction of Rivera's mural is in
the painter's autobiography, *My Art, My Life*.

RAPID-TRANZITLAND

The snake running beneath the Bay
 Is sacred,
   for it saves money & time
     & gas & oil;
       and when they drill
         for offshore oil
       and accidently hit
     the ruptured end of it,
they will say they have found
the Loch Ness Monster,
black as struck oil.
 It left its lake in Scotland
   by commuter tunnel joining
     Laplanders to Piccadilly Square
       in the flash of time
       flick of tongue
       takes.
         The Loch Ness Monster,
         tired of electric shocks
       sent down to find it,
       decides to migrate
     to the Bay beside the City,
   courts the two bridges
and could not make up its mind
which is more beautiful.
Both lady bridges
died in the earthquake,
 but the Loch Ness Monster
 now lives in the sky
   overlooking Quintana Roo.
   Californians always were quirky

From *Woman Explorer*

and believed anything
before anyone else
knew it was true.
They've renamed the monster
"Quetzalcoatl"
because he's half snake.
The snake flies
in their sky.

How else could it be up there
if it didn't have feathers?
And so, Californians
worship Quetzalcoatl
to reassure themselves
they're there
and to keep Quetzalcoatl on high,
which Quetzalcoatl
is happy to do.
His tail regrew,
and they don't need any subways
in their submarine place.
They simply float about
the sunken gardens
of ex-supremacy.
Back on land,
people of other states
still imitate the fallen place,
have a highly developed
rapid transit system,
and dump all the cars
in the sea.
That's where Quetzalcoatl,
son of Kukulcán,
serves the people of Quintana Roo.
In his godly way
he shoves scrapped cars

aside. Soon
they form an island of rust.
Once a year, Yucatecos
  slow-motion over to its base
and praise the feathered serpent
for piling those cars up
so perfectly
they will not fall over.
  Select Yucatecos
  climb the pyramid of cars,
    and as they reach the top,
    their heads lift out of water.
      They die there
        In sacrifice
        to the coming year of cars,
          for their lungs
          have adapted to water.
          No Californian lives
          without a gill.
      The survivors of the quake
      started out with snorkels,
      but Quetzalcoatl taught them
      the joys of inhaling water.
    Someday the pyramid
  will become too high,
  and unless Quetzalcoatl
makes the heap of scrap iron
lean another way,
Quintana Roo will be crushed
under auto metal.
Californians live
  as best and well they can
    under precarious burden
      of cast-off cars
        by their side—

the very cars
their ancestors
built and sold
beyond belief.
Most acts in the past
were done in the name of Avalanche
who inhabits
the land above sea.
It was her footsteps
made the thunder
that made California break off.
Avalanche laid eggs called
nuclear power plants.
The first one hatched
in a puff
that made the earth
open up.
Out of Avalanche—
Avarice, son of Avalanche,
brought an end to California.
That is how
the Loch Ness Monster
lost its tail and became
pie in the sky for
brine-laden people
set among seasquid mist
and hoarfrost fish,
who call themselves
Yucatecos
and founded their first city
called Quintana Roo
where Avarice
could not reach them
but affects them nonetheless.
Leakage from other eggs

seeps into the water;
soon water will be
deathly to breathe.
Even Quetzalcoatl will die.
Then the ex-Californians
will move On.
That is why
they're building spaceships,
imagining signs in the sky
from Kukulcán,
father of Quetzalcoatl.
No use sending Quetzalcoatl
to fight Avarice.
The latter's seeds
are already planted.
His destruction will be fertile
a million years.
So the Yucatecos
live for every minute
ticking away undersea,
worshiping the serpent,
and worrying about
the junkpile next door.
Next thing they knew,
inhabitants of Nevada
were throwing commuter cars
onto the pile of cars,
replacing them
with something faster
and more expensive.
Or had the people above
gone back to the land
to live simple
like the Californians
of Quintana Roo?

All in all,
it is all long hope
　　in a little while,
　　for they say Earth
　　　will return to the serpents—
　　　children of Avarice
　　　　and Avalanche.
　　　　　But first,

　　　　　that pyramid of American autos
　　　and commuter cars
will topple,
creating a tidal wave
　　at Nevada;
　　　and everyone will say
　　　it's because of Howard Hughes,
　　　Nevada landed next to California,
replaced its casinos
with caryatids,
　　eked out a living
　　on a limestone bed,
　　　grew crude rope
　　and drank from a barbed plant—
ecstacies of which
husbands
of tequila widows knew.
　　Nevadians' lungs
　　　soon converted
　　　　to gill living.
　　　　They saw their wrongs
　　　　　and cleaned their houses
　　　　　and changed their clothes
　　　　　　four times a day—
　　　　　　　and wore pure white.
　　　　　　Beside Yucatecos,
　　　　　Mayans lived and shared,

grew wise,
and worshipped the ex-
   Loch Ness Monster overhead.
   A new pyramid was started
      beside them
      made of bodies of those
      who had succumbed to
      nuclear power leakage.
   And they took Howard Hughes
      to the summit
      and impaled him there.
   Others they took up:
   Liz Taylor,
 who was visiting Nixon
 when the tidal wave came;
 those bad golfers
 Frank Sinatra, Bob Hope,
Sammy Davis, Gerald Ford.
   They rendered their fat
      for use in lamps undersea
   to remind people
 of the end of Avarice.
 & tho that beast
   yet roams the land
   above the sea,
      the creature
      is yearly
diminished,
   thank Quetzalcoatl.
   Quickly now, people
      catching on faster
   than streamlined trains
 of the Bay, make
 history into poetry.
   Say it in the signs

over the straps
   of the fast riders.
      Gerald Ford
         said we could learn
            from Red China.
         Learn from your
            Mexican brothers and sisters:
            give the government
         of the people,
      the oil. Give Rockefeller
      social security;
         he's 66.
         Thoughts finally arrive
      at realization
      that furtherance
   of Bigfathers
was fate of all our effort.
Greed is no more innate in us,
Diane Wakoski, than war—
though the seeds of it
   are well into the land,
      now that they are
         in the soil.
      O Quetzalcoatl,
   let us live out our days
   without Avarice visible.
Keep the slow creeping thing
   at its lowliest.

CARACOL*

Let us build
a pyramid spreading
ray in this country's city
see if there won't be a run on pyramids
Not a volunteer pyramid not a slave pyramid
Not a paid one but a soul pyramid a true pyramid
good as Chicano Think what we would learn from
Egyptians' triangles in the sky Pyramids of Egypt
upon us Let's make it Mexican style a little uneven
a little medieval Mayans had their high while Europe
had its lights off Mayans stayed in the sun polished
it up every night How they dreaded to let love out of
sight We don't have to prove we have hearts It's in
there bumping City of Solid Poem let us build a pyramid
of seven tiers and call it "Where the Magician Lives" Make
the mountain hollow and call it "Beloved Hunchback" Put a comb
of jewels on top called "Lascivious Moongoddess" Let us have a
step for every book read and a falling off place every day Lay
snow across for the Hermit Let the blond sunpowered Fool be me
Let the sun over the edge let stone cut it into a living thing
Look up at the light and say Light I love you Love Let sun light
cities spreading ardor round this town Look out our foreheads'
temples' windows at all the heart around Keep the observatory so
open anyone can be alone with a lens system of trees each leaf
makes a tiny print on earth of bird Windmills churning the Mexico
of our souls Old wells stirring bones of those who died for no
Colorwheels of aureoles evince the mind's Rosetta In colororgan wind
let us build the invisible every layer nearer let us build a pyramid Begin

From Woman Explorer

*To read the poem, find a stone that "feels right"—large enough to just fit the hand.
At the poem's conclusion the stone is to be lifted in one hand into the air and let down
just hard enough to make the floor or ground at the site of "Caracol" sound—but not
hard enough to do damage. Leave the stone where you placed it.

LOVE IS A TEMPLE OF TURTLES

Pull a lock-o'-blond hair in Mexico for luck;
what luck, free-to-care poet on a trip
should love a starling.
Wish well, April of Mayans
setting fields to their fires.

Are Mayans not birds going about business?
All of us leak albumen; everyone eats eggs
as starlings nip suet from feeders.
I well wish bird suck monthly egg I drop.
Luck-o'-love poet after intense naturalness:
Blackhaired starling, dart center of intent;
iridescent darling, needle through to sun.
Sky smoulders color of starlings' innate
smokiness.

Birds up north agitate a mating,
tamp cotton nap and nest straws
while Mayans set brush fires
to make the stone turtles of Uxmal sweat.
Call naturalness of intensity "luck"
and sweat of immobile turtles "tears."
Tears are rain, iridescent and sudden
as shadows over turtle eggs, some taken.
Care-to-free Easter here,
children out seeking colors in the grass;
Dangerbird, put thy lips to my beak and draw
in eggshell sky of that turtle of temples. t
                                     o
Love, O love's carapace rainbow— r
                                 a
forever falling upward deck-o' - T

182

Fire-Rimmed Eden

return to the lost land
of quintana roo

TEMPLE

You came to me in a dream by you—
you had a pyramid in the middle of your chest.
That single-centered orb
     had the power
     of a third eye.
When I lay by you—there were two.
I wondered where the third went.
In dream you came by me—
I kissed your pyramids and observatories;
     sequestered,
encapsulated in the sweetest chamber
ever orbited.

From Woman Explorer

THE BONEBODY JUNGLE

A poet must eat
a dog and a cat.
Aztecs ate themselves:
how they disappeared.

Quicksilver cat
squeezes in and out of
the apartment
like a thermometer drop.

The dog narrows
at squirrels in the park.
What good is a squirrel?
If you can't catch

'em, you can't eat.
What to do—
cook a dog and a cat?
the cat's endless belly

and the dog with pet worm
that eats half the food.
Hunger has made its home
in my heart.

Feel its feather duster
shoving furniture-lack
around in there.
It goes up and down

my body like a tree.
Monstrous rodent

hoarding hard lumps
in my heart—

not fit food
for dog and cat and poet
to sink in our teeth.
The squirrel's

not doing well
in a winter
that's already autumn,
but works away.

Body hints
at graveyard.
The poet's bonejungle
body articulates

how little
separates us
from animals
gnawing a hand.

TEMPLE OF THE DWARF

Bought a mop from a blindman
for twice as much as in the store.
He looked so straight
and tapped so tall
I bought
the finest mop.
Crumbs glommed to it
in the dark. It meant
good luck like when
I bought my Mayan hat
from the hunchback in Mérida.
A string went around
so any hat
fit every head.

The man who walks
head higher than his eyes
better be blind
or it won't come true.
What a wish
is privilege
to play with here—
to believe a hunchback
good luck, make
double sanctity
out of the both
crippled and blind.

The hunchback,
the one with more than luck,
sells so many hats,
he's well-to-do.
Would you trade
the blindman's height,
strands of mop
borne erect at his shoulder
for straw of hunchback's hat—
the role of Munchkin
in an Aztec movie—
the distinction
of having a pyramid
named after you?

CHICANOMACHO

Don't
treat me
like that woman
going about claiming
she's direct descendent
to Montezuma and Cortez. Don't

point your penis at me because
Cortez cheated on Montezuma;
resulting in a quickie-
divorce. The world
is bellyful
up.

IN LAND OF LIVID CHILIES

The
Mexican
government
will
not
rep
air
the
ten-foot
penis
sticking
out
of
the
ground
at
Uxmal
because
it
is
an
embarrassment
to
the
Land
of
Walking
Penises.

RITUAL

They made the sacrificial victim

wear wings   wings drooping

further   and further

the higher   he climbed.

A great   featherweight.
To touch ground meant "all free!"

AT UXMAL THEY ARE

Rebuilding a pyramid
one block at a time   carried up on
     the head of a stonesturdy Indian.
     While he goes up,
his double comes down;
both heads busy   with
     when day is done.
     Neither looks down nor up;
stepsaws   by heart.
60 lb. blocks on their heads
     give them bearing of priests
     burdened with feathers.
Where impositions pivot,
they move their
     millstone skulls
     in pillar state.
Their necks   serve
as altars for the brain. Sweet
     beehive brain's forced dormancy.
     Circumstance   balancing on the
ball of foot. Civilizations
opening in their sleep.

ADULT EDUCATION

I couldn't take a class in self-defense for women because
I couldn't bend over and touch my knees. Class was held
in a gym where sweat reminded me of standing in the shower
with my clothes on, the water running (because a shower was
compulsory) but never touching. (I didn't want anyone
to see my barely breasts.) C for attendance and deceiving
P.E. teachers with suspect cropped hair. I couldn't take
beginning Spanish because it was held in an ex-high school
building with green walls, and the teacher made me know I

knew I was slowest. F for not attending. F stands for
Fine-with-me. I already have bachelors, masters, and 3rd
degrees. When I teach English, the only lack of freedom
will be *no cacique** in class. "Cacique" does not mean
"no army pants for women." In Spanish, a cacique is a
ruler. It's not that he knows too much. In English in my
class, a cacique is a man who dominates conversation and
other things. What if a woman dominates the conversation?
An A for favoritism.

Fire-Rimmed Eden

*In this poem "cacique" is to be pronounced "khaki"

MAYAN LOVE

Squeezed dry,
you told me
in your way
you loved me

(Access to the body royal,
rivertide slakes bitter.)

How could I love an utterly
an utterly
udderless lemon
in a falsie onion Way.

(Don't want your money, Honey,
It's not a Mayan's way.)

From *Woman Explorer*

IF YOU SEE FAYE KICKNOSWAY, TELL HER

Where I go, poetry goes. You can't tell me
Mayans are not so exotic as to be extinct.
I have to make up their kingdom to go with it.
I mean, how to carry on exotic stories with
enemies of Mayans if they're not known?

I'm mean. Where I go, poetry goes.
Into the forest, body crouched in encroachment
where woodhairs spit rainbows back at the frog
of my croaking sores and victory happens
in certain light and only in California.

On the other side, you miss everything so
busy swipin' at me with those duodenim eyes
and pointed nostrils sniffing out the viable,
capitulating symphonies at every wipe. In false wound,
I play dead in the blood of my rainbow.

Whistling César Franck from fortifications
of airmade suspicions, my watchtowers are a
cacophony of imagined forays into enemy camp:
sneakin' out the back, lookin' over shoulder;
their swords like a bundle afire on my back.

Clouds over head are boulders' testimony
of my defeat. They'll be stampin' among
intaglio in their tents tonight, snortin' dust,
fingerin' exotic instruments while I imagine
offenses, swoon on paradox. The Happy Martyr.

Do not tell me imagination is not exotic and
does not exist. When I create love so esoteric

you can't see it—give her my name.
Where I go, poetry goes. 'Tis my namesake.
When I wee, poetry tinkles, whole toilets mate

in orchestration complicated as Mayan counting—
and as treacherous and as real, among you,
Humdrummers 'n Dreamers. Where I go,
poetry swells of piss n' vinegar. Dingbell
aura of yellow sounding bullfume out de pores.

Where I go and when I go, poetry perspires
like hiccupping green wristwarts of a non-smiling
Swede with her wild Mayan goose drives 'em
nonexistent into the city of the moment of the
Mayans. In a certain only California light.

                    Signed,

                    Suit o' Swords

AZTEC SATURDAY IN GOLDEN GATE PARK

Happiness is sitting in the sun on a park bench.
I'm honored some black women sit down beside me
talking about putting gumbo in a plastic bag.
They start to talk to me while a spider trembles
on the edge of a page I'm on about Aztec ritual.

One woman is from Louisiana: Baton Rouge.
"My father grew up fifty miles from there." "Really?"
A white man comes along with a Great Dane
that gets in a fight with a great Irish Setter.
My dog gets in it too, little lump in the clay.
We crash from the bench. Snapping, snarl
entwined furies spread us apart. The woman

with the red dog has a chain, is able to pull
him away. I re-leash my dog. You would think
the man would take hold of the choke collar
of the Great Dane, but he wants to show
how well he can control his dog with his voice.
They dash away—gone. Happiness settles
back on the bench, but it's not the same.
The spider's vanished or smashed. The man

with the Dane jogs around in a giant circle;
which means he comes right back to us with his
monster when he didn't have to. I hold my dog
and shout at the man, "Arrogant, aren't you!"
He smiles and shouts something I don't hear.
He names me "Babe." Then is he gone for good?
If I could only have said it then, I would've:
"Without a big dog, how big would you be?"

The women and I share our disgust of the enemy
who has shot us with adrenalin and wrecked
parkbench comfort of sun benchwarmers want.
Even a Great Dane is a victim of such men who
use their dogs for their penises. A Dane

is a great animal—as any animal is—and
should be allowed to remain. A great place
for Danes is in the country—country cousins
instead of city enemies of my dog who had a
hard time adjusting to letting out his little
shits on cement. The place for such men

is beyond my vocabulary. Persians built a city
for murderers, walled them in together,
facing themselves in everyone around.
I go back to Aztecs with savager heart.

A MAYAN IS A KIND OF OFFICE WORKER

Mayans have entered the City of the Moles
through a mousehole in the side of stone
and are reassembling the possession of parades
of movies of sundown over our eyes.

Background bakes; sun sinks in. A writer is
an office worker, underground. A Mayan is
a kind of chocolate butterfly you won't like.
The brain is the best organ music in town.

When the Mayan goes looking for her heart—
thought, imagination, ideas see out from
cinemas of love against corduroys of clerks.
Mayan Walt Whitman hung up his strange shoulder

alongside brains' folded bumbershoots.
Mayan writings of Paul Goodman, Susan Sontag,
Hannah Arendt, Bertrand Russell, I. F. Stone
are world alive. (How did they live their lives?)

Keystone of the shoulderblade is a working head.
Why is wisdom Mayan? A Mayan stays sane
by interpreting Moles in terms of Mayans,
by being Mayan all the time.

A Mole remains an office worker. A Mayan is a
kind of chocolate butterfly savored to the taste
of writings on the tongue: why wisdom is Mayan.
The sexiest organ of the body is the brain.

THE MAYAN STREETCAR

In San Francisco
the streetcar
with letter X on it
is the Mayan streetcar.
It only picks up Mayans
and an occasional Aztec
from Los Angeles.
See them skimming
the tracks of Market Street
with sacrificial instruments,
all that zigzag of color,
pulled-back hair,
and eyes the insides of
bottomless wells;
double-vision peering
out at tripling buildings;
remarking to each other
in chocolate language
concerning strange going-ons
out there in space.
X is the only streetcar
in town that doesn't
give transfers.
No one gets out
at corners.
A Spanish priest
once accidently
boarded the Mayan streetcar
and was tossed off
with his stomach
on a cord

From *Woman Explorer*

bouncing behind.
Perched atop the stomach
was a hooked-beak bird
with the insignia
of enlightenment
hanging from its neck.
Don't ever get on
the X streetcar—
they are riding
to the end of the line.

LAND OF LONGTIME-NO-RAIN

Part I The *Other*

Mayans
have landed in San Francisco.
Bubbles from rain.
skim down the alley

plastic spaceships
slide along.
No miniature people
pop out.

Mayans know
not to step out
in mind-dabbling
play of sequined rain.

Come out, Mayans, come out
of your closety
spaceships, enter
bejeweled ruin,

your Japanese
cameras flashing
at a native
in silvery sunshades:

close-up
of a mouthful
of pointy teeth;
the flighty creature

shows you
her motorcycle.
She bats *her* eyes.
You go for a ride

Wind capes up.
Something You have never
seen before
wings away in *her* eyes.

Smitten.
you escape to a tavern
where fake
angelmusic's playing.

Lynn, this is not
the only that is all.
Do not lose
sight of sound of rainfall

at the edge of
Epicenthus.
Pattering
sewing machine

operated by
a blackhaired woman
related to Mayans,
right now in Chinatown.

A sound
drowned out
by other
sewing machines.

Rain
neither seen nor heard;
only felt,
walked out into.

Weary trek
on bent legs
to a little living space.
Peel back a Mayan

and what do you have
but a black-haired woman
who is hurting
all her life.

Part II Suggestion from Outer Space

What
the black-haired woman
and the glimmering
sunlit fairy array

(count me in)
and the Mayans,
and all others
of us whose money
is going away and not coming back—
could do
is STOP.

WORK.
LIKE.
WOMEN.
DID.

ONE.DAY.IN.FIN.LAND.
glimpse OUR STRENGTH
as it lands
in San Francisco.

Let *them* call us
Vampires.
Demanding
of appetite.

Part III How the Book of Women Began

A stranger
turned to
the Swedish Mayan
and said,

"I see
a female bible
by your side."
"Yes. The only thing

missing
is tenderness."
"Tell me of tenderness,"
the Mayan said
to the fey stranger.
Alike as Martians,
the stranger
could not

and continued
carrying in her
scared jeans
the migrant dream

of belonging.
The Mayan kept
asking everyone
of tenderness.

It grew in fragments
on the page
inside the eyelids
of transient eyes.

The scared woman
found out
she could write,
and the word

got around:
there was

tenderness . . .

And they spent
their lives revising
new, improved
female bibles.

the book of women

(After reading Susan Griffin's *Woman and Nature: The Roaring Inside Her*)

POPOL VUH
SACRED BOOK OF THE MAYAS*

From *Woman Explorer*

The poet waited a year
        It did not rain.
to know a woman
        from another place
It did not rain.
        of the sun.
Forty years not knowing
        she was learning
to edge
        the curved earth
of her fingertips—
        the bowl-juggling-
melody-woman waited
        (there were two)
With her scraper
        to scour the well.
The other women
        made a drawing
of lightning in clay
        It did not rain.
(There were three.)
        the slow tuning

of another's trails,
if they could
squeak like earthworms
                loop through
ground, move curds,
                make the hanging
silence
        pourous.

The lips of the soil,
                if they could,
open
        the day *it did not rain.*
(There were four.)
                Dry bundles knot
in slowly creatures'
                systems.
It did not rain.
                There were many
with dry mouths,
recite, blind
(There *are* many),
                if they could:
"There are no women in this
sacred book in my hand
but who hoist the burden of sunlight
like straw on their backs,
about to ignite."
)Men must become them.(

Chant,
        say in unison, "Like an earthquake
about to make a world, "
                whisper, "I am
become displaced."

       The
   slow
       turning
 of
       another's
tales.

*The deliverer of *Popol Vuh* is to wear this poem in front of her face, supported by some kind of elaborate headgear and not so close that her eyes cross, and she is to imitate the curve of parenthesis marks simultaneously (with right and left hands—hands raised at either side of the height of the poem) at places where they occur in her reading of it.

HISTORY OF WOMEN IN 25 MAYAN
WORDS OR LESS

Objectobjectobject
Ornamentornamentornament
Artifactartifactartifact
Diggingdiggingdigging
Kneedingkneedingkneeding
Grindingrindingrinding
Hurtinghurtinghurting
Togethertogethertogether
Huddlehuddlehuddle
Hubbubhubbubhubbub
Gigglinggigglinggiggling
holding water on their heads,
sling-draped foreheads holding
more of it, elbows holding bowls,
close, compact, centering,
Gatheringatheringathering
Searchingsearchingsearching
Burstingburstingbursting
Bloomingbloomingblooming
Learninglearninglearning
Luminousluminousluminous
Illuminatedilluminatedilluminated
Breakingbreakingbreaking
Changingchangingchanging
Makingmakingmaking
Celebratingcelebratingcelebrating
Rainingrainingraining
Recorded in San Francisco's Chronicle:
as I finish this the 28th and last
day of February, 1977, at 7:55 a.m.,
It started to rain.

MIME

I am the invisible conversationalist,
a female Pepe with the Cantinflas face
who falls foolishly, deliciously
in love with you.

Foolfunny crumbs on my face,
eyes colliding with
the pie of love,
the meringue look of Charlie Chaplin,
I clasp my cookie heart and can't talk.

From *Woman Explorer*

PORTRAIT OF FRIDA KAHLO

A schoolgirl,
she taunted
Diego Rivera
scaling the skeleton
lumber scaffolding
of vision.
She poured
water on stairs
so he'd slip;
he was too heavy
to fall.
She would not
take her eyes off
him as his mistress
glowered at her
as he painted
"Creation."
Newly wed, she dreamed
goodbyes to her family.
Years she was
on her way to
the City of the World
as she called it—
San Francisco;
went there
with him.

A woman, she stood
in front of him,
shielded him
from four assassins
so astonished they

could not shoot
nor move
her.
She nearly died
of many miscarriages;
her pelvis
fractured,
her uterus severed
in a traffic
accident.
She was determined
to have a baby
by Diego Rivera.
A painter, her body
felt
in a million pieces.
This is a tribute
to an unfrayed woman.
This is her painting:
FRIDA KAHLO
WAS NOT AFRAID.

BLUE IS THE COLOR OF SACRIFICE

All my life I have been a beginner painter.
I see red.
What to do with it?
I am awkward;
I don't make it good.

It keeps turning blue.
Certain men you say make you see red
redder.

Our sight tempered
by our different lives as an artist.
You turned the color of feelings, painter,
into words.
And I agree with you:
red is a favorite color
when we both see blue.
Anger is an art
women are working on,
to name the painting red
but know it is men.
Such combinations
do not cancel themselves.
Sacrifice and rage
are peculiarly together.

The end pages of my new book
are purple.
Among Mayans old
as limestone,
purple meant zero;
meaning, my book speaks
of old days when

hermaphrodites abounded
and red and blue made black.
To paint the right picture
takes all my life.
I am a beginning painter
who wants to be a real painter:
Mary Ann Hayden who
on March 2, 1977, let people know
she did not like typing misogynist words,
but had to, to work.

Write the spreading
dye of the purple mollusk's
death.
Tell of invisible hermaphrodites
and women,
rainbows lilting from their lips.

WATER

We watched a movie of Mayans waiting for water
while liquids rain in us in touch with the sun.
Men going out and not returning while we swallowed
our popcorn. Women and children brushing against fire,
eyelids roasting like pages of holy book, and our eyes
puffed and our cheeks dried. Leaders huddled with oracle.
He consulted the inside of a dried-up rabbit, couldn't
tell a thing. Nuggets of corn stuck in our teeth.
They said it was the one that must be gotten rid of—
that wasn't the charm; they killed many that weren't
the one. We say it is sunspots forcing hundred-mile
fireballs up in Azores; sinuses' dry canyons,
saliva receding, tongue stuck out in salt. Speech kaput.

Joints rasped, muscles clamored, eyes screeing in
their sockets, blood peaked at the nostril. I fell asleep
from this dream. A sleeve nudged: the promised rain.
The magic man took his own heart out of himself; it lied.
It didn't happen, the man they thought wise. Hard life
it came, montage the rain in banks in hail in drain;
douzzled fires, drove dirt down gulleys of gladness
heaped up in tear-caked rivulets. We women watched rain
all through the theater, felt discomfort. Popped corn
dropped on the floor. We rose, relieved it wasn't us
walking out under a cinema sky overlooking something
unreal, unbroken night after night, stars like kernels of corn
Opening up in a glowing everdark field, unending of blue.

Fire-Rimmed Eden

THE AVON LADY STRAIGHTENS HER FACE FROM AGING OF SPANISH ACCENT

Grandmother of the sun,

beanshaker carver   of green stones   jeweler engraver

sculptor wrapt   cabinetmaker   she who fashions

green or beautiful plates, she who makes green vases or gourds

powdered smells   scent   Ms. Smith who fashions silver

with a hammer   her mouth and eyes   worn of wood

Rainface   cornshaker sunrise   grainshaker: sing :

completion

The woman of wood glows   obsidians

From *Woman Explorer*

                                        Sunperson
                                        raps on objects
                                        changes shape

The granddaughter of the dawn   grown lately

her Spiderweb skin tells of precious lines the sun placed there—

                    the windswept overhead,
                    the wisdom of that last woman
                    of a tribe being founded.
                    Thy reigning face of knowing!

THE MOMOL VUH

From
        the first day of spring
    on page 88 of *The Momol Vuh*
                    from pg. 88 of Delia Goetz
        &
Sylvanus G. Morly's *Popol Vuh* from the English from
the Spanish from the Latin from the Quiché. Into French.

Fragment

Languages-get-together women
of new-word-eliciting
   gathering a thronging at the pipehole
  of that first woman Dawn
She touched Gloria
    and the applesky shone on them
   Mixed they call to the others
 in spreading light
they liven and name
Earth earth

Yesterday Swallows Today

Yesterday swallows
from Argentina
entered eaves
in a once-a-year language
of wings entering flutes.
Expectations
fluttertongue
a California town
dotted with swallows.

Nahuatl* words'
Featherworking
entering under
Spanish tile.

*The Aztec language

OLD WAYS

Old ways
are no place
to begin. Liberation
is not Tehuantepec.

In wisdom a woman
puts her same
finger to the map,
and the place is new.

HEART OF HEAVEN

Is the human heart
once removed
from itself.
Worn by women
best. And some men
lately more.
Stems and
pipes
and
pumps
and
blood
and
loving. most.
and caring.
tend. removed.
brought back
and thrives.
Mouth to mouth
ourselves.
Of molt.
and bone timbre.

OBSIDIAN WOMAN ON A GREYHOUND

She looked like a chattering bird so hunched,
so much the "little old lady," I hesitated to sit
beside her; decided why not—am I ageist or something?
She was reading a newspaper, didn't say anything.
I spoke first. She answered she was going to
Medford to her brother's, went on with the news,
alert eyes behind glasses, perched on every bit of it,
even the sports page.

She knew the migrant workers in Europe book
I was reading of the oppressed in Switzerland.
She pulled out Mark Twain's *The Mysterious Stranger*
and read for as long as I read. When she started
Lysistrata, I knew this was no little old lady.
"Where you from?" "San Francisco." "I see you're
reading *Aristophanes*. I did not expect to sit
on the bus next to someone who likes literature."

"Yes, well, my husband is a scholar—just for fun.
I'm not into it as much." "You must have had a
college education." "No, I've always liked to read.
My husband and I have marvelous arguments—for fun.
I should say, 'we discuss'," she laughed—"and,
if you could take only five books to an island,
What would they be?" "Moby Dick," I floundered,
"Emily Dickinson, Shakespeare, the Bible—Diane Wakoski."

Mark Twain was one she named; his cynical one banned
all those years. We got off the bus at some place.
I wandered toward the stores, heard this most loud
Whistle I didn't turn to see. There were fresh men
on the bus—on the street? Wasn't me they were

whistling at—hardup smalltown men. I heard it again
and turned to see the Grey Power woman whistling me
back to the bus.

"Where did you learn to whistle like that?"
She stood uneven in her flower pattern dress, canary
coat, bent-over back, shoes taking shape of her feet.
"When I was little. Isn't it great? I always wished
I could whistle as loud as my brother through his teeth,
but I had to use two fingers. I plant them
to the sides of my mouth like this." She never
talked much; she talked wisely.

I talked more. What she knew flowered from her like
eagle flight. She was the perfect companion for me
if she weren't married to a man who owned the perfect
library. She said she wished she had worn her jeans
and shirt, hadn't a dress on in a long time, it's a
bother. She went back to *Lysistrata*. I interrupted
to tell her my fears about sitting next to a talkative
person on the bus—

that I had informed a friend that morning that
I wished I could reserve the seat beside me for an Aztec
or a Mayan. She told me she had Visited the Mayan
exhibit at the 1933 Chicago World's Fair many times,
and what she remembered best was obsidian; and that
I didn't look forty years old—I looked twenty-five.
And she asked me to tell her what I knew about Mayans—
and *oh my*!

SISTER JUANA INÉS DE LA CRUZ

For Frances Jaffer

Part I Colonial Mexico's
        Poetess Laureatess

Teach me to read;
don't tell Mother.
I will surprise her;
I am three.

Mother won't dress me
in schoolboy guise.
Thank God
for Grandfather's library!

I cut lock of my hair
for every fact not learned
for I am a scholar
not wanting beauty.

Beauty's in books;
the bride of God's
Cell fills up with
scientific experiments.

Lute, flute, easel,
Cookbook: married
to the clutter of learning—
They take these away.

Books are gone;
I become sick

from it. They bring
my dear things back.

I settle arguments
between nuns;
interrupt study to
word rhymes for church.

I Wrote the Bishop
to question
that women not
question men.

The Archbishop
and all the superiors
told me none of my
mind's business.

I rid myself of books,
my cell of instruments.
To learn is a sin
I sign in blood.

Never another book!

Part II Mt. Popocatépetl

To cross those ridges,
create these passages
is that lovely
sister learning.
    "Sister" in Spanish
    is "Sor." Sor Juana Inés.

As a child
she could see

one of Mexico's
highest mountains.

Aged forty-three,
our sore poet
attended nuns
suffering plague.

A mountain symbolizes
asexual learning.
In Mexico,
death is feminine.

  It is hard
    to pronounce
an exploding mountain
snows lie over
like the buried learning
of Our Sister of the Cross.

Part III Tehuantepec
    and Beyond

  In Tehuantepec
  the women are taller

  and more handsome
  than the men.

  Should a woman
  put her finger
  to the map
  and never come back?

  Of Tehuantepec,
  Eugene Fodor's

Mexico says:
"It is a grubby place . . ."

"As a village
Tehuantepec stands
as a great argument
against women's

liberation."
"The women . . .
howling at each other
in the foulest language."

"Tehuantepec is a great
disappointment." (It means
a man wrote it.)

In the index of Carl Franz's
The People's Guide to Mexico
under *Women*
it says: *see Girls*;

under *Girls* it lists:
travelling alone, body
searches, in cantinas,
whorehouses.

In Tehuantepec
women dominate men.
". . . the girls climb up on roofs
and hurl fruit at the men below."

ladyland ownerlord

QUINCUNX

Symbol of move><*meant for women
who inherit land after their
husbands who owned maguey plantations
drink themselves to tequila deaths.

Drunk on cactus or female succulence,
leave Death behind, my darling,
ride with me into the new fold
of the maguey stalk.

Partly sad "tequila widows" with
lots-o'-change; protected plants
spread eternally green fire
from which spiny liquids drip.

Ride with me off guarded ranches
where once a spark of flower smiles out
an endless century and after your whole
system of barbed brilliance is given up.

Your salty wrist caught in time!
Bottle got a worm; the best,

* This symbol is hand-drawn in the original book.

From *Woman Explorer*

my darling, fortunes twist.
Together fighting gladly free of twiny
fences and ropemade fleshly leaves.
Drunk on intelligence, ride with me,
my darling, into ensuing action
of the unfolding maguey's

      spikes)   (labyrinthine

          H

          e

        Heart

          r

          t

      of)   (formation.

EAST OF THE AZTECS, WEST OF THE MAYAS

A Country Lies North in Shrouds

Know California is an island of black Amazons catching
conquistadors and feeding them to lion-footed sphinxes
with eagles' wings and women's heads that bite armor,
spit out bitterness like bullets, and pick their teeth
with the swords of conquerors. A 14th century Spaniard
no sooner wrote a book about it than many a conquistador
set out and disappeared.

                                    Enough men
were kept on the island to keep the population going.
The base metal was gold. Gold bracelets, gold cages,
gold griffin collars. My gold car aimed onto gold
pavement out of estranged Los Angeles, fireballing down
gold vistas, foot on gold gas petal while gold radio
plays gold memories, "I Jus' Wanna Go Home."

From *Woman Explorer*

THE WOMAN WITHOUT A CITY

Egypt is Mexico, the golden-hearted queen-o'-Californee
discovers mixed skin of cities' north star; gold city of
all skins, heart steers. San Francisco is only one stop
in a year's poetry set aside to learn Spanish. Sailing
out of the city of lost angels, she gives different
pronouncement to all that passes: words' "musica poética"
zing. Tingle like gold promises on skysigns orient us:

San Diego*	Salsa
Buena Park	Honda
Bolsa Ave.	Loyola
Los Alamitos	Sepulveda
Palo Verde Ave.	Marina del Rey
Santa Monica	Pacifica Hotel
San Gabriel River	Montana Ave.
Los Santos	Moraga Dr.
Los Cerritos	Ventura Blvd.
Atlantic Ave.	Sacramento
Alameda St.	Ventura
Santa Fe Ave.	Van Nuys
Pasadena	Reseda
Ford Granada	Panorama
Pepe Lopez Tequila	Mission Hills
Dominguez Hills	Balboa Blvd.
San Pedros	Sylmar
Del Amo Fashion Square	Mojave
Gardena	Pico Canyon Rd.
Redondo Beach	Valencia Hospital
Hermosa Beach	Santa Paula
El Segundo	Val Verde Park
Olmeca the Head Tequila	Casa Royale
Gaetano Margarita & Daiquiri	Mission de Oro

La Cienega Blvd.   Café José
La Tijera Blvd.   Ft. Tejon Campgrounds
Ronrico Rum   Palomas Wash
Las Vegas   San Francisco

To name these, blood spilled over each. Years set aside
to learn a city's steps run red. To learn the world
in any language is to understand an explorer has no city.
To defuse power along camel-wedged years, she learns of
unions, multinationals, what work means, uses of women,
what servants mean. To turn a mountain of devils
around de-pyramid it, is journey essential, thought critical.

231

From *Woman Explorer*

*Give the Spanish words Spanish pronunciation.

THE MAYAN TAPE RECORDER

for Roma

There is inscribed on my heart,
"Owned by Mayans
 recorded by Mayans."

Metal is precious to work with
and takes a workmonth
to replace.

Soon, perhaps, metal
will be gone.
Mayans go so far

as to say a machine
is not a thing
but a person

with a name.
A tape recorder
is sacred,

Resonates
earwaves' exchanges,
's an artifact

of our time, more than.
a chip-off-the-old building.
I can hear futures'

"oohs," "ahhhs"*
over ancient jungles
of beetle transistors,

sea snail resistors,
solid-state hawks circling
o'er ruins,

plastic cruciform discs
rotated into shape
of movement of

clouds sounding like
gliding pearly seagulls
at dawn slowed down.

To use it up overnight
is economist Veblen's
"conspicuous consumption."

Last night I dreamed
we waited for the story
but the teller*

went into the woods
and did not return.
"The *forward* will not move."

Someday an archeologist
will find "Holy, holy, holy,"
on every heart

From Woman Explorer

*This line is whispered.
*The little girl who crossed herself before reaching into the cookie jar.

inscribed, that is gone.
"Holy, holy, holy,"
teethchant haunted waking

to the REALREEL
of the attendant
of the tape recorder.

234 *You are becoming*
a tape of history
recorded on bowls by women.

There is no abandoning
keeping pre-Columbians
alive.

MADE IN MEXICO

I am
my own
Mexican maid,
and I treat
her like
red hearts

on a pepper tree
that might not
produce
if you don't
tend them
just so.

I pay her with
shining gloss
surroundings,
and she can
stop.were.king.
anytime and

dwell on light
and distances—
the miniscule
in my
kitchen hold.
She works

extra
for nothing—
for a song.

Holidays,
I prime her
with candy

and rompope
and let her off—
not easily, but early.
Bent of my

Swedish shoulder

against
singing wheel's
happy turning
she rearranges
boundaries and
space, like

a cleaning
lady cleaning.
I own what I can
care for,
I care for

this maid.
By my
hands' ache—
hers,
in her own territory

and time
attend.
Diamonds,
faucets,
the muscle of
mind—

uncovered facets; hers,
new-to-me,
improve
mine.
The Mexicana

and I own
our own
land. How
the ground
feels, O and
the house

on it! she
flutters about,
her Swedish heart
opening up
to mariposas,
her privileged,

busy hands
alighting
flower chores,
exclaiming,
"Precious yellow-
hot morning

sweat
is mine
and sweet!"
I'm my own
Mexican maid.
She sings while

she works;
her own things

she's scrubbing.
I treat her as
I would myself—
exotically,

royally,
carefully as
dual monarch
butterflies
interlocked in
a garden afire.

When she
gets uppity,
we get uppity
together.
When she turns
on me, I

become a slavish
red pepper

glowing in a
dazzling house
demanding
things get done.

GILDA OF THE AMAZON

I had trouble
distinguishing you
from other blondes
in the movie.

What is that
with camera—
weighted neck?
A peculiar

twist to light
made natives
recognizable—
and you, a distant

lean stranger
signaling
by way of hair
a distinct village.

As if blondes
were towers
and bodies
were air bases,

Rapunzel
climbs down
with Amazon.
"With straw on her head,

what is she doing there?"
"Sprouting."

From *Woman Explorer*

"With gold on her head?"
"Slowing down."

"Something's
different about this one,"
(sed about blondes)
said Amazons,

whistling objects
in the sun—
and let her
in their design

to look backward
or through skin
scintillations O,
allowing loss of light,

a sunset glimpse
of again twin
flutes secreted
in holy hut

intoned
how blondes
found themselves
swinging their manes

flaring in shadows'
rippling arrows 'midst
bows of male bodies
scuffling.

A toss of light,
and you were all of

a forest of women
around the edge with

red-ant, ant-black hair
of blondes
haunted by people
they have loved.

Asserting swagger-
maze, *she*
climbs down
the amazed hatch,

unwinds flag
of the lopped breast,
the ^ quiver
of poised • mirror,

wood-stretched rainbow-
handles + cross—
Mexico'scape of Swedishcave—
sweet pitch of

off-colored hair
fit over like
arc connecting
histories draw again
eye
        ^-> hair ->
        •-> mirror ->
        +-> handle ->*

* In the original book, there are hand-drawn symbols on these lines.

matings.
In dust
from dance sweat,
blondes part air.

¡O *pilota*
chela blonda!
¡*Mechón de la mente!*

¡*Cabellera de la cerebra!*

¡*Tocaya de luz!*
¡*Asombrosa de la luz!*
¡*O corazón Amazon y*
cabeza heroica!

O familiar stranger from afar!
O gracing return! ¡*O astronautas*
a avistar en jungla!
¡*O sol y pájaro-mosca sola!*

Creo tu quiera me necesitar tu.
Quero tu, pero no necesitado tu.
Creo ésa es de cerca amor real
y por qué la idéntificación

con tu—porque conocemos
éstas cosas.
Blondes are treated
unrealistically like gods

see one pilot
of The Yellow Order
to the other as
they open banked clouds.

S.O.S. radio contact reports
United States inhabitants
having increasing
failing English

engine trouble!
Half Valkyries
holding up
California on their

cricket heads,
true blondes
come down
to gilded earth,

give Saint Teresa-type
flying! !lessons.
C O L O R S < A R I S E <
I N < C O R O N A S <

FIGHT OF THE WHITEBIRD
FROM MEXICO

They adulate your fledgling nose
in the color of another country,
Exotic Bird with split teeth
I'd like to plant gold between.
Your flight-rimmed iridescence—
your eyes' layers of azure hum—
your whelming feathers rise
and stir astronomers in persons.

Pilot of the single eye
at the side of the head
pivots above Earth, transfixes on
what catches, is caught championing
starchambers for children.
Breathless to dive, alight my
writing hand, ruffled windcreature
in your pride of motion, silverfright.

Adored Nordic return of farewells,
fear-to-the-quick colored Othertime,
Aztec Venus of longfunny name—
Scrambling Egg—Crawling Stomach—
Winged heartfall—tremor of birds
outside the window pull southward—
Quetzal! Quetzal! Quetzal!—
travel immortal . . . *In pale life*
                    they fly you
                    to Hollywood,
                    in a silver
                    of flight . . .

YUCATÁN BOUND

Mayans in boats won over China
by trading their eyes for scarves;
the Chinese tried out their English
on them and liked them.

While everyone else was eating,
you were filming
familiar people
eating foreign food,
sighting the continent of winding walls
mientras una china sonrio a tu altura:
while a Chinese woman smiled at your height.

In Summer's starry October auburn sky,
you held a camerawoman Chinawarm
and ocean baggage full of film.
The sun moved from spectator to participant
over tiled roofs of a Seattle
no longer the same latitude
as Manchuria and Mongolia.
Your ebony hair turned Autumn
your eyes became the Lord of the Dawn's eyes,
only quieter,
to make the movie human.
Tu película revela humanidad:
Your film reveals humanity:
your eyes more contained by fairness;
dawn devoid of lords.
The masses more hopeful
you held in film,
filmed foreigners eating food.

In Mexico, owls
are the message bringers
mientras en español atora en mi garganta:
while Spanish crows in my throat.
Like an owl with camera in your eyes,
you flew to the top o' the Wall, took
the temperature of the climate of the Yucatán.

In this our time: *how women lived—*
sailed away from darkling Mixtec eyes— —
into orb of light concentrate— — —
Quintana Roo! Quintana Roo!

CLITORIS LOST

Lynn Lonidier

Clitoris Lost

Cover of *Clitoris Lost* by Lynn Lonidier.
The cover is a computer-generated collage by Robert Berner.

The order of some of these poems has been modified from the original book.

CLITORIS LOST

a woman's version of the creation myth
a take-off on john milton's ordering of a heaven, earth, and hell

Finishing writing <u>Clitoris Lost</u> on the Eve of the two Great Powers' decision to share each others' land for future nuclear test sites as proof of "good faith"—turning caring people palpitatingly graven and keeping Christ from rising—the author dedicates this book to all feminist revisionist archeologists in every field and in-between, and especially to Marilyn French for her <u>Beyond Power</u>, a resounding tome for change!

Eastertime, 1987

<u>And in memoriam Karen* and Robert+</u> . . .

---

* Karen Brodine (1947-1987), Lynn Lonidier's cousin.
+ Robert Duncan (1919-1988).

"arguments"*

READING OF THE RATTLESNAKE

To Tina

Such a dangerous thing
for two women to do:
you sitting there translating
Spanish for me sitting there
—two squeamish women alone—
reading a theory about
how geometric patterns on
rattlesnakes' backs
were the foundation
of Mayan civilization.
You speak of people in Mexico
meting out land by the perfect length
of poisonous snakes; how Aztecs
settled on a bed of snakes,
got rid of the snakes
by eating them.
The book states pre-Columbians
read the stars by rattler designs.
I show you by flashlight

how the city shed its skin.
A Spanish street sign now reads,
"A Girls' Gang."
You tell me La Raza teenage girls
get together and design their own
low cars with their own
vibrant pipes, fanfare rainbow hoods,
fur-lined cave interiors.

And I tell you about the fifth-grade
girl matriarchy among Chicano-Latino
children where I work. O it's
a dangerous world slowly
being infiltrated by diamonds,
curving rectangles on the
rattlesnake's back. (La Curva
is making major decisions!)
I listen to your beaded tales
unwind a string o 'jeweled
heart-truths.
The shape of a bead of a rattle
is that of a heart; each one
proportionately larger in size,
like a pyramid,
like a city,
like sin.
Sin turns into quiet pets
on our laps. Loving words,
two women on a couch unflinchingly
touch pages picturing snakes.

CLITORIS LOST

When I'm with you, I feel like I'm with an eunuch
sitting at a table ordering food with you.
It's like each others' limbs we're ordering—
they ate. Two eunuchs keep finding new restaurants
to take each other to. When we paint the town
eunuch-red, I recall masses of Vietnamese people
in a mindfield thriving on poetry, not war.
Until recent times, the Vietnamese were obsessed
with looking for the right words for writing
forests of love feelings, rice paddies of honor,
prostitutes of chopsticks, ache of the missing
teeth of ancestral eyes. Poetry grew in a land-
'scape mined of tooth.

An eunuch who has lost feeling is a contagion,
a walking plague of sex; two eunuchs cannot
quite lose their feelings, just as somewhere
the Vietnamese still approach words reverent
as two eunuchs with all their feelings intact,
bottled up like poets in wartime, one poet
reaching to the other to say, "Just testing."
The other said nothing. Two eunuchs frozen
in causes. One who draws analogy with Vietnam;
one whose son may go to El Salvador. They hug and
they separate; the son and the mother; the poet
and the other, in a nation made wooden. "I'll never
speak to you again if you go to war." Eunuchs
write poems during war, which is, so far, always.

Two eunuchs is what it is like for one woman
to tell another, "I care. For you." The impact
strained as a shell-shocked planet of inhabitants

proceeding to a nuclear fate of mechanical chemists.
Two eunuchs who live in a land of the biggest
stick, grow fat eating restaurant food: two gross
Japanese wrestlers sent to America to pop.
What a match, circling one another, continuous
favorable positioning—one swollen "gay" woman,
one swollen woman "heterosexual" hugging one
another, swelled like American cattle,
our idea-laden tongues eyeing each other, pondering
what are women where are we when were they?—
clitoris lost in fire-rimmed Eden.

FEMALE IMPERSONATORS
AND HUMORLESS FEMINISTS

Out!Woman!Out

Throw the word   "woman"   out   It is a bag they inflate   that man
of womb   they stick fake hair on   that wooden fluff of viciousness
they swear is us   that sack with sex parts carrying around picture
of water   The dumb clothes fe(males) are seen in are   trappings
when you learn   they came from   the mailman

I laugh to be alive at men resurrecting idea of us from nightly
redeemed imaginings   They imitate dumb holes in clodhoppers   pawing
their way toward   animal stage of ridicule As if   the carcass of
cloth t'was Christ   how they strut at the promise of   cinched waste

I dare a man be me

Let female impersonators dress in men's clothes   research pre-
Mediterranean cultures   glean female history the likes of which
sends   them into falsetto   "Shake out this rag before the storm
breaks"   I want to see a man do more than   "put on"   I don't want

to be called Womb-Named-After-Man   I'd rather be me   a relaxed
transvestite   enactment of a female body alert to its mind   I want
to laugh and show life at scientists amazed to unearth women's
minds work faster and more accurately than men's   Purple Cow: Phone
Home

!In Intelligence Out!

A crone in the air   with no name   conducts with jest   a dish   a
spoon   a cow   the moon   All things   spilled   stay in the pitcher

fly   in the wake   of   mimicry   "Wake"   once meant   "humor"
"Humor" once meant   "moisture""fluid""wet""wake"   "Humor" now means
"adapt to or comply with the mood of another" 'til violence BECOMES

Yes Virginia There   Is An Utopia   In   a   sea   of   brainfluid
alight   a   lost   island   where   trace   of us   is   being
dug up   S(he) checks in at Intelligence Inn   carries her own bags
to a disquieting room papered with   whimsy of urns

256

CLOSE ENCOUNTERS WITH THE NETHERKIND

This poem was born in the wake of a man's fist
aimed at my face. *Paradise Lost*, he missed
and hit the doorway I stood in the frame of,
as hard as he could. The doorway stood;
I didn't blink. An excusing small woman
tried to restrain "Superstar." He pushed
at her, passed us on, threw a metal chair
at the room, kicked a metal wastebasket like
it was a football, and slammed and banged and
went on. Big Hero. Mover of Molecules.
"Preciousness" of the Fireworks Fellows
of Neverheaven. I left the room while
the patron woman stayed to lick his shuddering
at womanform. That was yesterday. Today
I call on his army—the police—a protection
of a joke—a formality in case he gets physical
again. I have a witness: the scared woman
who by clinging to my male co-worker deterred
him to keep him from hitting the target,
so far. Is whether he avoided hitting me
or missed hitting me a question For Blindness?
I heard when one is In danger one becomes
detached. I felt as an observer in the face
of a man's fist aimed at my wake, like
a black and white cork dartboard, mirror inside
a mirror inside a mirror showing fissure.
Caught in imposed history, a deer inside
a forest is dropped at the flicker-dent
of a finger like it didn't matter
I was the wastebasket; I stood as steel.

I feel dizzy thinking of him coming at me,
his grimace the face of a Contorted,
Gaping Ego; the Violent Home of My Job
at Close Range. Later, another woman, my boss
will say he's sweet and could not do such
a thing, and you have a personality conflict. (Or,
Death is a difference in style.) I'm the cause
of this man's killing ways, this thirty-year-old
she had planned to make a man. This Son of
a Policeman is smaller but stronger than I.
Irony is, I was angrier than he, and taller.
What's maddening is working around a woman
so competent, it's having a man for a woman
around: how he sees me. What pisses me:
four years he's fiddled and twiddled At Home
on the Darting Range of My Job. Ladyboss
lets him play; he trips me up at my work,
Think of us as The Drone and The Drudge.
The Infernal of His Glow, I provoked him,
but he devastated me. I was first and
hold my strength, and he knew it, and
that's why he is so afraid as to just miss
the infernal of his goal, and I know it.
How can I stand to work with the man?—
He's half creature; he believes women have
tails and are called mermaids. I <u>know</u> women
have tails and <u>are</u> monkeys. I am of
the Vulnerable Real Gorillakind. Wondrous.

"GO, SPEED THE STARS OF THOUGHT"

—Emerson

"Adults are like children and must be led." —Nixon

I found myself

I found myself accessory to people in a night of a roomful of sleep   259
knowing even   the people outside   could not move their heads
and wondering when my next poem would come I slept winter deep and
woke to the emotion of words that must have played a movie of
THE BRAIN in my night
                    I could say certain as morning: the brain
is not flat but round
                    My brain began to work as well as the best
brains I announced   to those I thought had the best brains   They
did not want to hear of   NEW WORLDS   They argued for hours
I saw them   illogical   myself   so sure   I took my brain
in hand
         like a globe
         to show them
                         "See the inching-up sail of a ship"
                         For these
nothing could horizons life (Silly Girl)   But I could not forget
vistas sighted   not beyond the curve of the earth   but in us

Years the years the years my poet's eyes could see beyond IQs and
otherworld maps hanging from stained ceilings and worn-out blackboards
Me the teacher   children just plain charting the truth for:
OUR BRAINS ARE CREATED EQUAL   CHILDREN THINK AND
                                        WRITE AND
IMAGINE
EQUALLY WELL until CUT OFF   at THE EDGE   of   FLAT   sea

Clitoris Lost

"In nature there's no blemish but the mind." —Shakespeare

if you cannot imagine your brain round( )

Think of intellect as a set of gold keys in your head (!!!)   Years and
years and years of keys in endless combinations   Yourself
in possession of entry   a five- hundred-year timely called
"Spreading THE RENAISSANCE Around" A GREAT AND
                                        DANGEROUS DISCOVERY:
                        intelligence
not unfolded in a simple act of genius like a napkin on a knee
but with a dust cloth   with the hardest work you've ever done
willingly in your life AND YOU WILL NOT WANT THAT WORK TO
                                                    STOP WHEN

THE SAILS SWING FULLROUND

        There is no such thing as the heritability of IQ,
        since heritability of a trait is different in
        different populations at different times. —Lewontin

The world's in our heads is the excitement!!!the freedom

A peopleful of room!!!is the REVOLUTION!!!MY BRAIN IS YOUR BRAIN
hopefilled!!!THAT EXTERNAL KEYS ARE NO LONGER
                                    NEEDED!!!gives life
to this room!!!It is REVOLUTIONARY!!!to begin the world with
your own poem
        THERE'S ROOM FOR EVERYTHING THERE IS TO KNOW
IN YOUR HEAD
        THE BRAIN IS NOT NARROW
but   o   c   e   a   n   i   c
The slowness of humanity is it has not acknowledged its INTELLIGENCE
the cargo in the hold
        The sea escorts delicately-painted figureheads
pretty but deathly-empty/ the rest of the ship follows

260

Fire-Rimmed Eden

in unconscious   hand carved journeys
Talk about children cheating: figureheads of inventors of IQ tests
who did mind-delineating research to further ambition (their own)—
there's books being written on how *THEY* CHEATED   IQ tests *are*
                    leaden-footed   administered
TO HOLD US DOWN
SCIENCE is now unearthing dinosaurs it thinks were quite intelligent
and moved faster than scientists dreamed!!!O LAMP OF LAND!!!SkulL
GLOWS!!!with ITS!!!MUSCLE THE ULTIMATE MUSE ALL MUSES   261
                                                AT ONCE:

        Calliope

            Clio

                    Euterpe

                        Melpomene

                                Terpsichore

                        Erato

                    Polyhymnia

            Urania

        Thalia
ART LITERATURE SCIENCE singtogether   Chant: Chorus: Clamour:
WE ARE THE MOVERS OF INTELLIGENCE INTO OUR EYES
                                        The forehead
is the mast
        (advantage)of(ship's peak)
        (unraveling)of(crow's nest)
Your hands
upon the polished wooden wheel pointing the mind housed by a ship
about to unload THOSE SHINY GLITTERING!!!THINGS!!!TAKING
                                            !!!SHAPE
IN OUR HEADS!!!OUR PRECIOUS!!!TONGUES!!!ARE
                            LEARNING!!!TO SPEAK
    O CHERISH SUNHIT BLACKNESS!!!PRISMATIC FEATHER(!)
    IRIDESCENT HUMANITY DARK AS CROWS THAT OCCUPY
                                        SHORES,
    THEIR SUNSPOT EYES CASTING FOR GOLD AND BEYOND

AND BEYOND THE SACRAMENTS OF BIRDS THAT
                                APPEAR BEFORE LAND———
WINGDIPPING———   ———HONOR THY BRAIN
a parrot   a rainbow   a virgin shoreline of parrots flexing their
rainbows

262

uncovery

APPEARANCE OF THE ARTIFACTS*

Archeologist Sir Arthur Evans huggled the Jugs
then photographed the 1900 A.D. positions
he found the 1200 to 8000 B.C. artifacts in.
He divested a temple of underground amazements—
design of a snake's back running along rainbow
architecture springing ripple effect upon
the Mediterranean; he wasn't bad—like
a halfway lover, mined women's history
city-deep in earth, like a divining rod
down to virgin rock, tapped place of worship
of the Goddess of the Double Axe; whereafter,
waist-cinched ladies oiled wheels of griffins
and King Minos kicked about.

Sir Arthur found a row of round clay disks
in the bathtub had picture-writing on them.
Cookie cutters, whisk brooms, and fish drawn
between a spiral-shaped line read from center
to edge or outer to inner—no one knows
one's own maze of ear. Sir Arthur believed
the library had fallen from the second floor
into the queen's bathtub. He saw pre-
Mediterranean culture in terms of royalty
". . . an English dinner party," and named
the place, "The Palace of Minos at Knossos,"
where snake invitationals were the rage.

He with a flair for rocks had male artists
fill in faint frescoes with images of Egypt.
Idea of books in a library on the second floor
landing upright in a row in the bathtub, was,
by later archeologists, smokedream of a pipe.
Keepers of the sacred, packing their trust,
grabbed armfuls of books then plunked them
into the tub for slight protection, caught in
ensuing tremor of abandoning how a British
gentleman put the Golden Age of Women
together again.

*From excavations on Crete, an island south of Greece's Peloponnesian peninsula.

A PAINTING OF LADIES' NIGHT AT THE GRANDSTAND TALKS BACK

Sir Arthur Evans says:

"Were these ladies perhaps pointing or beckoning to
favorite champions in the arena beyond?"

The talking painting says:

"They were pointing to lady bull grapplers
who threw their heels over their heads, gripped
the horns of bulls and allowed themselves aloft.
Even Wheaties of Champions, whispering in milk,
can't compete."

Sir Arthur Evans:

"The raised hand of the first lady being seemingly
indicative of surprise at what she is hearing."

The painting says:

"She's the one talking. Her hand
does acrobats of thoughts while she catches
breath for the next elucidation."

Sir Arthur:

"These scenes of feminine confidence of tittle-tattle
and society scandals take us far away from
the production of Classical Art in any Age."

The painting shows

Clitoris Lost

women absorbed in profundities like how to make
music of bodies and people, jewels.

Sir Arthur Evans:

"The body of the second is thrown slightly back
with her hand raised in front of her face—
she is quite shocked at the scandalous tale!"

The talking painting says:

"Her advance turned down by the other lady,
she's raising her hand in protestation.

Sir Arthur:

". . . gay Minoan ladies seated in animated conversation
between the piers and pillars of the Grandstand."

The painting takes a look at itself—
sure enough—there's the "gay Minoan ladies."

Sir Arthur:

"... far from being veiled their bosoms are at most
barely covered by a diaphanous tissue."

The painting ascertains from a dictionary:
"diaphanous" means "a see-through blouse."

Sir Arthur Evans:

"These Minoan ladies indeed seated in the interspaces
of the Grandstand present a marked contrast to the others
from the fact that, so far as these posts of honour
are concerned, there is no admixture of the other sex."

The painting's had it up to here with men.

Sir Arthur Evans elaborates:

"The men are treated in the most summary way,
only the head and neck with the surrounding collar
being rendered while their eyes are indicated
by mere dots."

"Artistic license,"
the painting surmises.

Sir Arthur deliberates:

"In the case of the women, on the other hand,
their complete figures are reproduced, whether seated
or standing, their eyes moreover are fully outlined, and
full details are given of their brightly coloured robes."

"Was I commissioned by women?"
the painting asks itself.

Sir Arthur Evans:

"The lively nature of the conversation between the lady
to whose coiffure this net belongs—and her neighbour
on the right at once strikes the eye."

"Shades of saffron!"
exclaims the talking painting, turning menstrual.

Continues Sir Arthur:

"The latter points her statement by thrusting forward
her right arm so as almost to lay her palm

Clitoris Lost

on the other's lap, while her confidante raises hers
in amazement. 'You don't say so!'—the sense of the words
can be supplied, though we may never decipher the language."

"A kind of communication peculiar to their day,"
the painting offers.

Sir Arthur continues:

"It suggests the intimate converse of two confidantes . . .
[The next pair] are engaged in a very close tête-à-tête
talk, the right arm of the second lady being laid
on the other's side as if to arrest her attention."

"Captivating thesbians of their day!"
the painting exclaims.

Sir Arthur Evans:

"On the other female figures or fragments of such
in this series, the bosoms regularly show two mere dots,
indicating the nipples. In contrast to this,
pendent breasts are here clearly outlined—a matronly
touch. May we venture to suppose that we have
a mother giving social advice to a debutant daughter?"

"Spare me!" the corrective painting responds.

Footnote:

Sir Arthur Evans has as the frontispiece of his Volume III
of The Palace of Minos at Knossos which deals with
the *Grandstand Fresco*, a painting of two women
with flounced skirts and sea-tossed hair, holding hands,
gazing into each other's eyes beneath a fresco of

blue dolphins beside spirals of pillars and
delicate urns arbitrarily set here and there
and drawings on the walls of lady bull dancers
and tender female caretakers of snakes. One woman has
the other set down her jug on the floor beside herself.
Two women gesturing, "Let's lie down together,
lovingly looking into each other's eyes beneath
'The Fresco of Blue Dolphins' beside spirals of pillars
and delicate urns arbitrarily set here and there
and pictures of pet snakes radiating out from the Goddess,"
say the two ladies beneath a fresco of blue dolphins
beside spirals of pillars and delicate urns arbitrarily
set here and there and paintings of lady bull dancers
and priestesses with flounced skirts and sea-tossed hair,
holding snakes aloft, say two ladies holding hands,
engagingly looking into each other's eyes
beneath blue dolphins . . .

Sir Arthur Evans says:

"Such lively genre and the rococo atmosphere here
bring us nearer indeed to quite modern times. . . ."

"Although the two women are nearly the same age,
'tis the scene of a mother planning her daughter's
Coming-Out party," the captive painting bleats.

INVOCATION

In Cretan cypress forest clearing   salt-heightened eyelid priestesses
away stark-eyed with snakes and tower heads   Skirts swallow wind
Breath of seasight rustles clitoris in anemone harmony

Farmlands smoulder artifacts   Men loosen dirt from conch shells : a
crystal vase : a clay dove : an ivory gaming table : the Swinging
Goddess : Blue Monkeys dug up by doubledouble-edged Man with a Handle

With mighty skirts spread and breasts starting the world   women
embossed in ritual upon gold rings   step in a whirlpool o' poppy pods
Sistrum's   tintinnabular   given over to unearTherers   notegatherers

EMBARKING UPON THE ISLES OF SAFEWAY

Removed from the mind of my Crete,
people jimmy-jammied in the aisles like
Cracker Jacks aiming grocery carts up to
each other like they had glommed onto
a major traffic accident standstill snarl.
Are people jam or are they accidents?
Because Safeway store is not using four
out of twelve check-out stalls and
treats us like cans stacked up to fall,
can we behave as if we're not in a box?
People in the three fast forever
check-out lanes are like churning cattle
in three ceaseless stockyard stalls.
I hear me moo: "Why don't you open more
check-out lanes so we're not crowded up
with grocery carts against our elbows on our ribs?"
People seem relieved someone is expressing
something in the fast check-out forever lanes.
The grocery checkers turn toward me
with benevolent disregard. I'm not a nut;
I'm a salty cracker, neither safe nor Cretan—
distinguished by my carton of milk
and two cans of dog food.

Acknowledgement of quandary, fleeting,
I witness faces glaze over like
overheated frosting-coated cakes.
Painstaking bottleneck conveyance trickling
us out to evaporate between a crowd
of parked cars makes me find my voice among

a blur of bottles and beeping, automated
price-reading machines. I ask the clerk who
to complain to about overwhelming congestion.
"Nobody in the store," she says.
Does the mean we're not here
or there's no one to complain to?
"Why not open the last four check-out lanes?"
"There aren't enough clerks."

"Why don't they hire more? There's plenty
people looking for work—and obviously,
they're needed." "Write a letter
to the main office down the peninsula."
"Where they depend on computers, you mean?"
Safeway headquarters is probably
an impenetrable fortress and how convenient
its distance as we creep along
in cretin style, a tagged and banded bunch of
vegetables on a rotating-around counter
of Cheez Whiz, Sugar Pope, Pampers, Ding Dongs
Oriental-Flavored Top Ramen, bags that are Glad,
Chef Salto's Frozen New Fresh-Bake Pizza,
temporary paper towels for wiping one's island
hands on another kind of our Aisle of Creep,
Cosmetic Puffs, Pepperidge Farms' Chocolate
Star Wars Cookies emanating from a store for
minority people who've never heard of "The Force."

SISTRUM

A musical
instrument Isis
set in motion in Egypt
to ward off Greed. Enfeebled
in museums a few examples are left
to memory. Round and made of strips
of wood Has a handle Is held aloft in
side is a hard hollow ball Inside the ball
four harder objects like four dice(air!earth
fire!water!) which when set spinning inside the
ball rotating around the cage hitting rounded
stats of wood create a hyena sound Quickens
hair. No one knows its sound like the bull
roarer rushes air cracking crackling shock
o' snakes in lovely motion O as Hecate's
golden sphere twirled by thong o' leather
shows its sapphire center—hidden past
hidden future(oracular)hidden presence
Created in the shape o' the path o'
the moon Rattle circulates the sky
our ancient sisters used to set
themselves alive We won't pass
imagining its sound Wheels of
a lion-headed woman-driven
chariot drawn by lions
(revive)'til once the
sistrum
sings
the
sistrum
sings

BACK IN THE SADDLE OF SAFEWAY AGAIN

Halloween day, all Safeway store clerks are dressed
like cowgirls, bandits, Indians, belly dancers, and E.T.
A teenage girl in the other long fast check-out lane
catches my eye because her lowered head does not
hide tears dripping onto her t-shirt. She is black,
with the physique of an Amazon and the bearing of
a terrorized child. I expect her to put her thumb
in her mouth. I notice a young, tall black man
standing up against her, his hand on the back
of her neck, squeezing. Happy Halloween!
Imagine someone intimidating someone in the middle
of all these waiting people. Or are they a team
trying out for the best wife-beating couple
at the Midnight Ball? And are we sheep in clothes?

I spy blood spots I hadn't noticed on her t-shirt,
at the level of her nipples—and speak up
for everyone's ears: "Leave that woman alone!
How dare you threaten her like that!"
Why doesn't anyone speak up or do anything?
They aren't looking; some must know.
The man answers with bullet breath: "None of your
damn business! She's my wife; I can treat her
any way I like! She's mine!" His hold tightens
on her neck. Tears are silencing out her eyes.
He nudges her hard: "Stop it! Stop sniveling,
Big Baby!" "Big Bully!" I answer him back.
A man ahead of me shakes his head; he's the wise one,
and I'm the fool to interfere. We're not sheep—
we're cretins in a time that defines "cretin"
as "subhuman." Does not to be mentally retarded

mean not to have compassion? "Shut up, bitch!"
the man who's mistreating his wife hisses back at me.
"I'll get you outside Safeway. I'll tell my wife
to beat you up! She'll do anything I want!"
"Pick on someone your own size!" I answer while
everyone in the fast check-out lane chooses to act
the part of the Living-Dead. We're not cretins;
we're great pretenders; it is Halloween.

I'm thinking, if we all jumped in, we could hold
him to the floor; not forever, of course.
Shut your mouth, or I'll close it for you, cunt!"
He's thinking how he can further get at me.
We're at the same place moving at the same pace
in each of our respective lines. I wonder what
I'll do if we exit Safeway at the same time.
"Cunt—Bitch!—Mother-Fucker—I know . . .
you're a lessie! Mother-fucking lesbian!"
(Only lesbians speak up about battered wives?)
A matronly black woman in line ahead of me
caches over to utter, "Don't bother. It won't
do no good." Lines continue to check-out.
While my beltless super maxi-pads, cloves, aspirin,
spare ribs, milk, two cans of beer, cat food, and
strawberry jam are rung up, an elderly white woman
at the edge of the check-out lane leans toward me,
whispers, "I'm so glad you said something, dearie.
That pair lives on my block; you can't imagine
what it's like to see him treat her that way
all the time." I whisper in the checker's ear,
"Would you call Security? A man who's just
beat up on his wife in the store is threatening
to take me on outside."

Here comes Security dressed in a baggy red and white
polka-dot clown suit with a big crimson smile
painted on his chalk-white face and a billy club
attached to his waist. He has no gun.
He should've dressed as a policeman for Halloween.
"What's the matter?" I tell him. "All I can do
is walk you to the edge of the parking lot."
As we pass a little music box carousel
of horses playing sadly to children outside,
I further describe the incident to Security
and wonder what I'll do if the couple follows me.
He remarks, "Funny, I and a clerk just discovered
a pool of blood in the aisle between the milk bin
and the food freezers; we couldn't figure out
how it got there." Now he knows. As I exit
Safeway's lot, clutching groceries, the clown
waves his big-gloved white hands at me.
"You should be safe now." Sure. I'm shaken.
All the way home I keep looking back.
I don't see them. They could be following by car,
find out where I live, make trouble later.
I'm lucky the man didn't attack me physically.
Speaking up may have meant nothing more than
asserting my self-respect. How could people stand by,
let what happened happen? The man may have
taken his anger at me out on his teenage wife later.
How dare she cry; how dare she bleed; how dare I speak.

Months later in an aisle at the Cretin Safeway store,
I see them. She's looking down; he doesn't remember
me. Both with sullen grim looks of abuse.
The teenage girl is neither crying nor bleeding,
merely mute, automaton-like. The safe way of
America's murders is to slowly over years
do in captive Amazons being treated like Baby Janes,

bone-bit by gristle-nipple knuckle-bit, alongside
stacked meat cross-sections, Pillsbury's
Tunnel of Fudge Cake Filling & Glaze Mix, Swiss
Pudding Bars, Party Pride Mini Pops, Froopy Fruit,
Juice Paks, Heavy-Duty Wisk, pink Hostess Sno Balls
and Ho Ho Cakes, Nabisco Cheese'n Bacon Snack Mates,
Larry's Two Original Frozen Poor Boy Sandwiches.

THE SWINGING GODDESS—SALLY RIDE: FIRST AMERICAN WOMAN ASTRONAUT

                             the   the
                     the swinging swinging the
             the swinging headless headless swinging the
       the swinging headless goddess goddess headless singing the
swinging headless goddess headless swinging says   her head is missing

Without her head archeologists surmise the swinging goddess the swinging
goddess   may be nothing but a child's toy child's toy   How could she
be a goddess   without a crown how could she have a crown without a head
The swinging goddess is using her brain to swing high without a head
without a crown

Archeologists with heads on acknowledge   pillars on either side of
the swinging goddess's swing   each support a dove   and   such signs
indicate Presence of the Goddess Aloft

As the figure swings   the wind sings a little song out of her missing
mouth
        O have you swung lately
             you
       have you have
           you sung lately
           in the skyday sun a woman's in the sky today,
                     sky today, sky today,
                     a woman went up in the sky today,
                     easy Evie over and out.
                     She went yes! out of the house
                     and u-huh! above the garden wall,
                     like a necktie on a lady,
                     straight up, yep! Eve slipped
                     through bible night trying to

net her like a housewife in the sky
She's the wide-eyed newborn
floating about the starry clime of her origin—
Libyan air returned to forest.
Get yourself a man, Man,
another man, yep! A man for a man, Yes!
As he retracts his rib, centuries-slow Adam
births compassion beyond what he's fucked lately, u-huh!
The weightless swinging goddess
steered him off his perch
and out under the moon   to touch
his finger   to another   man   and Eve   without him
lives to find female
flying
companions   New earthfoundlings explore awe

Most expectant happy landing says the swinging goddess swinging the
swinging goddess swinging the swinging headless swinging the the
swinging headless goddess headless swinging the the swinging headless
goddess says goddess headless swinging lately swung lately sung sings
on an ocher island   in an aqua ocean

THE LESSER OLD GARDEN'S PERVADING ODOR

(Inspired by the *Saffron*-Gatherer* fresco)

Little non-feminist female gold frogs in the boggy saffron garden
of Yore   still amazing go Croak-us Croak-us Croak-us

The Argument   whether the head of the creature happily picking at
crocuses is that of a young man or   a blue monkey   has been
abated by a Cretan museum   hanging   two versions of the
painting side-by-side

In both paintings   restored by a 20th century male artist   the body
with the head missing   is that of a monkey   Why turn   monkeys into
men when actually   they're artists with hair on

The head of a man on the body of a monkey makes monkeys not artistic
but dangerous

A man is a monkey fingering crocuses   much like boys monkeying
or monkeys toying with the ripe sides of female baboons' rainbows

What temptation begot is   a modest blonde girl with stays on   about
to pluck a lemon from   an olive tree seeded herself by the hand of
The Oldest Goddess WHOSE HAIR WAS DUSK

A woman consorting with wisdom   causes   fruit   to rot   and
The Argument whether Adam was a monkey or a man   turn murky

So many of us   proves   sex is a blue monkey   Top to bottom portrait
of an anal-retentive

Our fathers our grandfathers and their fathers abstract-painting
a world   about to be peeled through layers   of wars

Fire-Rimmed Eden

God is a blue monkey in a business suit travelling aboard Agent Orange
Airlines to Washington D.C. to ascertain how many more flaming bananas
he can finagle out of Bonzo the Neanderthal Man

Monkeys in long black attire and hats on aboard a jetliner bound for
The Promised Land at Dawn stand in aisles and—spit curls aside—pray
in spite of insistence   of stewardesses that they sit down

The ride is bumpy but as long as the jet keeps catching up with the
rising sun   men who made up God—and to the wonder or consternation
of other passengers—keep jiggling and bounding and falling about
in difficult show of obeisance to all they've reaped paying lip service
to The Red Monkey God Whose Veins Are Filled With Whiff of Saffron
                                                                    Death

So "Precious" It Has only begun   to fade

Men trying to imitate baboons   doesn't mean they're not   beautiful
It's looks that count and what we can endow them   chime the little
non-feminist female gold frogs with stays on   in Today's Perfect
Victorian Croak-us Garden of Yours   not Mind

Clitoris Lost

*A spice rare as human essence collected by hand from crocuses

WOMEN ABOARD MOONBOAT

For Felicity, Who Asks

<u>Men are beautiful but choose not to be.</u>
<u>That is The Hell</u> . . . If there was a Cretan Paradise,
why did the men finally turn against the women?—
they didn't. Unlike the ground-hamburger-home
of our time where any utensil becomes lethal
in a kitchen hell, the double axe of the Goddess
was not a sword but an all-purpose utensil like
a kitchen knife in a time when men benefited from
being lyrical and women were melodiously omnipotent.

Paradise ended twelve centuries before Christ
was borrowed from three sides of a woman holding up
glint of a wine cup in a palatial field of lilies.
The House of the Double Axe fell to the North
"on a spring day with strong south wind blowing."
Bronze men stormed an enshrinement festooned with
fruit and beads and flowers and awe. Seven thousand
years of ocean as Protectoress filtered down cracks,
leaving snakes as question marks.

In Cretan art, men's limbs sway a merry blending-in.
They're beneficent as a fourteen-foot well-fed python.
Mutuality is not a bore but an obsession; Paradise
is a pseudonym for the pleasure of complexity:
women efforting to learn the angel-glance of history.
A Garden is a sophistication and should tempt
like red-apple wisdom of pursuit of the taste of
3,400 year-old olives found preserved in a cup
denotes a communal-arrayed moonboat winging home.

Fire-Rimmed Eden

REASON BEING A TWO-EDGED MOON

Reigning ice,
needlepoint life
women cling to.

Secrets
folded
tight.

Waterdirge news;
tune of Zeus
on TV.

In the dark house
books open
whorl-shell,

centrifugal
stone bodies'
original glow.

Hear of,
while women
type & harp & behave.

Houses fall to
misused sea;
baby cyclones born.

California
house trailers
grandstand—collapse.

The land broken open.
Archeologists chip out
the hidden half.

Stone speak
bone smile
bless polished scraps.

Language of the Lost
is beginning
a Paradise of Altitude

opposite furled brows of gods;
Lydian sidelock springs
seawave hairdos;

happiness
involving as
the sistrum's ratch.

A Greek word,
"labrys" meaning
"double axe"

later meant
"labor."
Wisdom-glimpsing

women
dipping in
in any direction.

POEM FOR THE WOMEN'S
PHILAHARMONIC OF THE BAY AREA

Eighteen years
I haven't worn
a dresssss . . .

    An orchestra
      ought to look
        like a rainbow

        and ssssssound like
          sssslipping on
      of

        sssssacral
      quilted
      sssssskirts

        poignant as
          conch shellsssss
            differing

        sssssummoning
      expanding
        pitchchchchchch . . .

      (dresseses
    of
  priestesses).

ISLE OF LESBOS

For Janine, Who's Been There

Retsina sings the throat
like horsehairs pull ribbons
from the bodies of Aeolian violins . . .

At the Sappho Hotel heterosexual couples
glide along banisters like it was Tennessee
Williams' town. They're dressed risqué in
gowns and ties. A slightly decaying staircase
and "We're drinking pine trees tonight!"
make for slight depravity.

Women go there alone, in groups,
looking for Her. Between Sappho's poetry
and a Mary Wollstonecraft novel
love remained quiet between women
two thousand four hundred years.
Sapphotown is restless, keeps moving.

Two other towns with the same name
espouse life—Greek women in black winding
and haunting white walls resonant
in milklight. Word has it
She didn't jump off the cliffs of Leucadia
for love of a sailor.

Smile unearthed, Her town is buried.
You'll find much of Her under a pile
of pottery fragments—intact—
one thousand years later than Minoan

priestesses and two thousand six hundred
years earlier than We.

Knee-high boots and a permit,
Her dusty heart is Yours pounding
to dig down.

on the isle of crete

CRUDELY-SHAPED MAP OF CRETE

Fire-Rimmed Eden

   Have you O been
   to the O Isle of   Crete
in your head lately   where the
dittany plant O that eases birth grows rampant   lately in your   head
where houses and streets are shaped uneven in your head lately   have you
been O to the Isle of Crete O on your head to see a mouse's face
sticking out of a crowd fascinated watching the tip o' the mouse's
tail curled O around a reed O have you been to the Isle of Crete O
                   where cypress trees were turned on
             end O for pillars O to hold
             occasions high

CRESCENDOING EARTHFOUNDLINGS

I await you, Tiara of the Tilted Head—
Lady of the Hooks who gives away
National Geographics like they were
centerfolds from her soulheart. They are.
Worlds in Miniature. And the gypsy
harpsichordist who has my *National Geographic*
with the Minoan Goddess pinup, under wraps—
Give Us Back Our Golden *National Geographics*!
I awoke you, Shard Counter with Camera Vision
dizzied by frozen believings.

By such rumblings cause conch shell intonings
in the California cold. Three blasts
by the purple snail spire mean I await you,
three-sided "Homo"—Triumpherant with endless
string of interests and loose clitoris,
her dance corded with snakes, mind vacillating
between pinstripe pantsuits and cooperative
anarchy. 1980s women "heteros"—uncoil
even more and deepen; these women of those
men of such forbidding.

OCTOPUSSY HAS A HIGHLY-DEVELOPED BRAIN, JAMES, AND HAS ESCAPED YOUR BRAIN

James Bond gets the idea

he knows what's good By good I mean   he senses   where strength lies
and it is oasis-like and inviting   but he's no dynamite stick for
cracking the unconscious where octopuses lie   He thinks   he's an island
without men   He thinks women who untangle his treachery   are an island
beholden to the fantasy of his conquest of lesbians

From Russia without love

came Myceneans   Those horror hordes from the North sliding over
the
continent with their pointy beards and penis-splitting swords   entrenched
themselves in strongholds: paranoia holes: tombs for home-sweet-homes
Yet couldn't ward off doves consecrated horns trees vases   moon on
the Mediterranean   making Myceneans   less murderous

United States pretends it's Egypt

perhaps no one receives more thrills from attending a British heroics
movie than   small dark men   Large dark men peck next   The American
Dream is   to be Ancient Egypt   Indisputable in finery Indestructible
in corruption Infallible under the Sun of Absolutes   Deathbound in its
exoticism Slavering in its slavery Undeniable in its bones cache

California is the capital of madness

in madness is sense of Chaos born of an Anarchy to be Day itself revered
What making!What marketplaces!What trading   Between Greece and Egypt

lies an island with women and with men   where matter is thought   sacred
where humans take responsibility for happiness   New-emerging leaderless
land   is my idea of Paradise

Crete lies somewhere between Russia and America

where peace existed six thousand years and several centuries without
spy business suits wearing bionic wristwatches scaling its lack of walls
for no fortification   No heroics save to grasp bulls by the horns   take
to the air and land on the other side (if one's in shape) on one's feet
leaving the wondrous animal on the side of She-Who-Helps-Things-Grow

No gods no goddesses

no record of leadership except giving thanks to Life regarded as
delicate   island people endeared again and again in picture   Picture
no marriages no marching no armies no riots no arsenal in Cretan artwork
Communalizing is no miracle No accident lesbians serving women children
minority people with   verve and fervor of nuns having sex

Eternal curious interest in caring and pleasure of relating

no wonder   my miracle mother   in old age   with defenses down   dying
showed fascination   the first time in adult life   for people around her
No coincidence at least a third of eight hundred people arrested for love
at Livermore Lab Nuclear Weapons and Testing Plant protest last June
were lesbians   The world turns toward this island

This island is timely

this island invaded America without weapons of   deathbond   nature
Insurmountable presence of such history Word of Crete or Legion without
army   Viable "workable and likely to survive" or "to have real meaning
pertinence":   Anarchafeminism   quietly viable   enters rocks and
harrowingly thrills   to the mirror   to the 'morrow

A CUP-CONTEMPLATING OCTOPUS

(an octopus clings to a cup contemplating an octopus contemplating a cup)
Delicate tentacles fastened to   smooth sides   Mantle to liquid have
you (divested of moon) lately taken hold clung sucked embraced attached
jettied-out affixed siphoned reversed yourself you your octopus eyes
looked back reversed yourself swum back   returned

In driest of moon man-night have you partaken of the disappearance   of
the swinging goddess her sepia ink Ladies have you entered lately   her
squid body that speaks in heaven of tongues that reaches to fifty feet,
lately   saying have you reversed yourself have you swung back returned
clitoris peaks scudding valleys of oceans   manifest of moon

THE PYTHON CADILLAC

For the Lindas . . .

"When I was little, my grandmother had a well
and in and around the well lived these small snakes
called 'racers' or 'chasers.' They were harmless
but when you approached the well, they'd become
aggressive, start running after you.

When Grandma saw how scared I was, she said,
'Chase those racers right back. They'll run at
you, but if you run at them, they'll turn around
and run the other way.'—and it really worked!"

Mediterranean Snake Admitter

To admit the beauty of a snake,
give it a room of its own.

Place a statue of a woman holding lightning bolts
on a ledge in the room.

Put a low table made of red clay in the room,
table balanced on three legs.

Fashion the top of the snake table with four
evenly-spaced, intersecting troughs to form a cross.

At the intersecting point of the two sides of the cross,
hollow a hole for the feeding dish of the snakes to fit.

Place the snakes' food in shallow terracotta bowls.
Leave out barley kernels, honey cakes, milk,

grub worms, and pieces of cheese.
Make a hollow clay pipe with holes for the snakes to crawl

up and out onto ledges where each can rest or eat or bask.
Call the pipe, "snake tube."

Line temple floors and hall archways
with the notched plume ornament.*

Design the flounced skirt of the chryselephantine goddess
or the borders of portable hearths,

or The Tomb or the Tripod Hearth
with the ornament of the notched plume.

Paint the wave and dot pattern arterial red
and the background a deep tawny wheat white.

Recognize the rows of waves with intermittent dots
what you're creating is not a notched plume

but the design on the adder snake's back.
Know the adder also as the "cat snake,"

but it solely eats lizards and mice.
Learn the fangs on the sacred adder are too far back

in its mouth to seize the limb of a human
and deliver a deadly sting.

Research that the adder is no longer found on Crete
and the adder was once endemic to Crete.

Fire-Rimmed Eden

---

* Lonidier drew the ornament here in the original printing.

Regard the adder as the Mother of the Sphinx.
Observe adder marks on wings of sphinxes and griffins.

Be assured the way priestesses held their snakes,
they loved them.

See the snake gazing up at Her fondly?
Feel that if a snake appears, it is a long lost

intimate ancestor, and you and your garden are
entranced with the new skin of its entrance.

"One time I was at a friend's, and we
were walking in the countryside. My friend
had seen that we both had staffs to carry:
wood sticks. And we came upon this huge snake
stretched out across our path. It was as large
as a boa constrictor, and it wouldn't move.
My friend indicated it was harmless, but neither
of us chose to step across it.

He said, 'Place your stick near the snake
and pound.' So, we did; we started pounding,
and the snake made a movement, inched forward
a little toward the woods.

We kept following, tapping the soil with
our staffs. The big snake kept reacting to our
vibrations and would move a little each time,
not try to escape or turn on us. It was implied
that the snake liked the shaking of the soil
the rhythm of it, maybe even our presence.

We passed through the wooded area and be-
came aware we were approaching a river, its

current rushing. The snake kept moving toward
it, bit by bit in a straight line. Pound,
pound, pound. When the snake reached the edge
of the water, we thought it would turn and move
back, even become aggressive toward us, to do so.

But no. It reared its head, raised up its
front half, almost like a cobra, glimpsing back
at us like a final comment—a kind of farewell
gesture—as if to survey our inability to move
forward, transcend the situation—then slipped
into the water, and in an instant, disappeared…!"

The Cadillac of Snakes

Get that Python Cadillac off the road
and into the field where it belongs, Girls.

· It's yours—much bigger than it needs be
but for beauty.

Who needs traffic blocking traffic, Girls?
Not the Python with Cadillac exterior,

not the Cadillac with Python interior.
Methinks the sly, slimy qualities we attribute

to the human's lower "reptilian" brain
are more in our much larger, higher brains—

that portion of the brain that waxes lofty
and makes some want to run for political office.

You know, patriarchy that cakes the snakes
and makes them extinguished?

Like the San Francisco garter snake
on the list of endangered species.
I mean, what snake has ever run for president
or viper tried for vice-presidency?

(The Three-Leafed Clover as a Club

Saint Patrick driving out the snakes in Ireland
was the beginning of the end of ecological sense.)

Decry the loss of the natural enemy of mosquitos!
Aspire to cast aspersions with an aspergillum,

which was horse's hair attached to a handle,
dipped in water and used before Christianity, to anoint.

Get off the male freeway and onto the trail
of a gliding star-guiding.

She's got lightning, Honey. She's got honey cakes, Baby!
The Python Cadillac's line-streamed to go!

By starting her, you get going,
her starting yourself, you get her going.

Storm up a swim, cloud up a run, her heart beats
in your mirror, reflective glass steams her hiss.

Like children skimmering heat, she skitter-wafts
scaly night. No man dares snatch her.

Her hand or pocket holds venom in a tube.
She knows to use it, to throw, to tower like

those live dead women shaped like bells ringing so hard,
they bowl you over while fork-tongued slither-snakes

entwine and wind them to a stately high,
an impenetrable height O of Priestesses like boas

with arrows, girding their elongated stride.
A snake rings your peaked hat, Priestess,

sticking its head out in front—a third eye
at the level of your forehead, onyxing wisdom—

Your limbs lithe with snakes, three snakes
rimed* together to make your hair braid.

Get that Python Cadillac off the road
and into the fields where It Belongs, Girls,

much broader and longer and profounder than Beauty.

Proof Sheet of Lynn Lonidier with her pet garter snakes.

*Forerunner of "rhyme." "Rime" also meant "to harmonize."

INTO THE LABYRINTH OF CREATURES FANTASTIC

Palac stre chd w th spin ings nd urns,th pi ch of female fr scos
      of seacrests aliv

          The god of th sea co mand d:
          "Bul , fal li ht in loy wit th king s mate."
          Th w ite bull cau t the d rk ey s a'blindin .
          The que n nd te cre tur
          She bor a chil ith th he d of a b l,
          the body of a man
          Th k ng shu th   monst r up n his bas m nt
          b t cou dn t allay w isper ngs.

     (
    clim rs in ston , nes led ga nst
    te tos ing ead oft bu froz n
    in sculpt
)

Gr k   sa lrs tol of a maz like san tuary nd bul s
kept n co rty rds.

       story stre ch d of und rgroun pas ag s.

    ing Minos kep s v n teenag oys
    nd s ven teenage irls -fo rteen pe pl   xact—
    t c rya fo rte n-foot pyth n to he danc
    of teir s crif c .

Ariadne's Clew Box
Lit l cla pot
wit a slit
in one nd
an a hol
n th oth r to
<u>mak lov and breathe in.</u>

Ari dne s cap urd
und rgro nd but fin s
er way out.
Skein o wool
sh unwin s the deep r
she finds

       unwoun wool
ba k to its b gi ning
b for King inos
made up hr tre ch ry
for his Palac of Mino's
spr ng hous cle nings.

inoan cl y anim ll shap s rest n in grav s,
  sea-creature array on pot ry:
   , tid l tang an spume,
      . . . spew M noan—
          His nam   pplied to
all wom n-b lon ing th ngs.

<u>Read,</u>
<u>rea everythin yu can</u>
<u>on Cret 'til moon a quir d cowhe d ni ht gentl scals</u>
. . . mily i kinson's angel glanc . . .

paradise regained

CRETANS CONVERSE CLOSE

tell me what you said   and again what you said what you said   tell me
and again what you said what you said again tell me what   tell me
you said*

SAINT ELMO'S LIGHT

Saint Elmo's Light is when I
met you and heard rumbling like
treetops, church spires, ship's masts
gives off (aura of halos)
       (   )
       (   )
       (   )
       (   )
       (   )
      (   )
              an old-fashioned hidden sensation
              in modern times. "Saint Elmo's Fire":
              a visible electric discharge (((corona)))
              sundering my vulnerable already eyes.

---

* In the original print this poem begins and ends with a small hand-drawing of a
musical element indicating repeat.

DAISIES, LAZY SUSANS, STRAW FLOWERS?

Looking at you looking at wide angle of crickets,
water, motel room, snowdog, white clothes, my own:
white flecks deep in your polished roux-sienna ring
and mocha blouse—tremulous white cast to every
thing on The Spit at Inverness, I couldn't.

(I was cooking.)

What flowers those flowers in all states of
golden being, outside the eggshell restaurant window.
We weren't the best dinner guests (impossible to
fit the size of night into a motel room);
our spirits pulled past those tame stars in
the window box.

I kept shifting scenes—the biggest bed
and smallest white furnishings ever. The curtain
opened on my feeling your thoughts playing
with daisies, Lazy Susans, straw flowers (what
are they?) in varied stage of openings and
closings. (Narrowing motel room.)

In all shades of openings and closings, I shall
call them "Looking-at-an-Angel White-as-
a-Rabbit-Down-The-Alice-Hole" and hightailed
my peach oyster car and love-wired self
out of there, imagining your moon-wired self . . .
and orchids flooding Inverness.

IN CRETE ONE LIVES TO LOVE TO LIVE

Paradise regained

You eat fast I eat slow
I sleep nights, you days.

You're a "sex pot"
I'm an "it."

I want to be with you in
a room on an island where

I sleep fast you sleep slow
you eat nights, I days.

Without a brain, honey,
I doubt you'd feel your heart.

Paradise is a room on an island
of continuing defining.

When one feels this much love

When one feels this much
one should be allowed to
        —as an aside—
to lavish and language in deliciousness
and fallowness of completion
be nursed and lowered into bed
—our mushroom flesh alleviated and luxuriated
lower half's staggering lips' musk
our liquid beings secreted into

a hut with moonglow we absorb
'til white wave intervenes,
separates us from death.

Annunciation of Time
moves our catatonic bodies,
and eyes swim out of sight.
Each to her separate hut, slipped mead,
dreaming honeycakes under pearhalf
peachhalf moon, 'til each one
threads sunsets backwards and forwards
a built-in secretion that makes us
raw and cranky as protection
                    —snake-dehibernation ready . . .
When one feels this much love
one should be left upside down.

Lovesick

Our society
is the sick part of love

saturated
unsatiable.

In Crete
children
drop
flowers
over
our
exposed bodies,
and adorned brief
men in lithe musculars
bring sautéed

new-caught fish
that fleck
like petals
on our compost tongues'

motionless
feasting.

Light sleeper

I am writing this so light won't enter her fragile cave
while I am away brightly breathing.

I wanted her to know the insides of my novel and red bucket
before we dug up the sun—and not throw sand.

Poets are ridiculous, bowled-over romantics,
defiant, only slowed by a beach.

Tears in a cuff of wind—she refused to say,
"It's all right, I still love you."

Wavelet embraces two umber figures
in all the world's sunning, all the whirlsome day.

I left my heart in Berkeley

I had secreted my heart into my pocket.
You can look for it though.
Locket knows the dark of a day
terribly beautiful to have you.

Night tripper

I awoke; you asked me to kiss you:
I couldn't find your lips, so sleep-turned

was I on my head, tried to enter the headboard
a number of times thinking it the way to the door.

"Languaging"

You create lines without making/showing them.   All I can do is listen
to/Willie/Nelson/languishing/vacation/music/   —and doing dishes—
n endless Western stream/Housekeeper-absent-minded/tucking the edges/
f tv city/and vocation into/a cream-made bed.

Poems never written

"Poems," you said, "never get written."

They mosey in,
throw their Stetsons in corners,
ask, "What's for chow?"
stretching their crude stocking feet
over seamless flowered upholstery.

They reek with "Bury-Me-Not" Whiskey
and "Don't-Fence-Me-In" Snuff
chucked in their dreamlessness.
The sheriff whiffs out
the swinging doors.

They hightail it outta there,
mining their gold teeth with picks,
gauging their tether distance
with a kinda "hoss" saunter
into the gunpowder sunset.

Wallpaper town
posts pictures of them;
their prairie twang

echoing words of hipgait mystique
in the center of zeros.

The reward is the memory, hankering.

I came home

I came home
and was startled by white daisies.
Three fairies had visited my house—

"I did the dishes!"

"I left a note which 'Yyn' was hoping for,
didn't expect to find
and found right away!"

"I made the bed and left a flower
the color of my love on the pillow!"

"Whyng"* didn't have to do that.
All day at work people kept interrupting
thoughts of you, insisting
happiness a dream.

*"Whyng": a cross between "wing" and "yang."

Habits

I kept feeling old urgings of hurrying home to take care of the dog,
and, realizing I didn't have to, felt the panic of his void.

You brighten the corners around here, placing mysteries on tables,
his grave curve filling up with dried, thrown-out flowers.

I'm thankful for fairies, and the cat misses observing
your angelfur dog with curved strungbow and shaft of love-eros.

Exercises

Certain days should be face days certain days breast days certain days
backrub days and other days of Clitoris-in-Crete days head daze mind
daze too dazed leg days hair days air daze lip days heart daisy
Have-to-water-the-yard days When-did-you-get-home? daze
Birdie-Cat awaits the Great-White-Dog-Artemis-In-The-Sky-Daze.
Dewdrop,
Bye*

---

* In the original printing this is handwritten.

beginning sunny us

higher learning

BRAIN DRAIN

Brain curled cobra-like in a pan on the floor where we MuddayWhensday
Fryday died in the formaldehyde-lingering firmament: SCIENCE   Years
I'd put off that man that class   that brain belonging to   the unclaimed
"I-do-not-think-therefore-I-am-not" lying entrails outstretched to
pallid students in paler smocks   holding stance of the Anatomy Lesson

Brain leaked a puddle   mirrored our heads' island aspect   Flood-stuck
graves   Storm cloud sans electricity   Cauliflower gone out   Fungus
rumpled base of a tree   did not grow nor make the one in my head STAND
OUT   Misery piled there   commiserating requisites   the professor
pointing out parts

Brain came unwrapped in class   grey linings aimed at skylight   Old rope
trick: ESCAPE   Slippery little mystery of a professor   head swaddled
and kept   inched upward while we lay huddling   pained as worms   across
a place of learning

YEVTUSHENKO YOU SHTINK

Ruby liver Moonrock giblet Panbottom riches enough to coat a king   Poet
prefers a bread-wad packed bird to a question-mark shaped swan   Time
and Rhyme and Drink stand out on board the Good Ship Santa Albatross
leaning to glory   as sail & bird & hand flap in the sea's sore throat
Poet Know-It stands with turkey lard about the neck   hunks formed from
mouth gorging on heart   hang foul   wet-feathered from an oiled neck
croaking   "yes   bedeck"

MY MIND IN COACHES DRAW UP

The feeling of a mind in a book   looking up "erudition" and "verdigris"
turning the talisman "You-From-The-Blue" o'er and o'er   Verdigris
means surprise on the flesh of an angel

Rattly steamer trunks strapped to the (skull)Erudition on iron wheels
"wings" above the plain   OLD MASTER TEETHMAN'S
                                        CRIMSON-LINED CLOAK
spreading O'ER

Once Bitten does one rest   or file one's teeth   become one of those
sycophants atwitter at the castle over whether Count Dracula rides in
the coach   or is driven

NU-TO-ME-OLD

(ik-sipí-ənt),* <u>any pharmaceutical substance added to a prescription to get a desired mixture</u>.

"Excipient" as inert word (the bitter of the unknown) as-in-"medicine" added to resurrect breath   "Excipient" rings upon the tongue brings rivulets from ruined towers of Latin Flotsam rising above board

<u>Excipient</u> "the only soap carving of its kind floats up from the leaden book" Peculiar curved wood   sea-shrined   lapped ashore   Vitamin C vitalizing isles of information

Excipient! Excipient! Excipient!   A civilization's bottled message slapped ashore   Resonant coined gold hammered   into the architecture of thoughts

(i-lik-ser),+ <u>excipient old land hewn with inhabitants set upon by savage other shores</u>.   "Elixir": Breath/Heady clearing   made named "New Foreverhealing Wornfound Land"

Clitoris Last

---

* In the original printing, this is handwritten.

\+ Also handwritten, with an accent over the k and a tilde over the e.

PERSON

(For Jody A. Person)

I will not make a movie of a woman with a shaved head in pants and hard
hat on   kissing a man in a dress checking his lipstick in the mirror
They turn away and strip   and turn around (tahdah!) and the man is
a man   the woman a woman   The poster is of a monkey
mounting a human

Don't introduce me to people who'd advertise me on a stick in the
production of self as sellable soul   If you're "for the people" don't
favor connecting you to me   by connections when we have separation
in common   Call me Recluse for not wanting to meet anyone like you in
the Vampire Forest

I won't drive you ten miles to the airport having never met you before
having offered to take you (feminist) a short way   Don't monkey don't
ask Yet you ask and I eke tremorous refusal resenting I don't have no choice
to avoid entering the burning hoops of refusing your attempt to make me

Your friend,

Lynn*

Fire-Rimmed Eden

---

* Handwritten in the original printing.

HER MITTS

Scratching about in high mountains   nose up to nectarberries corpulent
as I   as mean as   lovely as a bee-tuned breeze   the year curled
(bear in log)   not to sleep   but with a good book in a foreign tongue
about   edification of appetite   To come out of the cave   stand in
the shag of former whoring   blinking at the beehive sun after reading
paw-to-mouth bestseller "How to Partake of the Out-Of-Reach Bough"   313
takes as long as a bear's got

CHARIOT

The tarot told me   soon as I wear my underpants' holes out   to
beat a bloke path out of the world under   Trust the blond stranger's
gentle armor   whirling ever

Under canopy of stars with dark glasses on   sphinx   link   at feet
of chariot as if   burden was the beast of motion   Giddyap!Sphinx Get
me South

to shifting hieroglyphics underworld   Drop Chariotess off at
Discernment's door   where facets off fountains   thresh dizzy over arch
artifacts' hard-squeezed ciphering   luxuriate in shadow

EXERCISE FOR ENGLISH TEACHERS*

Rather than don boxing gloves( )choose to turn   and let
armed foe of knotted arms   pass   Turn and pass   and turn( )
as the Chinese greet dawn in courtyards   at Great Wall gates
their( )limbs flowing their centered torsos moving circles
let the sun up on the body arcs' outlines rays coming( )off
formalized Tai-chi gestures done with deep( )breathing called
(The Flight of the Bird)( ) If Bird adept should be set upon by
crouched figure   knife in hand( )the adept turns the knifer
becomes part movement of bird thru space( )ground below and sun
above   Flight( )of the adept's hands in the shape of doves
takes the cat-o'-nine-tails creature (he is his own whipping boy)
by turns( )turns and lets him pass   and by passing   face-on
meets dawn playing on knife( )blade   taken up( )in rays
prisms( )and rainbows( )dazzling metal   the same as
the figure standing( )doing( )deep( )breathe( )ing
( )Dawn glows upon the arsenal's dark thrust frozen( )
frees   the Burning Book manifest in the (writer's)( )

*The Ground rules

1. At each point ( ) appears in poem, reader is to take slow, deep breath
   and gently, audibly let it out.
2. Word "hand" is to be pronounced in the exhale followed by final deep
   breath.
3. If poem is read in public, audience is invited to join in with the
   breathing. The reader should indicate moments of breath by slowly
   raising her totally relaxed (palms down) hands and arms in the air over
   the poem. The apex of the gesture should be synchronous with the
   moment the lungs reach maximum intake. The hands and arms are
   lowered as the air is let out, to an at-rest position with no air in lungs.

Addendum: Where one needs to in the poem, it's all right to breathe in
the Western culture way ( ).

The ( ) in the original printing are hand-drawn ovals.

HISTORY LESSON

In 1492 America discovered Columbus

I watched your cowboy knot jump on your neck foam mount your mouth
fluid with civilizations   weighing questions midway between sandwich
bags and fluorescence White spit glint and dry   11:10 the fountain
turned on Heads turned A student whisper-guessed you drank heavily   315
Shy at life   comfortable in history so concerned with what you
handed us you created permanent embarrassment You left the 19th
Century high up   your fly open a shirt-tail tucking-ins neatly
covering your part You had daughters You   cleared your throat

Awaiting an A a B or   C

Each lecture the building let out a gunshot sound that hit across
other buildings We never knew why pressurized air was escaping the
basement At the break you lit a pipe wandered out of a room
giddy with the gap in your pants In 1942 you laughed as fellow
officer cut off a dead Jap's penis Today laughing haunted That
1973 day you entered the 20th Century too young for a senile prophet
fly still undone we were there uncomfortable as memory   simple
as health

NIGHT RUN

Town dark without gas stations lit up   and my gas
guage low   A chocolate soda to keep me running

Signs saying Gas Open 24 Hrs All Night Never Closes Gas going so fast
the dealer lost count below those cold observers   the stars   He
addressed me as from across the Sahara: Grants Pass is closed up
There's one open in Ashland until one a.m.   Otherwise forget about gas
until morning in Redding forget central Oregon

How do you pump gas how do you fill it all the way   Nauseated by new
nightmares overflow covered my hands ran down my arms got in my mouth
A day-person I like to travel by night with gas dripping out my tank
After two stops I couldn't wash gas reeling off me   Forget the
central organ

By morning the gold on my gassed fingertips vanished   I knew I was
in California by dragonflies' bluegold bodies breaking on my car and
sulphur moths buttering up my windshield   There was gas again   I was in
the unisex restroom contemplating pancakes   a tank of gasoline—and
somebody clean my windshield   Forget the central ore   gone

I VAN GOGH, YOU GO GAN

In arena   two masters stand empty of spectators render the gnu in the
clearing   different

In the turning of the powered sunflower   Gauguin's gazelles Van Gogh's
bulls   work

                              Gauguin's insistence the   317

tiger's striped road   meet Paris dusk of lion   Vincent's obsessed
idea of ear   waits to unload oblivion on Gauguin not wanting to hear
they hunger

Clitoris Lost

I DEAL

All I could learn I could learn in a cave   Instead I'm thirty
novelists in a dark hall listening to the passage Man Loves Woman
I associate learning with lying in bed   my lover and I reading Dante
off the edge   We don't always make love like books but cuddle a world

Pet dragons we hold in our heads for fire   let go   For the world under
the sun needs touching   I go to school to learn school is a relic
for a tongue of treasure   Thirty novelists in a dark hall turn to
action   to sight themselves   in fancy (Dick Tracy calling all cars
                                                        Falli

                                             n

                                                g

                                                 o

                                                    f

                                                    f

                        continents

                                     falling

                        off continents

)

SPECIAL SHOW FOR MR. NIXON
AT DISNEYLAND PLANETARIUM,
SWAMPLAND, FLORIDA

VISUALS By NASA SOUND By Mafia

Mr. Nixon wants to know

Think of earth   as not even a gnat in a night of New England fireflies
Think of yrslf Mr. Nixon son of Quakers think of yrslf   as star scum
Not the movie star kind but lying against a giant star pulling into
itself shining more than our own one billion tons of matter in a
matchbox blowing apart with POWER<FORCE<GLORY of one million
                                                            million
million million hydrogen bombs goings-on   primetime

You can't think of it,
human can't think of it,
poem can't light a match to it,
nor faith, a candle.

Mr. Nixon does not want to know

His mommy said her son might not make good presidential material   Say
it doesn't matter we're all made of stars   We'll all go together down
Superstar Lane   Sunny growing HOTTER BRIGHTER SMALLER

We will fry,
the ocean boil,
the sun swell,
turn red,

Clitoris Lost

swallow
mercury venus earth mars
and shrink
vibrant red,

white,
then electric blue;
shrink earthwise,

the Great Scientist sed.

Mr. Nixon think

There is another system out there like ours   another Nixon   The sun
turn into an earth as it cools   another accession of presidents
gravitating toward axcendancy   Everything free and scientists Will Be
over easy on your Supernova egg crisp earth toast coffee black sky
Science hired to deter   the sun turning super needle blue to white-
dwarf   dull red to black-dwarf drifting with other dwarves & diminished
unlit planets   it HAD NOT CONSUMED

Mr. X, you knew all the time you understand

You've made your plans and x-acuted them since we are all going to go
anyway hand over head down Supernova Land   The Japanese learn fast the
Arabs learned last but longest   To quote Agnew's friend Frank Sinatra
"As long as you're born you might as well have a good time" comet-
tailing the sign above his bar: LIVING WELL IS THE BEST REVENGE

STAR POWER BABY

Car lot,
Starlot,
People Power,
Star Power,
Star Power, Baby!

Gollygoshland

If golf clubs Winnebago's and fiberglass boats don't go now they'll
vanish into vapor later until   we're out of   galaxy   Don't worry ice
invaded North America four times in a million years   Primeval forests
took over the Poles   Nixon tainted the pyramids   by visiting them
Be gratefulThankfulyou Uncle Walt for this preview of attractions
Gratefulforwarning us something worse than A Bombs and Communuts:
Nixon
above telling us we're sin and the monster below is Earth

What it must be like to work for Nixon

At Disney landhappy end Kissinger will keep shining armored care
of us   His lily strange glove   deprive horizon's forehead of its
jewel   Like the Cyclops' eye screwed out of its head   Earth turns back
to careening unmanned beginnings

MISSION ACCOMPLISH

Parasol and smelling salts afloat the luggage rack   canary weightless
in a cage   they let a lady volunteer astronaut man the first flight
headed for the sun   singing I sea the sun and the sun seize me

All the vaporized lady volunteer astronaut could do was spy on all
those good forces in that other world whose temperatures raised to
the sun's   emit daylight   singing Icy the earth and earth   frees me

RHETORICANDY

What is this thing called Eye-for-an-I-and Tower-of-Babel-for-badtooth-
ayer   rapture sits in high-swung chariot Hermaphrodite drives called
facing-the-fleeting-stone-countenance-of-wisdom-embraced-by-a-sphinx-
enrapt-by-a-lion-weighted-down-by-breasts-with-wings'-waving-oar   for

See of the moon they say where sands wear duncecaps for some enchanted
starting evening sea of pyramids of waves the curved moonboat rocks in
name of clay the guide a stranger points to pyramids around that rock
this point

TRIUMPH

The black owner of the brand spanking new sport scar   the man so badly
injured   he couldn't wiggle his toes when the ambulance driver asked
the   man who'd totaled his car   other passengers thrown from the car
all the man with white Triumph with panelled dash asked was   where was
his hat

IN PROVINCE OF PERSON

In 1927 ice Siberia archeologists convinced to dig to what in 1908
                              (meteor or Martian)
entered the earth in miles of waves   made the forest and its
creatures   flame   1985 earth wondered what pulled the Dali land's
cape twenty-five miles thin   1991 they raised money to dig deeper
2021 their shovel hit something   2025 a crane hoisted up a glowing
disk   which turned black holes of archeology's eyes blue
A 2045 invisible shield was erected between It and them   In 2078
sunbeam penetrated the light inside the disk inside the light

2079 a representative of the world reached inside the year inside
the ex-glowing disk   extracted a piece of paper which had capital P
inscribed on it   Beside the P was a pea like the princess slept on
preserved   as if   centered in pyramid   The pea was X-rayed and found
to be   a seed   The plain pea was placed on a pillow in Kiev Museum
World people streamed to point   not dreaming   Martians had hurled
pea and paper to earth for when we could conceive Martians took a pea
                              (irritant or tear)
of ours   to start a P-patch on Mars   Green grows the yew-on-earth

OLD GOLD

What's so good about gold

It's pretty   Mayans liked it   Spaniards took what Mayans liked
 and lost it   Grab it before it always goes away   Know it cannot
leave this earth except by way of Martians   In the gold forever
what would Martians do with gold where gewgaws are black holes
ladies do not lust   and anything that shines is ugly   If we gave
it to Mars   we would declare war on Mars and Indian-give it back

Gold is good   God is gold   a crow's eyes spy

It's nice   People aren't so kind   Even Mayans pushed each other
off pyramids   A tourist climbed one and couldn't get down   There
are no Army helicopters to rescue Americans where gold has passed
from ground to knife handle   She got down   coaxed by the tour guide
Tourists with soft feel for gold   remarked   a Mayan's profile
resembles a lizard's   It's people that's harder to like than gold

All people agree on gold   Who agrees on anyone else

What kind of creatures   were Mayans   Miniatures   scurrying over
jungle paths before snakes could hit their ankles   The tour guide
theorized how these squat folk   fit stone   What kind of legs and
feet they had   to build two-foot high steps so narrow Americans
have to walk sideways to the top of the ruins   Gold is good everywhere
In the teeth of badmen everywhere   see the good gold

THREE KINGS OF OXIDENTAL

One brought wood,
One fixed things,
One helped carry.

Uncle Caverobber got money to go everywhere   trading hand-me-down
clothes from the States with Mexican Indians for Mayan artifacts
What he couldn't sell surrounds he and his wife's   love   life
His doing to natives not one of my aunts will admit what   All dote
on impossible-to-read postcards from Europe

Unfun Uncle Conscience announces Third World people will arrive a
night at my first uncle's bedroom to get their golden arms back
(Arm rhymes with harm)   His homemade mottoes leaden the table:
best way to learn Spanish is to join the grape boycott organizers
Do not eat wine or drink lettuce   done us one more time

After the dinner part of my departure   wives of the three uncles
play Scrabble   and tie   I wash   listening to Third Uncle Eye-At-
the-Top-of-the-Triangle   dry   Dishes pass faster while Spaniards
make Mayans climb pyramids to empty headslings full of earth
'til temples are covered with dirt

Conscientious uncle's head buried in an environmentalist magazine
rises as My Uncle the Sun   In Actuality Uncle Most Serpentine asks:
couldn't I make one thousand dollars last longer than ten days
by taking a slow boat from Miami to the civilization an other uncle
helped carry off

A niece is cursed that judges uncles equal   The three uncles know
what good books say   At Mayapan   capital of Yucatán   miles of
ancient wall surround 3,500 mounds   Each potentially houses
fragments of sages: Righteousness is the same as pilfering   The
Left hands the Right   Who helps most around this house   is King

PYR▲MID

Is there a pyramid to be had in the world: On the breast of Temperance
and the skirt of the Charioteer   In the windows of lamp reflecting sky and
gown of the Queen of Cups   The robe on her back   and water at her feet
End of each startip   and triangle eye of her crown   Word T A R O T in
the Wheel of Fortune has a pyramid etched between   letters   A chalice
is but a pyramid and inverted   pyramid   A drink from   the Queen's cup
A pyramid is opposite dichotomy   Is something to challenge   Kings at
the end   rest in pyramid   Who Kings do   do in   before they're done
is the question

In the original printing the triangle for the A in the title is hand-drawn.

america blond reentry poems

POEMS OF A RED-BLOODED AMERICAN GIRL

At the Log Cabin, Pine Creek, Oregon

Through planks laid across
the second story level,
I peered at my second grade teacher
changing out of her bathing suit
and wondered why shaky floorboards
weren't fitted together, nailed tight.
(I could fall through.)
I saw a black triangle of hair
over her place.
(I know what a triangle is,
my heart beating fast
at the chances I take.)

A Porcupine is Good Protection

I walked the porcupine around the block.
It still had quills.
If a dog came along,
quilts bristled.

I lay down
and let the porcupine
crawl all over me.
I was regarded as a wonder child.

Killer of Butterflies

I liked wobbly feel
of frogs in my hand.
I put them in
and kept them,
then let them go,
wondering if head and hands
would sprout warts.

I caught monarchs
and tiger swallowtails.
Their technicolor came off.
Land born,
I dunked their pantyhose heads
in a jar of kerosene.
The butterflies broke apart.

There might be
one perfect dead one
I'd take in the house
to show around,
then put on the windowsill.
Was I trying to put it
back in touch with the sky?

Handfuls of sulfurs
and buckeyes, I didn't even
bother with plain
white cabbage butterflies.
No one stopped me.
Were they so desperate
to keep me occupied?

I lay on the ground
among butterflies.

Green and brown camouflaged
bombers flew over me.
I sang "God Bless America"
all the way to Arcadia—
Louisiana relatives.

Honking the horn
in every tunnel, ducking
my head under every overpass—
three thousand miles
to my cousins' BB guns
—there were few butterflies—
I had a slingshot.

I was so impressed
seeing redbirds; mockingbirds
I had never heard before—
they shot at.
I went back to Lakeview
Oregon, began to become
a butterfly.

Venison

They brought deer home
in the trunk, on fenders,
hoods, and roofs
of now classic cars.
There was a smoke hole
and salivations' hankerings
curling from the earth.
Nothing tasted better
than a strip of smoked deer
handed me by the womanly
mother next door whose
name I used to call out
before I could pronounce it.

OUR GRAND RAINCOUNTY COUNTRYMOTHERS

Finishing reading homosexual poems in robes:
St. John of the Cross wedded to Christ on a bus,
I lifted my head to a sign on a worn barn wall:
"FOR WEAK WOMEN, DR. PIERCE'S REMEDY" and wished
a picture of it for women back home
with the camera I didn't have along.
Where was the piercing man could enter
the trouble the pale women were having
entering the dark at noon in farmhouses,
by wood stoves, lifting iron lids, placing in
crumpled news and kindling, arranging
teepee fashion, carried-in wood they cut?

Her single footprints left marks in the wet.

Water roils in the iron pot on the stove;
onions sliced and carrots cut in and spices:
Bent to her kettles, the woman of many children
"tolerated" her husband's blunt approaches.
Expect he's dead. Roof grows straw she
could fix, if she wanted. She's strong in her
wellborn jeans (outlasting God and some
long gone doctor with a penetrating look).
When the soup ropes and laces, she calls
to any visiting children, grandchildren, or to
herself, spooning into bowl and centering it on

a spidermade doily of rainbeaded sunthreads.

WOMAN SEX PARTNER ENTERPRISE
DREAM

I was at a dance hall for gay women. It was late
at night. I noticed a line of women forming in one of the
antehalls and was told the line was for women who wanted
another woman for a sex partner for the night. They would be
paired off and given a small cubicle room to have sex in, in
some remote part of the building; I got in line next to
Dorrie Jackson who goes to women's bars every night. The
line grew long and curved around. I was holding a card with
my name and address on it which was attached to an extension
cord.

Men were in charge of the Woman Sex Partner Enterprise,
obviously for profit. I wondered whom I would be paired
with. Some of the women were attractive to me—some weren't.
I looked around and recognized a few sycophant women: bar
regulars. I wondered if the men would use any selectivity in
pairing us. I was taller than most of the women. Another
tall woman was ahead in line. I thought I might be paired
with her. I began to feel uncomfortable about having sex
with just any woman.

The line was moving rapidly, steadily past a man who was
recording our names. As I went by, I looked at a page he was
using to pair the women. Nothing was on it but their names
and an occasional doodle or simple drawing beside a name.
The man asked if I wanted to make an identifying sketch be-
side my name. I realized he might use the sketch to find a
partner for me (One woman had a flower by her name.) All I
could think of was the two overlapping triangles in reverse
to form the occult six-sided cabala star to cue the man to

find a suitable sex partner for me for the night. But as
thought about it, I concluded he wouldn't be cognizant of
symbols. I began feeling frantic.

Women were being loaded into modernistic rail cars which
had rows of seats built in ten to twelve across. The rail
cars were transporting the women to their rooms where they
would spend the night with their partners. When the rail
cars returned, I tried to find a passenger seat by myself.
Jackson seated herself next to me. As we were riding up to
the rooms, I was embarrassed to see Angela Steiner, the new
girl friend of one of my old loves, come into the dance hall.
She sighted me among the women seeking sex partners for the
night. Now people I cared about would know to what lengths
I'd gone. I felt angry with the women I'd loved who'd re-
ejected me, resulting in this end. I felt I was being shipped
to Siberia. I felt claustrophobic about being put in a room
with a woman I hadn't chosen, for the purpose of having sex.

I suddenly realized I didn't have my name and address
card anymore. I looked through my belongings. I must have
lost it in the Sex Partner Enterprise line. Dorrie asked me
what was the matter. Then looked for my driver's license.
I'd lost or misplaced all identification.

MY BELATED VALENTINE

I found my valentine
in the trunk of my car.
What was she doing there?
I'd say she's buried.
I put my found valentine
under a pyramid
to keep,
preserved,
perfected to a T
until feelings come free
of her knotted body.
(I found out
what was she,
wasn't.
The same as archeologists
unscramble the Singing
Statues of Thebes
their song but
". . . air rushing
through pores
of stone when
hot rays of the sun
suddenly expand it.")
There's love
in a history that housed
scarabs and tarots.
(Mostly,
we write valentines
for ourselves.)
More than once a year
occasion comes.

OWED TO JOY

"Just as my fingers on these keys make music" —Wallace Stevens

Budget cuts poetry music and P.E. out of public schools
Women P.E. teachers of America are being laid off
unfortunate because they are all gay   which brings them
in their imitation jock stances   ever closer to Beethoven

Beethoven was a revolutionary   his mother a servant with
fingertips muscular as musicians in   sounding palace kitchen
Beethoven like a winning team   striking awe as they enter
the arena   plays heroic across our eyes

Women P.E. teachers turned out to pasture are in training
to be Beethoven   They don't need enlarged foreheads tossed
hair scowling countenance legal hassles syphilis and lost
hearing   to moonlight as the I scream man

The fingertips of a sonata are in women P.E. teachers of
America's heads   Their horny protruding tennies match
those of the emperor of human concerto—just as my fingers
on these keys match Susanna's feminist   fist clench

MAYAMOUSE*

A curve-backed Mayan sleeps on the floor of her San Francisco apartment
to straighten herself out at night   Years ago I read Diane de Prima's
poem about picking spaghetti out of something or off the wall or floor

If blood is found on the floor of my apartment   it's not ketchup it's
not my blood   It's mouse blood   a stiff thing with a split belly angled
through the window by my cat

I bet there's more mice and rats in San Francisco than pasta strands
cooking in all the pots at once in San Francisco   Enough to keep my cat
killing

Italians are running the city where the curved-back Mayan's first words
upon returning to a city that makes me feel it might protect me and
my cat's rites

Deprived of Mayan rights   Women I still don't buy that female
accoutrements of love and longing's apparatus   is a box   Or river-
stick and hole-an-ocean

Jill Johnston told me she wanted   a harem of women in the woods
Pictures of it are in her latest book entitled *How to Manipulate Others
or Fun and Profit*   I quit every movement and join the ocean   when

<u>we are the chosen</u> gets voted in Moral: Don't hold your harem up to
Lynn Lonnie Dear, Jill John Stone cause under my Lois Lane clothes I'm
Mayamous   I'll rat on you   When <u>we are the chosen</u>   gets in
                                    sailor goes to sea again

*A second version of this poem is in *A Lesbian Estate.*+

+ In *A Lesbian Estate*, this poem is titled "Minnie Mouse in Levi's"; it is on page 158.

DREAM OF THE PERFORMANCE

The audience listened while I read my poetry. Then
realized none of the equipment, had, been set up for the multi-
media part of the evening. I hurriedly set up screens and pro-
jectors but couldn't find outlets for the projectors. The
audience grew restless. Some boys kept unplugging the projec-
tors while I was trying to run them.

I spoke to the audience about the woman artist whose work I
was presenting. I thought I had their approval in presenting
work not my own. However, as I talked, I noticed the two tiers
of audience were resting on flatbed rail cars, and the rail
cars started to roll away in opposite directions from the per-
formance area. I had lost the audience.

ROBERT AND JESS DREAM*

I was at Robert and Jess's house. Jean was with me. I was
eager to show her their aesthetic interiors. I was surprised
to notice the paintings on the walls were not the ones that
hung there previously. These were of inferior content, sim-
plistic in form, and amateurishly rendered.

I was hesitant to go upstairs without Robert and Jess, but
I knew Jess's paintings would not disappoint us. However, as
we entered his studio, workmen were dismantling it. Not a
single painting remained. I asked a workman what had happened.
He told me Jess had gotten a job as a social worker for fifty
dollars a week.

---

* Robert Duncan and his lover, the artist Jess.

THE CANNIBAL CHURCH OF SPAIN
COMES EATING AMERICA

From the Chronicle of the Conquest of Hair: What beautiful lesbians
Mayan women hewn of rock would have made   The men   too if they'd
been friendlier and saved their priests' hair so matted with blood
it couldn't be combed (No one shoeless n' shirtless allowed in)

What beautiful Mayan women lesbian men split from rock would have been
before a freak sun rose from the West   blotted out sun glyph of sodomy
in a midnight of hair: From the Chronicle of the Conquest of Ass
(Nothing is allowed out of California these days   NO ONE NO FUN)
                                    (Salvation awaits
                                    blinding books by
                                    lesbians becoming
                                    beautiful Mayans)

Clitoris Lost

EMILY DICKINSON THINKS SHE'LL HAVE A TALK WITH HE THINKS HE'S WALT WHITMAN

For Gay Pride Week Poetry Sharing, 1978, and in protest over the impending demolition of S.F.'s Gay Community Center to make way for a parking garage

I am interested in cocksize   leather pants and the Paul Bunyan of the night for reasons of Emily's   You are interested in dresses bouffants and high-heeled mannerisms that have been identified by feminists with being
                                                                                    oppressed

Sometimes with my voice I imitate you imitating what you think "female" I kept quiet when you told me gay women are repressed and haven't caught up with your signal system for getting the kind of sex you like

> I remained silent
> 'cause I'm
> the silent type.
>
> I waits,
> I watches,
> I jus'
>
> takes things in,
> honey,
> lik' a mystery.
>
> I got royaling
> arounds
> inside

'cause
I'm one of those
thinkin' girls

been waitin' for
the sun to shine
on all.

Watch out for weighted years
of silent types.
I shall say somethin' tonight:

A red flag in the right hip pocket means just that: a red flag.
The key chain hanging from your belt loop means getting off on
the longest run picture show: "The Above and the Beneath."

I happened to be handed a cute newspaper called <u>Gay Sunshine</u>.
Such precious light falls on the gist of one who says about another:
<u>This writer who just wrote a book about traveling was not exploiting</u>
<u>young Third World men in Latin America. Well, there are overtones.</u>
(What <u>Gay Sunshine</u> meant was <u>Central</u> America: central to America.)
The critic continues: <u>What the author is doing is dwelling on complicated</u>
<u>nature appreciation. Isn't it great to get back to clouds and bodies?</u>

The book tells how the author gets Indian boys to lick him
The nickel (haha oldboy in-joke) so they can go to a movie.
You say there are, no sides to a trick? I say each side
of a coin looks different, but we're not money. Hungry-looking
boys seek more than an author's plaindick face. Nor do they

love literature. Some fatherliness going on here, you say?
Put those boys in his shoes and the Americano out on the street,
and see how Daddy does. Will they take him in, snap him bare
with his legs apart? (Note photo of him in <u>Gay Sunshine</u>: fully-
clothed.) Will they pay him trickling centavos to have sex,

hang around while they go after likenesses of pretty young flesh
of themselves? Not a look or dime will author get. May children
who poke his white face with begs grow into Third World poets who
read of the lean life nonstop 'til dawn. O say can't he see there's
to no Third World gay men poets reading tonight? Are they too oppressed
to sing twilight's last, too new in their boots to make poetry prance?
What is Emily to say to Walt this night of laymen laywoman poets
gathered together to celebrate our tropic hearts? Show her gaypoets

in wheelchairs, elderly mariposas who didn't make it up steps, every year
made more accessible in virgin adventure of caring. ¡O Cuidadores de Todo!
Gay brother, you say off the page I am   quiet & unimpressive   I'm saving up
to celebrate our same shoulder applied to the wheel to prevent the deaths
of kindness (providing   other plans for us   this loft of butterflies
darkened   stacked with autos   don't happen)   It is rumored next year
Susan Griffin will get together with Allen Ginsberg   <u>There's fireworks
between us Walt</u>

ELECTION EVE 1980 AND I IN MY NIGHTMARE

I'm a Martian who has landed on a strange planet   at a time the unknown
inhabitants are turning   against themselves   I don't know English
I'm going to learn Spanish   I go around asking ¿Perdón, como está?
How old are you? Are you well? ¿Habla Español?   Do you like
where you go to school?   They look at me strange.

Some of the live ones braid their hair on the sides so I start to braid
my hair on the sides   Signs   individual expressions   I'm learning
the inhabitants are very busy preparing for love or war   They have
no time for terrestrial extras   They overcame curiosity when they
found out   it costs

The atmosphere on this planet smells like the insides of pockets lined
with a few dollar bills   and only males   have pockets   Think I'll
head home it's late   I fire the rocket   rev the pedal   I'm not going
anywhere   The blonde girl who speaks invisible English   can't lift off
from exhaust fumes of money   The dreambank of an alien reads "zero"

Clitoris Lost

CUBAN ART EXHIBIT AT THE MISSION CULTURAL CENTER

A French Swedish Martian set down on Mission Street
and entered a building with the words
"Furniture Store" spelled on it.
There's no furniture.

People are standing around rows of pictures
drinking and conversing,
but she can't understand them.
The Martian has a *Beginning Spanish Dictionary*
for Advanced Space Travelers and knows
very few words.
The people look and look at the pictures.
She goes along looking at the pictures.
Each picture has words on a label beside it.
The Martian can only read two words; they are
very revealing: Tinta China : China Ink.
The pictures were made with ink from China.
Spanish-speaking people have history.
What are Cubans doing with ink from China?
Making beautiful pictures.
Back home, I'm going to make a picture called,
"A Blonde Martian Looking at Art and Drinking Wine."
I'll work hard to make it look like those
"Tinta China" pictures back on earth,
in the furniture store.

THE HAIRLESS DOGS OF CHINA

Slaughtered with the eunuchs,
the whimpering hairless dogs—
darlings of aristocracy—
stabbed or torn apart;
throats cut, spines snapped,
their piglet bodies
flung squealing by laughing
revolutionaries and landing
in a splatter; their insides strewn
from one end of palace to another.
Secretly, someone hid a few pairs
in caves. In 1981,
sixty hairless Chinese dogs
are left on earth to cradle.
The skin of hairless dogs of China
is like human skin; it perspires.
Scientists are pinpointing
precious chemistry of the
murmuring hairless dogs of China.
Kept close and cuddled through
the history of China,
these sweating nude dogs
secrete a substance which cures
and prevents arthritis and rheumatism.

"... WHAT GERTRUDE STEIN
WAS TO THE 1920s ..."

for Dorothea Oppenheimer

Who wants to be fat
and look like a man?
Who wants to walk funny like a hat on her head with Picasso   chugchug
in Red Cross trucks   and rescue doughboys' hearts   Who wants to own dogs
blackball friends who do not with wood hammers hit wood balls the way you
do   Who wants to   will her sweetheart everything   her relatives win
back later   Who wants   to be a female   feminists found-out-later was
chauvinist Who   wants to sing "Song of the Lonesome Pine" over and over
à la scratchy Victrola Who wants to be American Dream Woman when you're
Europe, broad and
heavy and deep

Fire-Rimmed Eden

the cyrano poems

DO NOT PIETÉ ON ME

My body does not measure up to a mountain,
but Michelangelo's knocking around in there,
chipping largesse sensibilities out of
ordinary granite of sheerest possibilities.

"My god, you have so much feeling, so much feeling,"
my violin teacher remarked on the odd lament
winding from my fingers until it became his refrain.

The smartest, best woman friend I ever had,
a lover, in fact, who knew better, felt it anyway:
"Lynn, you must have less feelings in your breasts
because you have lesser breasts."

"No, actually, petite breasts make for monstrous feelings
like marbleated bodies you seek on the ceilings of chapels
I find acid-eaten away in subways."

My body is top heavy with violins.
Life's body bigger than clouds, raindrop build-up.
There's a Botticelli housed in my body.
The right thought in the left body.
The only boyfriend I ever loved who loved me,
told me I was wrong for him
for not having enough meat on my bones.
He was drunk and I was gone.

My last boyfriend. Who needs them
when you've got an army or cripples and deformities
at your side. The uglies will win because they (the others)
do not see notsee as Nazi.
And besides, we have Superman on our side.
I am, in fact, Superman. I may look like Clark Kent
with glasses on, but Michelangelo's housed in my body.

That's why Emily Dickinson always meant so much to me
besides baring love of a girl doll upon her prow—
she's plain of face, and she has no money.
"Not attractive" to put the-mob-within-her heart politely.
Why a heart becomes your own when you consider eating one.
It's no plain-Jane tidbit of a lady cooking Valentines tonight.

I love a pretty face and hate the arrogance that lies
like a second face just below the first.
I hate the glassiness privilege makes
of perfectly-chiseled faces—not all, but most—
given enough strokes and years. I hate my worship
of icy shine of pretty faces. A pretty face
reminds me of my own.

A dancer with an, of course, well-shaped body once
lumped me with what she called "the beautiful people"
in her pecking-order shopping list of desire.
I was so superior an artist as to transcend physicality.
I walked away from her movie star collection of Hollywood dolls.
She wasn't a good dancer.

And you, Ariel, always looking for Superman,
surrounding yourself with Clark Kents without glasses on:
narrow sighted, robust, bearded boy-prototype gods
that got Walt Whitman handsome-hot at swimming holes
Americana later sent to Vietnam, whose baseball paws held

my violin hands like they were claws they could hardly stand
to touch during sixth grade dance class. They were stuck
dancing with me; I was stuck dancing with them.
They called me a "thing" and an "it"
while the teachers petted me precious. I had mine.
Clark Kents are not supermen but Michelangelos with
obscured sight and fake Superman credentials;
they guard with swords lodged in stone.
The Grail of Cuteness bores through me;
such privilege, 'tis poison served in gold.
"Hey ugly," the boys call to me from hotcars, "get pretty!"

Grotesqueries, the Gargantuan is my redemption.
Caliban of anger, the beast becomes a tempest
in a teacup, tastes lascivious.

My body does not match my mind. It is like a toothpick
in the wind, chipping away at infinity, giving it
form and sense for that ultimate art exhibit
nobody's ready for: The House of Mirrors inhabited
by the twisted, the invisible, and the laughing.
What luck, my Holy Quest that
flesh extends its boundaries, overlaps all flesh.
That Michelangelo is housed in everybody's body
is the tragedy and the blessing.

THE RED MILL

Sitting watching the Hollywood movie *Moulin Rouge*,
the heart of my teenage limbs standing, flaming.
I knew if I wanted the love of the older woman
I was attracted to, I would have to make it
as an artist, a great artist like Toulouse-Lautrec.
From then on I practiced the cello six to
eight hours a day. I would be a world-famous
Concert cellist. Toulouse-Lautrec was a cripple.
If he could, I would.

The object was to attract women who wouldn't otherwise
want me. Toulouse-Lautrec with foreshortened legs
and a paintbrush that extended on and across women,
leaving poppies and peonies in their place,
everything painted slightly crooked
to match his gait.

I practiced the cello and compensated for my thinness.
Skinny Bones put on fifty pounds around the stomach,
and she's a great artist, creating.
I played cello eight hours a day,
and the Roman in my nose went away.
I don't think she wanted to lose weight off her nose.

The plastic surgeon gave me a local;
it knocked me out. He said I was the first one
in his fourteen years of practice
who, with no memory, tried to save her nose.
I rose up from the operating table and remarked,
"I want out of here!"
They drugged me heavier.
The plastic surgeon said if he'd been a little further

along with the job, my unconscious protest
would have caused his scalpel to cut my nose off.
Thank god I knew not to ask for a turned-up
Hollywood nose. Without part of my nose,
I talk nasal; it's better than having
endless children hold their fists to their nose
as if I were a clown balancing a big ball on it.

As for thinness as a child I was so busy playing,
Imagining, fantasizing, I wouldn't take time
to go to the bathroom. I became constantly
Constipated. This may have discouraged bon appétit,
may have triggered an epic.

Imagination took over the cello,
or I wouldn't be writing of peeled-away
skin-layers of my life, the stinging flesh,
the mill of the burning hoops our bodies
churn through. Bruised and skinned; we are thrashed
into acceptable shape. The Red Mill.

Let's start a movement called "Flesh Liberation."

As for Toulouse-Lautrec, I don't recall him
ever going to bed with the lady. I think his legs
got in the way. I think the beautiful woman
invited him to dinner and took care of him when
he was dying.

I'm old enough to know I shouldn't have taken
Moulin Rouge seriously. It's just a movie,
a musical about a windmill—the bright colors
and the flailing.

ST. VALENTINE'S DAY MASSACRE

May Valentine's Day never come on a weekend again.
Then adults won't be able to celebrate it.
They don't know how.

It felt like Halloween without our costumes on
but scariness nearer.
Adults standing around staring at each other
like gangly children wondering if they'd be made
to dance with each other
at a party in the wilderness.

When people grow big,
their valentines grow big as
the unwieldy world of adult
hearts.

My first and last date, practically,
was playing Spin the Bottle.
I didn't understand what I or any of the children
were feeling.
We just did it.

Adults are so clumsy as to interrupt
the myth of love.

There's all kinds of valentines.
Some, a penny; some curly-topped chocolates
oozing satin, sitting in ruffles, centers
sucked out in cherry rush;
some in juxtaposition with Cupid's arrow;
some so riddled with arrows

they look more like Voodoo dolls
than true hearts blue.
Then, there's the prickly pear kind
not meant for anybody;
my kind of valentine.
And there's black valentines.
Should I wear dark glasses?

Valentine's Day aftermath,
the clocks in my house stopped,
and I was moved through centuries' ago childhood,
on up.

Days before, I used Vaseline
trying to clear my chapped lips.
Chewing on my lips
is an old habit, like old loves.

Adults are so clumsy as to interpret
the myth of love.

I tried not to chew on my lips
so no one would know it was my
cracked lips they were kissing
if the bottle pointed to me.

I thought of a variation of the game
so everyone would be blindfolded
except the person spinning the bottle.
Only the most popular person
at the party would get kissed.
I could kiss who I really wanted.

Straight men were going to be at the party.
How would I be able to kiss them?
I'd leave the party before then,
or may the saints take me.

Adults are so clumsy as to interpret
confusion of love.

352 May Valentine's Day never come again on a weekend.
Valentine's Day should only be for lovers and for
children.

BALLAD DE MI BARRIO

Howdyasay "homosexual" in Spanish   One adult dictionary wouldn't say
"Homosexual's homosexual" the other said en Español   Does that make
for a double homosexual   Let me tell you a tale of one that winds
labyrinths

I had to wait out the repeat performance of the Feminist Erotica Festival
to THE END because women were using my extension cords and light dimmers
but I was tired of seeing slides of vaginas   like smiling pap smears—
when you've seen one oyster you've seen them all—same said tor penis-
clams feet   I went to a Mexican restaurant to study Spanish   ordered
a Dos Equis and steamed tortillas

I suddenly heard this most gorgeous male voice belting some wailing ranchero
song de romantico   the singer   surrounded by mariachis   But when
Cordoba ended and they moved back I realized   the singer was a woman
a Chicana or Latina   the well-endowed long-eyelashes long-fingernails
kind that rules suburban households in Spanish soap operas—¡watch out!—
except she's wearing Levi's and a dusky long-sleeved angular sweater
and she has no microphone   Tremendous deep-voice volume The place
broke into applause   Even cooks and waitresses lauded this one

She sang on and on wearing her heartvoice   taking us into the sensuality
of Federico García Lorca's gypsy nights we're all missing   When she was
through   she straightened and fussed with her face   deadly ordered
coffee   looking worn-out from a weekend of love   or less   It was
Sunday night

I went back to the Feminist Erotica Festival   unplugged my dimmers
wrapped my cords went home satisfied The Singer of Spanish Songs made
my day   I'll seek her in the waltz of restaurants   She'll have this poem

On Monday   a friend I was exclaiming over the eroticism   of this singer
about announced "I think she's a he"   That makes sense   How could I
an authority on Rosettas   not recognize the overwhelming affirming
unction of the human vocal cords and the paradox of THE BODY-EROTIC
(CLItorisglotTIS)

THE LONIDIER CHRONICLES

Forget my father   Mother was so busy idolizing me I don't think I
got much help from her   countering life

When my period came   I went to bed to counteract it   But when I
started walking upright I found out I was   normal with the red

I grew up wanting to be idolized more than I was loved   Isn't that what
love was

I thought my vagina was too small to be a vagina   I picked up an under-
round filmmaker on the street   He was furious when   he couldn't get
himself   in me   Only with promises of later could I get him to stop
He came looking for me I'd moved away   He died young   His films move
about   above ground

Turns out I was extra virginal   I had a double hymen a doctor opened
right up   I had a hard time   coming out   in life   but HERE I AM

Father was a short dark-haired man   I fell in love with a short double-
dark man half-Filipino half-American Indian   We didn't feel good about
ourselves but   we fucked   wondrously   He respectively painted us

I made up my mind when I was young to act bland with people so my body
holds up IN INTENSITY OF POETRY   It was THAT or fastfizzle

I've given a lot to life I've helped a lot of people What life held
me   Being idealized got to be   passé   I looked for other pleasures

"You're looking for a mother"   "No I already had a mother"

"What you want is a goddess like any good feminist wants"   "No
goddesses don't help   with dishes the wash your job   You don't know

Clitoris Lost

what Nature is like until you've   tried to stay the sweet corners of
a house   around a maelstrom"

What I'm looking for is a wise woman like myself   Believe it or not I
like myself even when I look in the mirror   I can't tell what I look
like   but the reflection is unaffected   and slightly smiling   GIANT

What would turn me on more than wisdom is another woman   is a bevy
of wise women   Better yet   all the women of the world already all-
desirable becoming all-wise

"What about the men"   "They'll follow along"   Wisdom begets Wisdom
Given enough centuries   and disapproval   men will become desirable

As for this life finally I feel good   I'm Courting Life AND AM VERY
PARTICULAR   WHAT IT LOOKS LIKE

THE RIGHT WRITER'S CONFERENCE

I put on my man's outfit   and went to look at two old boy friends
in careless stride   on the street   in a gay men's neighborhood everyone
spoke to me "How you doin"   or stared   or both   A Black man called
"Hey She-Bear!   Hey She-Man!"   Another: "Hello <u>there</u>!"

I sat legs spread   in a café   I reached to the inside pocket of my
pinstripe suit   pulled out my father's cracked leather billfold
extracted pencil & paper and wrote "coke"   I'm surprised they didn't
give me snow   in a teaspoon   Everyone behind the counter was having
joy   dishes rattling delight   I made their day or week or month
I held the large coke   like a fellow   every finger in place in a
firm grip and downed it in quick big swallows   I wrote "check please"
I'd sat at the counter and left no testy tip

Clitoris Lost

I strode to the Writers' Conference   There was one of my X's leading
a forum   Important   Different rhetoric same tune   Lord-of-the-Fallen-
Earth   And the other one   looked at this strange   lady looking sexy
dressed as a man in a black hat with a color-flecked sprig o' feathers
tucked in the band   brim on tile over   her eyes OUTA SIGHT

Everyone stole glances at "Mystery" having fantasies   I went to friends
and gave them the eye   and a solid handshaking   Anyone who talked to
"the man" got an answer on paper   I stayed around long enough to see
how the one I loved   long ago   who had hurt me so   had fattened up
had an almost white head of hair   hardly   from aging   His hairline
had receded right   in the path of this soothsaying   Now he calls
himself   a magic name   but I could smell   the sleight scope   of his
change

Reeking of Fabergé BRUT 33 Splash-on Lotion   sweat didn't matter
heavy in my topcoat button-down vest wool socks floppy fly pants black patent

shoes variegated necktie white striped percale shirt angular-shaded ski-
glasses my Diamond Jim rings and one honey-colored curlycrown of an
indistinguishable Goodwill wig   I floated out of the conference   high
as the writer I am   one happy gold gypsy earring of a poet glinting in
the blue-dove sky   my Sojourn to Maledom gloating in me   a delicious
old gaucho refrain I!Yie!Yie!Yie!   whelping in my jackal limbs
In two close shaves in one blow my hyena bones learned what they learned

"THE KISS"–A DREAM

You were having another party   a slumber party   I entered your
living room   Only women were there   your daughters and several other
women   lounging at a long low table   You were seated in the middle
of a long couch   We were all in long flannel nightgowns   I sat down
at one end of the couch   and   after a long time   proceeded to reach
over and around you   to kiss you   As my mouth touched yours I realized
your lips were pursed in a tight refusal of pucker instead   of   a
ensuous kiss   You weren't angry   You were experimenting on me with
that kind of kiss   It was so funny I woke immediately immensely amused
still laughing about it in the morning   writing "of it"   and   "this"

THE TAKE-A-TILE HOME RESTAURANT

When you were in Deutschland I dreamed I was in a restaurant in America
where you had suggested   we meet   There were snakeserpents there
I abhor snakes   but these snakes were friendly   like   stretched-out
perfectly-still rainbows   They were the mascots of the restaurant and
had feathered pre-Columbian talking heads   The entire restaurant was
lined with the most exquisite gleaming tile   I remember being so
impressed with it and the painting on the tiles I   fixated   on   one
piece   wanted to take a tile home

THE DREAM YOU HEARD

We were riding along hills in gorgeous blue sky sun in an open-air car
We were "The Creation" in Haydn's billowing-waves music   elatedly
listening to a recording of your last week's concert performance

quipu diary by quintana roo

For the one good with number . . . the one called "Quipu"

*Quipu the Incas knot string records went ". . . beyond mere compilation of statistics it was used as a supplement for a memory of historical events." —Victor Wolfgang von Hagen

WHEN LOVE IS LEFT AT LIMA

In Peru I lived instead of wrote,
I watched instead of moved as a poet,
and the imaginary I carried with me
was from Mexico and fit well
like brightly-striped peddlers' bundles
brought from the Antigua train
to the streets of Lima.

My last love was so imperfect
I traveled to Mexico to escape.
Love did not stop,
and I escaped.

In Mexico City you placed
a round table between us, jammed it
between the beds and opened the curtains
at night so we could play cards.

Conditions are mucho mejor in Lima.

IN THE PERU OF THE MIND

I know people like me.
The problem is most people are repetitive
in their games and pride and knowledge.
I get impatient

and run to the mountains,
remain with an isolated tribe of Peruvians
with an average lifespan of 625 years.
Time enough for tolerance;

time enough to learn not to like power;
time enough for all languages,
all history, wisdom.
<u>Time enough to accept</u>?

THE GOLD MUSEUM

Grey garden museo at the outskirts of San Isidro:
guns, swords, armor, maces, slings, axes, cannons,

a ground level full of hate
and a basementful of beautiful blinding.

FIVE MILLION PEOPLE LIVE IN LIMA

You are a very private person.
With a poet, little is private,
all is honorable.
Poetry has to be personal to enter
the immortal double doors
of a creator-god who commands
occurrences be clearly recited.
I am writing this with diarrhea. Private.
Poetry is as private as a quipu rope.
No one knows what it says when they see it
but Viracocha.

DOS NOCHERNIEGOS: TWO NIGHT OWLS

I dreamed I was taping music some feminists
were making, but my tape recorder
wove tunes among their music instead.
They don't like my woof;
I awoke with bad feeling.

You were awakened by your voice
poking through sleep so loudly
it disturbed you.
I felt like asking was it your body talking,
did you ask your body what it's weaving?

MUMMY BUNDLES

We look for tapestries so ancient,
tiny round-eyed and open-mouthed and no-nose
creatures repeat themselves o'er and o'er in cloth
like a moan. Terror or is it comedy moves me
to look close at peanut-brittle cadavers?

Pizarro's remains in a church:
he sure has thick neck, arm, and leg bones
the size of my neck, arms and legs carrying flesh.

His overbearing demeanor has caved away.

He seems to be laughing like all bodies laugh
through ashes, memories, and effort at
upkeep of ornate cathedrals.

In warehouses in Lima they X-rayed
mummy bundles and found
all that's left

under gold masks,
funny gunnysack faces
and tight-braided wigs
is a dish, a pipe,
some feathers,
missing film, a camera,
a tape recorder, twenty
dollars' worth of soles,
twelve cassette tapes,
two sweaters,
and all kinds of messages besides talking.

ARTIFACT-BLINDED

U.S.A. museum officials label
a coincidence, identical symbols inscribed
on the pottery of Mexico and South America.

Pre-Columbian Peruvians visited Tenochtitlán,
and the pre-Columbian Mexicans visited Peru.
They shared coca leaves in the Andes,

Crossed arrows in the Amazon,
laid out their wares together in half light,
suffered separate betrayals at night.

They went back to their respective lands
with sacrifice and each other
written all over their faces.

The only case for the fact
Peruvians and Mexicans didn't meet
is Mexico had books; Peruvians, none.

Why wouldn't Peruvians use books
Mexicans gave them
behind museum officials' backs?

Maybe they swore off them like
I vowed I would not write a word this time,
not a word.

The hours filled with birds, rivers, clouds;
words not uttered,
continue in slumber.

CUZCO

A Peruvian town in the mountains so high up travelers
have to go down and down and down to get to
Machu Picchu.
My head felt pushed in; my body, ponderous; my breath,
in another town.

A desk clerk hands us Room Key 13.
My nose and my friend's nose blew bloody at Cuzco.
We were dizzy wind blowing through double panpipes.
We kept running into pure wooden tunes, vivid threads,
sheered existence; I got locked in.

Everywhere I travel with love heavy as two suitcases,
three handbags full of taping equipment, occult systems,
rechargeable batteries, and a complete fall wardrobe.
The object is not to have to stop to wash clothes.
We didn't stop; we kept on spindling.

PISAC MARKETPLACE

Down a windy gorge fifteen miles lower than Cuzco,
women wear men's hats, carry rainbow babies
in broad miles of brilliant cloth
and lay out potatoes to sell on alpaca blankets
zigzagged with pointy-beaked birds
and startled-eared cats.
In the dirt-floor church little boys make
sounds on hard-to-blow conch shells.
In open air children come up to me
wanting to sing into the "micro."
I play it back to a cacophony of booths
of broad smiles.

SACSAHUAMÁN MEANS IMPENETRABLE"

"Sacsahuamán"

People in the bus joke
the way the guide
pronounces it: "Sexy woman."

Tall-bouldered walls were smooth-rounded.
Not a sharp edge.
Not a penny could be placed between . . .

By the roadside a woman was working a loom.
A tourist tossed a coin out the window
at the calm fortress of a loom maker.

Under siege, Sacsahuamán fell quickly.

THE TRAIN TO MACHU PICCHU

A train that was made Alp-narrow
kept heading uphill backward
and rerouting itself forward.
Trains only travel in one direction at Machu Picchu;
only one train track to Machu Picchu.
Train windows kept unwinding the lives of people
in valleys and mountains—
barefoot women with machetes
and men peeing in sight of the train.
They come to visit each other,
lay out goods; they came
to live by the train—dogs darting
rapidly at the sound of it
the sound of it.

A gringo asked for a tamale at a stop.
It sparkled in his mouth,
and we were hungry.
Everyone warned him not to eat it.
He said it won't hurt;
they boil them in water like they do in Texas;
besides, this one has no meat in it.
We looked to see: pure sunmeal.

The guide explained the trauma of the country.
How land was given to the people
and it didn't work; people would only work
one day's need at a time; and now the land
is being given back to landowners
it was taken from, and maybe
they will really do something with it.

The guide said don't record this.

Plots for farming are rounded at the corners
instead of tri-squared like those in the States.

The ground the Incas farm is imperfect
and smooth like the hand has made care.

370 Soil is poor, mostly, but tendered, hand-shaped.
You almost dispensed pills to me by hand.

MACHU PICCHU

The smoothed-together steps of Incas
leading to the sundial.
No sooner do I get there
than some German men arrive at the same pinnacle.
I don't know what to think,
listening to their marked language,
their guttural tongues exclaim like children
over the sight of a huge stone slab
and an upright boulder
that marks time.

A daintiest snail shell
is lying on a ledge
of a five-sided window
in the intellectual quarters at Machu Picchu.
The feeblest contradiction of design
took precedence over a place
where ideas uncurled
delicately.

I am frightened to tell you,
and I won't be hurt.
I have lived so long,
wariness has fallen off
and I wander numbed,
to the tunes of high mountains.

SOL DE ORO

We have taken so many flights in ten days,
experienced so many raptures in ordinary
lives of a different people, we are made high,
sip coca tea—a stimulant—to come down.

A stronger type of coca leaf is legal to chew
past sponginess and can be taken anywhere in Peru.
Spaniards forced the Incas to chew it
in huge amounts to get more work out of them.

FOTO

In the photograph the man took at the airport
you are bundled up unrecognizable
and your eyes are hiding.
But he caught the accuracy
of the wrist's strength
of your own camera's hand.

—O cherished picture of
O female efficacy—

HEART OF PÁJARO MOSCA

Pájaro mosca /"Hummingbird"—the word
the five-year-old Peruvian princess
in the childcare center taught me.
"Lynn, when I grow up, I'm going to marry you."

The cooks call her "princess" because
she's from Peru, picks at her food,
won't drink milk unless it's heated
to the right degree.

A green valentine a child gave me
at the same children's center:
"Lynn your a good teacher.
your smart and
not dumb.
Love
Carmen"

MAMACUNA

A place of learning for women
at the Sun Temple overlooking the sea
where not a trace nor shard is left;
"José is Here," sketched in stone.
The stuff poems are made of.
<u>Tomorrow, goodbye.</u>

NAZCA SIGNALS TO SPACE

Lines on the land in the country say:
roads, mounds, fields, plains, chickens,
smart pigs, lovable spitting llamas; mestizos
slowing down cars, bartering for care; Inca-
Kola, Inca banana split.

I am so full—so stretched-out as Nazca writings—
I could die.

It doesn't matter that I won't see you forever.
In hotels when you slept, you slept so hard,
I thought you would cry.
The night before the morning,
tears welled like foam on a pisco sour.
The waiter thought I had taken a hot bite.
How could I and be an Inca I asked myself,
just a little saltwater turning into
silver under cover; glint of shiny absence.
Mysterious snoring soothed me to sleep—
so near the sea, so near the sea.

IN HALF PORTIONS OF SUN

"Mañana," we told the shoeshine boy.
"Goodbye."
"Mañana." Truth
keeps people apart.
We barely got out of Lima before
air traffic closed.
One day the garbage men were on strike;
another day, nurses; finally,
airline pilots.
We escaped by the skin of our feelings.
"Goodbye."
"Mañana."

Worrying my suitcases would break open.
I burst into poetry at Lost Angels airport.
hour awaiting flight, images came at me
like figures sticking out of woven fragments.
"They carried all they needed with them."
That is what you wished me.
Protection.

The Incas of Peru
had no record of writing. They tied knots.
When I see you again,
I will remember this to you.
Say it didn't happen, Quipu.

I gaze out the plane window
at hazy San Francisco.
What strange land is this,
what smoky valley lies south?

The banging 4th of July distances me.
I could not recognize names nor voices.
I'm on Lima time: to bed at seven, awake at four;
supermarkets pale the stomach.
I don't want to know what the news is.
The taxi driver told me the fare had gone up.
Going to the airport cost twelve dollars;
coming back, seventeen.
I sit with my dog and fix alleviate green tea,
return to the Trip of Double Happiness
otra vez, otra vez.

MOUNTAIN SICKNESS

Kaiser Group Medical Plan is a California joke.
A nurse puts a thermometer in your mouth,
says, "Leave it in three minutes."
A doctor comes right in and takes
the thermometer out. I say,
"But the nurse said leave it in three minutes."
The doctor says, "Oh, don't worry."
It takes at least five days to get test results.
No wonder I'm never sick, I could be dead.

Prescribed Pepto-Dismal did not rid me of diarrhea.
Finally persuaded the doctor to give me
the little white pills. He sulked, insisted
little white pills won't help. I plead,
"I want to feel better, even if it's temporary."
Was cured the next day, and, having passed all tests
for no organisms, still felt fourteen-thousand feet
high in my head like I did in Cuzco—like hurtling
through space backwards. Great for creativity
but bad for a public school district employee
(in increasingly narrowing atmosphere).

Returning, I learned of a woman
who travelled with many doctors to the Himalayas
to learn acupuncture and Tibetan cures.
They too returned high as kites,
ready to stay up there, quit work;
found themselves travelling to get together
as a support group six months after high mountains.
It's definitely a phenomenon and not just me.
My brain has altered. I called the woman doctor.

She advised me not to quit my job or do anything
extreme—gradually reacclimatize to sea level.

I'm not sure I want my feet to touch ground
when my head can really fly. My memory plays on
hard-to-blow double panpipes, heart-a-flutter
hummingbird spiral-tonguing-toots.
High mountain Peruvians have larger lung capacities
than we and five million more red blood cells.
Something to do with lack of oxygen—
rush of centuries' freshness.
I had mutated without adapting,
a woman without a land, suspended between
Kaiser Medical Plan and the real silver ring
on my finger of a hand that holds a redblack
bean in its palm to ward off evil.
Do you suppose if I quit my job
this magic ring acquired in Lima would cure me
of feeling ill from uncaring practices,
this strange land I find myself hyperventilating in?

fire-rimmed eden

EMMA GOLDMAN SEWING CIRCLE IN THE DAYMARE RISE

I DREAM OF A LOVER OF LONG AGO

I kicked you out of my house
but allowed you in my dream:
it's all right for a Black man
to paint portraits of Romans
in fiery robes, hardening forth.

You sat on my couch wanting to know
what I thought of your canvases'
tremorous feelings for
the human subject. "They
have no meaning because you

are cruel to your wife and child."
You resisted, then admitted it,
and sat in your ejaculation;
not sexual—more like you had
wet pants. (Water as realization?)

I told you it was all right
and woke, after enunciating
over and over, "Be kind to your
wife and child, be kind to
your wife and child."

ON THE TRAIL OF THE GREAT WHITE SOYBEAN

The Human Bean

Now science has discovered
the soybean is
one of our progenitors.
Yes human beings
stem from soybeans.
Some same basic
substance in a soybean
is in the breakdown of
our blood.
The walls of our cellstructure
trumpet, "Mama!"
Little question mark of a
soybean stretches upright,
stands up like a doughy breadfellow
on a tenuous taper of a leg and shouts,
"Greatgreatgreatgreatgreatgreatgranddaughter!"
Have you noticed how
a moistened sunlit
growing soybean
resembles a
foetus?
I never thought I'd see.

What the world's coming to
is enough to make
vegetarians cannibals.
Bean sprouts erupting
from grinding mouths, "Oi! Oi!"

screaming to get out, writhing, "Oy! Oy!"
falling fragments on the floor.
So, a string of life dashed
at the foot of humanist spread.
A veritable Moloch situation,
these half-
eaten, long-
lost, simplest
ancestors, ours,
oppressed:
"Free me! Free me!"
Like thinly-
spread belief.
"Spare me! Spare me!"
Who proteins us,
sparse,
expire.

The Avenging Soybeans

This is a soybean grown up,
answering the phone,
making money.
A soybean drives a Ford Pinto.
Now stop it, little critter,
get back in your grave of green hairs,
or I'll swallow you whole.
Don't make me choke.
You didn't have to have me.
You say you didn't ask
to be born either?
I wonder what would happen
if we mated a soybean
with a human, since they're
"of the same flesh?"

Little John Waynes with
tapeworm faces.
Stop the thought.
Step on a soybean, it'll
squash, juice like spit
in the wind, undistinguishable
as movement under a moistened cloth
in a box on a windowsill.

These are soybeans gotten politicized.
Soybeans stick their little heads out
and motion to the cameras
they've got under wraps.
They make underground films.
A feature-length about how
soybeans were left
in the sun too long
and grew into giant foetuses.
The huge soybeans went looking
for vegetarians.
The soybeans' giant stomachs
were really their heads.
Their foetus exteriors swallowed up
the vegetarians, held them prisoner
in their stomachs—one person
per soybean.
The vegetarians sat there,
feeling water-logged, shrinking.
The soybeans sat in the sun,
their stomachs lit up like thin moons,
and you could see the vegetarians
moving about like waning patients
under hospital bedcovers.
The vegetarians have lost their
features and look like vegetables

sitting inside soybean skin.
And the giant soybeans who
have plomped themselves
a great amount of space
on Earth, ruminate:
what's theirs was theirs
in the first place.

The Soybean's Cousin

Talk of soybeans
has made me hungry.
I'm going to go get
a nice, soft bean to eat.
I'll just eat one, so as not
to hurt many.
What I have in mind is a chickpea bean,
cousin to a soybean.
The chickpea I select has tap-dance shoes on
and is singing, "Jesus Loves Me."
How can I eat him?
That is how the soybean's cousin
was saved.
And to this day, he's a famous
traveling entertainer with stigmata
on his palms and through his yellow knees,
and I'm a meat-eater.

HEY NONI OH

Into the wind with a 50 lb. falcon (You said 15)   a hatchet-
conflagration of a hood-draped head   tied with fine   string   You
bruised like the princess rests on 20 mattresses (Or was it 15)
positioned on a pea   You hid from your mother   swellings
on your leather-bound wrist " " so she'd let you go galloping   <u>O</u>
<u>open field release o' poetry</u>   <u>Claw-released arm</u>   <u>held erect</u>
<u>awaiting</u> <u>the return o'THE FEEL O' THE CATCH O' PERFECT WORDS</u>

SISTER-IN-LAW

To go to your house
is to enter Summerhill.
A place for kids.
(Adults, bring hard hats.)
I start getting a headache
while admiring your son's
drawings of trains and trucks
across walls that become
freeways for children's brilliance.
Your daughter screams in her cups:
she's a starlet in her mirrors.
They're persuaded to take baths
early evening in hopes they'll
unwind. They parade
between their beds and TV
while you're back and forth
all-day weary.
Going to your home is like entering
a zone for constructing adults.
A sun place for timberline
kids. Children, I ache;
you make me sing, Paulette,* of
singularity of high mountain trees
stretching up—in a hardhat world.

---

* Paulette was Lynn's brother Fred's wife (Lynn's sister-in-law) during part of the 1960s and '70s.

EL TECOLOTE Y PESCADO EN LA PLAYA
DE NAVIDAD

I relinquish Spanish daily
because it's making me "mareada":
sick by the side o' the sea.

I embrace Spanish nightly
en l'arena del mar
a la luz de la luna.

"Mi cama" is my boat.
Estudio 'til the little light
gets tired.

In my peapod bed
I'm floundering
through fjords.

I study Spanish
to get home. Howd'yasay
"sucker" in Spanish?

"Foolsafe."
Yo soy
una especie

de sauce americano.
I am the kitty
in the whistletree

—O willow-rue,will-o'do!—
learning two languages
at once, like an eye

on each side of a head:
¡O guisante de olor!
¡O sweet pea owl!

The high-capped boat
is sitting in the sand.
The owl and the popeyed fish

dance in the dark
of high-kept shores
of my house of

Swedish borderleaf.
Cat's in the tree
and can't get down.

Song's at the back o' the year
in foggy frogtown.
"El sapo estaba de viaje."

The frog has married
the road, but the cat
wants home to the owl.

Estudio Español
en mi peagreen boat
nodding through fiords.

Oh play it,
banjo y guitarra,
the song at the back o' the book—

"All I Want for Christmas
is Snowflakes
on Palm trees!"

Sing it,
motley crew,
bring Christmas in:

may Sauce de México—
the sun as the star at the top—
grace your December.

Navidad, 1978

SISTERS OF THE GRIFFIN

Susan   Thanx for saying you could see my invisible Mayan identification
bracelet   as sometimes I wonder where the tourist trinket I'm on
a riderless horse that knows where it's going

Joanna   To escape stone creatures or home   words take a sailor to
the North Sea of her typewriter where Sappholand is jungle wrap around
mapped and tapped out   It's a regular rappers' reunion   to meetcha

Eat peanuts Susan while your poetry grows into women turning into wild
horses in reverse in which the cruelty in the animal kingdom is undone
where balking horses turn into Amazons   thereafter   Tell you a mule:

> I'm not a woman,
> I'm a secret woman.
> I'm not a man.
> Tell you what I am:
> an angel.
> Don't laugh;
> I'm not bragging.
> Heaven is 144°
> hotter than Hell.
> Can't an angel
> be a person
> and a Mayan?
> A ventriloquist
> angel, I write
> in imitation of
> the kind of angel
> not to tangle with.

Joanna I want to call up   the fabulous last century Fox sisters Maggie
and Katie   who went "pop" under the table shaping backbone to
liberation   For some reason, which no one understood at the time,

the children used to call on Mr. Splitfoot to make noises.
"Katie exclaimed: 'Mr. Splitfoot, do as I do';
clapping her hands. The sound instantly followed her
with the same number of raps; . . ."   A hoax but O what a way
for two women to earn a living   trot their double-jointed toes to Europe

4,000 years looking for love of a missing woman   traveler of the last
century   is no longer on her way to Egypt nightly   Meaning   bandages
of the mummy unwrap   insides found to be a seventy-eight-year-old
woman wearing riding pants and boots in the Yucatán
                              Stēlē:

                              World's
                              oldest
                              explorer
                              Edna
                              Robb
                              Webster
                              poking
                              around
                              uncovering
                              Edna
                              Robb
                              Webster
                              attributes
                              her
                              youth
                              to
                              finding
                              herself
                              through
                              Mayans
                              She
                              found
                              humanity

                    born
                    of
                    a
                    griffin
                    in Mindland

I don't know Mindland language yet,
but three raps of the big toe means
it is important for me not to always
say what I mean:

Mrs. Splinthoof, do as I do: (Clap three times.)
(Knock on wood thrice.) "Jo-an-na Gri-ff-in."
(Knock twice.) "Su-san Grif-fin."
(Knock four times.) "Kar-en Bro-dine."
(Knock twice.) "Al-lie."
(Knock once.) "Light-Light–Light–Light—Light—Light——— Light."
(Knock twice.) "Sha-ron, Bet-ty, Su-ki."

                              I had a rubber doll named Suki,
                              and one day she turned to me
                              and said something
                              I don't remember.
                              That she had a message
                              unaided by mechanical device,
                              that me and my doll shared
                              something scary (I was little,
                              I didn't know the inexplicable
                              had hold of me at the door of
the universe)—if you know anything about
   the Mayans—there aren't any Mayans
   the Mayans—there aren't any Mayans

BECKY, OF SUSAN

A twelve-year-old
with a too-big hat on,
the first
female
to ask me
to dance
in two years!
Doesn't she
know I've
turned down
queens?

Books
turn into
churning bodies
and first memories.
Having birthdays
between dances,
authors
are
waterballs
glimpsing, if willing,
origins.
Tending

writing,
I catch my head,
step with adolescence—
Traumereis and Reveries—
surprised to be moving
inside gazelle eyes(!)(!)

an entire forest
for company.

In some
dance

—rebellious—
the hat

will fit

the melodic head.

EXEMPLAR

In another life
you were
a nun.

Now, they
persecute
you.

To be persecuted
is to be
made a saint.

saints
remain
whether

wanted
or not.
Saints

stay
because
there are

so few.
The rest
"know not . . ."

They pull
at Might
in innocence

bring
mountains
down,

ignorant
of hurts
they aim

from harm
done them:
how saints

are undone.
Each person
is a mountain,

a volcano
of curiosity,
an intelligent

formation—
but raised
to behave

like a bulwark
thrusting
irrational

arrows.
True saints
don't think

they're
saints.
They resemble

resented mothers,
pulled-on
nursemaids,

ambulance drivers
caught up in sirens,
spreading

white sheets,
pounding hearts
to thud,

applying
a light
to the temple.

Saints remain—
not in righteousness—
but in answer

to lowland
living.
People clamour

to saints—
something foreign—
suspect.

It is a saint's duty
to be.
(Forgive

a moral Swede
for preaching
a Catholic

to continue
to watch over,
endure.)

A SWEDISH FAMILY WILL AND WILL NOT ACCEPT

A Swedish-*   family-   will accept-   a married man-
in the family-   disappearing- in Europe- Mexico- and Asia- for months-
and you know-   he is sleeping-
with kept women-   because-   he's the blood son-
with the most money-   and because-   when he's home
he can't-   keep his hands-   off-   other-   female-
family-   members-   and-   his wife's-   best-woman-
friend.

It will-   accept-   mixed marriages-   and mixed-
marriage-   offspring.

It would not-   have accepted-   my uncle-   who married
into-   the family-   leaving-   his wife-   when he-
was seventy-four-   wanting-   to live-   with a
twenty-five-year-old-woman-   who would finally-
not accept-   that he used-   judgmental-   aspects-
of a Swedish-   family-   as an excuse-   not to leave-
his wife-   So-   in his eighties-   he fell-   in love-
with a twenty-year-old-   woman-   who is married-
to an eighty-year-old-man.-   My uncle-   invited them-
to live-   in his home-   where he lives-   with his wife.-
Our family-   accepts-   their presence-   because
it pretends-   that my aunt-   appreciates- the
arrangement.

It accepted-   my traveling-   uncle's-   new lover-
his wife's-   ex-   best friend-   but would no longer-
accept-   his wife   -who had been-   one of the family-
for forty-   years.-   When my aunt-   or uncle-   or
my mother-   was asked-   how she's doing-   they'd

answer- "I don't know- I haven't seen her-
since she broke up- with our brother"- and silence-
followed.

Our family- does not accept- any in-law- Who
separates from- or divorces- any family member.-
I'm the oldest- and expected-most-of- cousin.-
My youngest- blood cousin- is Karen- Brodine.-
We both- write poetry- and fail- to make money.-
Karen's mother Mary- married into- the family.
Mary- was adored- by the family- she's beautiful-
charming- intelligent- a communist- and a dream-
of a piano player.- Every member- of the family,-
a musician- I remember- family gatherings- at
Karen's- house- where everyone- would bring
homemade food- and their harp or cello- or violin.

Scandinavian polkas- embroidered- the air- and
string quartet music- flowered- out open- doors-
all- afternoon- while we children- waded- the
stream- near the house- or wandered- backroads-
that border- forests.- At the call- of a voice-
we'd run- to the house- for all- that food- and
those crust-swollen pies- Mary made.- Karen- and
her mother- and father- picked- wild-berries.

When Karen's- parents- divorced -I remember-
Grandmother- saying- "It's Mary's fault."- No-
family member- saw Mary- again- although- she
lives- in that same- old surrounded-by-blackberries-
house.- Not even- when she had a stroke.-
To separate- from a Brodine- is to be- unfaithful-
to the family.- To leave- the family- is not-
acceptable.- Rigidity- harkening back- to old-
country ways.- Susan- Sontag, -a Swede, -herself-

says so.-   I'm hardly-   an exception.-   I'm close-
to the older-   generation.-   Grandma's-words-
stuck.

I've thought-   of going-   to see   Karen's mother.-
The day-   I completed-   this poem-   I learned-she
died.

*The pause for each hyphen-space is observed like a swift, silent upbeat.

INTO THESE OTHER WATERS

Not potatoes,
but faces
of a history
forming.

Coldplate workplace,
and my potato lover
relegating me
to onion time.

You having to make stew
of Emily Dickinson's
cabbages and kings.
The regalia

of human behavior
in the tarot cards.
Direst perpetrations,
inhumanly acts

done up in plumes.
The spectacle enters
the door in skeleton guise
of glazed shadows.

The dragshow
of the universe
shines
atrociously.

Karen, put the potatoes on.
In a fairy tale she enters
the ubiquitous forest
and all that is in it.

an arc, a maze, the facing

B.A. DREAM

I dreamed I was visiting the house of the woman I love and
loved for six years. She shut herself away in the main part
of the second-story house, which was another house, and yet, I
was in the living room of the house which seemed to be a second,
surrounding house. Coming across a photograph of her I used it
to begin to design a picture or her on the dining room table. I
used different mediums: pens, colored chalk, and strips of paper
and made a striking portrait or her. I knew she would pass
and it would please her. A few other people were there and com-
mented, what an admirable likeness my picture was of the woman.

When her husband saw the portrait, he began to tamper with
it. Then I realized I had painted his face—a Melvyn Douglas
face—into one end of it. He sat down on his face, and when he
got up, his nose stuck to the seat of his pants. Each time he
rose up, his nose would stretch as if his face would pull off
from the table. I consulted with someone in another room and
decided to leave. But when I reentered the living room, I
realized my love's husband had pulled off strips from my portrait
of her. I determined not to leave until I fixed the picture once
again. I left, gathering art materials, and when I returned, I
realized the table had disappeared. It had been dismantled and
turned into couches on which a number of men in business suits
were seated, including the husband. They were reading newspapers.
I realized I couldn't redo her portrait anyway because I no longer
had her photograph to draw by.

Before I took leave, I entered the house proper to use the bathroom. When I exited, she came out of the quarters where she was staying. I could see varicose veins on her nose, but she looked exquisite. I told her I was sorry I had caused trouble in her house. She replied. "Lynn, what would help you is to see the humor in this, to laugh at what just happened." I wanted to say, "I can and do find most everything funny, but not this. I'm serious about you. My love for you is serious." However, I didn't say this because her two daughters were with her. They didn't know of my feelings for their mother.

RUNNING FROM AIDS

I am running running from AIDS the same as you ran from competence
Mourners marvel you   were both   most popular boy and class clown
o' '66

Troubling me at your funeral: reverence for your lack of seriousness
That rot asked for the big league baseball score two days before death
sad America totaling

Your beam of smile   a harmonica with wah-wah pedal: your choice of
record to be played at the funeral   How come when you bought
my lesbian poetry and said you liked it/you didn't say   I'm gay too

It's not Gays that arrow-spread AIDS in America It's men   And
drug addiction and prostitution: forms of male oppression   I escape
to a gay bar with gold palm trees sandy muse and black sitcom

The bartender and I the only souls   He apologizes for a lack of crowd
I say I   prefer   quiet   having come from an AIDS funeral   He
says "oh the bartender here passed away of AIDS two weeks ago"

Next day I run into a friend haunted by the leprosy-looks of some men
at an AIDS clinic where she accompanies a male friend running downhill
from AIDS "Snowmen! *Snowb a l l l i   n   g   !

*Shout the words.

LESBIAN BLOOD COULD PAY TO PRINT A POUND OF POETRY

I had gone to a camp horror flick called *Buckaroo Banzai*.
That night I daymared about a heterosexual San Francisco
poet and publisher or poets, who always snubbed me because
my poetry's gay.

He finally showed friendly teeth, invited me to his
veritable country estate where he was to hold a reception
for a gay male poet. I wondered that the splendorous
view from rows of bay windows was partially fogged,

why the poet and his wife would want such a look at
nature. A number of poet guests had gathered. Suddenly,
the heterosexual poet/publisher grew hysterical about
the guest of honor, bewailing that he had just heard

the man had contracted AIDS. The heterosexual poet recited
all the therefore polite, social things no one could do
at the party. The gay poet arrived with his boyfriend,
their faces—swollen grocery bags with pop marble eyes,

gawky aliens straight out of the bucking movie.
They bumped about wildly. Because we were friends,
the gay male poet greeted me with a kiss to the mouth.
He and his boyfriend then leapt on top of the house.

The poets followed them there. The reception became
a roof party much to the begrudgement of the heterosexual
poet host who remained in the depths of the house with
his wife and their foggy breath windows.

MAKING JOHN JACOB FAMOUS

In response to a disfavorable review
and in light of feminist librarians
who select books of "favorable" review

Buggernot the man nudged by Juggernaut

What mindless acceptance of John Jacob Discriminating Book Reviewer

For

The American Library Association who said my poetry was   "surrealist"
WHEN ALL OTHER REVIEWS SAID I'm Gertrude Stein   Show me

I'm Gertrude

Stein   or surreal   Oh what page of what book you didn't really read
am I   not real: poetry as Cheap Sapphic Publicity

Surreal is safe it's easy to say   Surreal escapes   It is irrational it
startles   Surreal abstracts   It Is an excuse for not looking   It is
static   unchanging as a canvas of painted sea that extends into sea sameness
and does not mean   It is a woman librarian who reads 2,000 reviews
instead of one book on a beach in a month   How oppressive: Surrealism
Librarians Reviewers Lonidiers "excesses apparent in duplicate are are
fraught with a faltering technique"   (another free ad, Mother)

You're pure   Book Reviewer

Dear dear Man Sir Jacob Dear Mr. my my reviewer of "That Classical Lesbian"
who interests you as "a type of contemporary phenomenon"   wing-ed shot
down into bland landscape of of commentary over whether this "insistent"
She-Poet with navel hair on her face (I shall escape)   "is more interesting
than truly talented" or   truly interested than talented morally   or
two women's bodies doing something naughty as seeing and being immortal
Do-it darlings encouraging all canvases to turn an enriched lavender angel
labia hue

Moo-moo says A man about a purple cow Meow-meow says Purple Cow about making JohnJohn JacobJacob famousfamous   altering his fright with a figa uphis   Taught Man (I'd rather not C or B) holding F RUI T between his teeth (Godnose where he got it)*   making an A outa himself repeating his jawbone in the wind on paper

LESBIANS LIBRARIANS NEED TO GET
TOGETHER TO ASCRIBE THE PACKANIMALDOM
WORLD OF CRITICS LESBIANS LIBRARIANS

*A raised fist with the thumb between the index and third fingers. "The 'fig gesture' . . . its origin was in an order given by Barbarossa to the people of Milan to remove with their teeth a fig which had become lodged in the anus of his mule."—Magic and the Supernatural

TOURNAMENT OF CELEBRANT LOVE

There's Billie Jean and her husband, King;
there's Rita Mae* and what's-her-name;
and then, there's me and "E.G."
(I'm not at liberty to disclose her name.)
I'm her confidant. In this narrowing
circle, only I am allowed to
call her "Von."
What drew us together was her name
and my racket: "match"—"love."

We live in a house on a cliff by the sea
paid for by her wins and my love;
a house of honey dripping from
freshwater fountains, with eleven bedrooms
for putting up ten sets of tennis players
for a weekend's competition.

When Von's gone clubbing, I tend our
few gem plants and jewel-collared animals
that can stand salt air,
while reciting her promise,
"I'm faithful to you," to me.

She wears thigh-length white tennis
mini-skirts that I disapprove of,
that hold ball after ball after ball
in their folds, and loose-fitting
white terrycloth t-shirts so her opponent
will feel the full freedom
of her lean, mean serve.

At cocktail parties to raise funds
for the Florida winter quarters'
tethered set, people ask
what I do for a living.
I don't tell them. I say, "I'm recovering
from the long-distant Olympic trials
of Ulalume, and, with stricken eye,
recite, "Annabel Lee! Annabel Lee!"
Hearing that and seeing a dark bird,
they ask nothing more—
not even, "Who you with?"

I'm with E.G., champion tennis star
with straw-straight hair drawn back
in a rubber band from her face
like a slingshot.
I'm with the sleek look of body elastic.
She loans me the key to her animal Ferrari,
and I offer "Von" sweet snarls of poetry.
I'm given locker room privileges
in the wives' side of the clubhouse
in exchange for words that rhyme
with "ghoul" and "gone."

I'll give E.G. away, someday, take
The darling of the jet set, tennie groupies
to the bank. She's not reached her peak—
Big "E"—"Biggie." She's twenty-three:
"married, with double garage&rumpus room
walls of rackets for kids." I'll wait.
<u>What you've done for me, Honey,</u>
<u>I'll take to the nation, someday.</u>

Alone at home, I sit and watch
her flaring loins from a secret tv angle,

her let-ball teeter on the edge,
then drop. No one knows
my name is poetry. Anonymity grows
like mold on a green tennis ball.
And when I call her "Von"
on six-o'clock news, at eleven o'clock
you'll witness a star tennis player deny
she ever heard of "40-Love" and "Game."

I'll take her to the cleaners.
Two players in beaming white pantsuits
whamming the moon back and forth
at one another surrounded by woodgreen
benches, cement echoes and nationwide
coverage; two women facing one another
down in a court at Whimperdom.

A kingdom for a kiss, I win.
I win our lily quarters on a cliff
overlooking the Sea of Californee.
I win the Ferrari and replace
the panther hood ornament with
an actual falcon. And, E.G., the loser,
has to forevermore tread, oh, so lightly
the circuit of impeccable heterosexuals.
I admit, all this publicity
of the underhanded serve, has furthered
poetry immensely.

*Rita Mae Brown wrote a book about her affair with a woman tennis star. It's called,
Sudden Death.

TWO FOR MARGARET FABRIZIO

Resonance

Lion-faced winged revelers I was trying to figure out
whether the sash of your redblack outfit was from Mexico—
you looked so comfortable in an anarchy-knitted afghan.

The rose-stemmed object you threw into the space of flame
became a Japanese paper umbrella, umbra-crumpling,
startling someone.

The costume of the coals or the Chinese impersonator's
fireplace sucked   in,in   folded instant.
Wing-faced lion revelers breathed spruce of fire.

Wineglasses reflecting electric lickings inside
dusk-frosted light fixtures, the room became THE FUTURE—
harpsichord-poised on the shoulders of the New Year,

shawl-wrapped, circumspect: purpose-on-Earth is winged
faces of lion revelers, griffinhead o'er the mantle,
with wings for ears, sailing into the unheard-of night,

the gamelan voice of the man annunciating bell tones'
zenith at Chartres as the suntanned Muses roll in—
hammermusic !   lift of eyes !   "Reverie and Surmise"—

Hayseed and Saffron

> There was truth
> and there was untruth,
> and if you clung
> to the truth even
> against the whole world,

> You were not mad.
> —George Orwell, 1984

A guru
rides donkeys,
has a white beard,
collects people
around him who believe him
an alabaster amulet.

A philosopher
relinquishes
India import business,
her hair the shade
of saffron—resonance
pungencies pop out of Pan:

!turmeric!   !cumin!
!mustard!   !cardamom!
!cayenne!   tamarind exposure

of anarchist hand.

Gurus need pomp of adore,
serve worshipper pie to simple
treasure believers. Oh, Hayseed!

Ah, Saffron . . .
Beyond intaglio window,
     birds sing
         then

            listen to
        themselves
     having sung

BARBARA GRIER* AND FRIEND

To meet you was to   meet women from my childhood   the oracular eyes of
Norma Sanderson my piano teacher   the breeze of seamstress cook and
canner Floy Bagley   the magnanimity of Holly Fetch a police chief's wife
who took my mother in as a border before my mother met my father and
introduced them: Sigrid to Sampson

Holly Fetch announced she was my godmother and nicknamed me
                                                          Sammy Lynn
Fragrances of Bach and Beethoven floated out the springy screen door of
Norma Sanderson's greenhouse lent stature to crisp-lobed roses she grew
Both the Bagleys and Sandersons built summer cabins one of knotty pine
by itself at a lake one of logs all alone   by a creek where I played
naked   baptized by Nature

Forty years later there you stood with Norma Sanderson's eyes   and your
friend's heart was that of Holly Fetch   Safe in the forest I was shocked
out of my spell of disbelief   and wrote a poem   The surge of women from
childhood   Floy Bagley's kind shaping hands

---

* Barbara Grier was at the time this poem was written the editor and publisher of
Naiad Press, based in Tallahassee, FL.

COMMUNICATION IS WHAT I THINK

(Heart of fragilest gold, the smouldering turn-of-century
valentine and the kissing elephants postcard are folded away
precious.)

You took the romance right out of our lives, leaving
two individuals   with problems.   413

Beware of a band of tall, golden, ladies with sea spiny, flounced
skirts and snakes wreathing their torsos (you're as transparent
as a daphne), sneaking up and attaching a bumper sticker to your
car: VULNERABLE IS BEAUTIFUL!

Maybe we'll meet   as two tourists in Crete.
The wine sea   you keep insisting   is boiling red   after showing
me   loving blue.

GO GENTLY INTO THAT GOOD NOVEMBER

Aroused by Sappho's ease-stricken poetry
stride, how like her, you, I were, letting
rain break the world of the burst grape.
I intend to gather joy when you told of
two children crashing down the Fall.

Your birthday was in the drying and browning
month of my mother's death. I took how
Summer tossed your heart at me and made
a cornucopia of a snake, my crown.
Snake's tongue begathers Winter's sway.

When a forty-year-old tips into November
with sheep's hair: O Spring Girl who bore
breath of old news like parched touch or
maple tree held captive red—I shan't shake
like catalpa tree's (heart-shaped leaves)

lightning-struck look of loss. You get
only gentle words for your birthday, for me.
Go good into gentle November. Two children
with feelings big enough for history turn
greatly into Sappho's oft-felt violet Autumn.

FRIENDLY THE SNAKE

I dreamed Friendly was in a performance I was giving. My friends and I were making elaborate preparations, even painting walls.

Just before the performance started, I got Friendly, but let go of him a second, thinking he couldn't find a place to hide that fast. But he disappeared instantly under a wall surface. There was a projector operator in a room inside the wall, but I couldn't figure out how to reach him. I knocked on the wall to ask him if he'd seen my snake.

I started calling, "Friendly, Friendly! Here, Friendly!"

I noticed a small hole in the floor. I peered into it and saw Friendly gliding past the hole. Then his head appeared cautiously, up through the hole.

I was pleased Friendly had returned to me.

ANARCHIST WORKING DREAM

I was at the work place. The staff was getting ready to
meet. My glasses fell off. I couldn't put them back on because
the frames had come apart. I noticed a tiny screw was missing
that had held the parts together. As I began to look for it, a
man entered the room and announced he was a psychologist and that
the boss wanted him to observe us. Because there was consider-
able stress on us at work, we knew he had been sent to "help" us.

I was holding up meeting because I was still looking for
the screw that held my glasses together. My co-workers grew
restless and began to fool around. Our boss entered the room,
sat down and waited for the meeting to start. The workers con-
tinued to stir and fidget. When I finally attempted to sit in a
meeting chair, I noticed fresh globs of food spilled on it, and
I tried to arrange myself to avoid sitting on the food. My boss
was growing impatient.

Then I noticed the children of some of my co-workers were
in the room, climbing the furniture and adding to the chaotic
atmosphere. We never did hold our meeting, and consequently, we
avoided having to have the psychologist work with us.

I awoke from this dream with glee—with satisfaction of
accomplishment!

PORTRAIT OF THE LONG BOYS

To be read with a rattle

Owed to F.S.

Mr. F.S. used to like my college poetry,
but we grew up; he became a college teacher,
and—I learned through a feminist friend—
these days he dismisses my poetry as "lesbian."

Thank the feminists, (rattle) he's finally
become the minority. In the good old days
my name was Girl-Running-Scared, and his
was Hot-Shit Hates-Queers, Could-Kill-'Em.

Dress, Crossing into Cross-Dressing

Here stands today a lady poet's odd stance
in a strange outfit in a man's land. (rattle)
A forty-seven-year-old woman has come back
to haunt now that you've finally opened up
your haughty-boy buns to a two-way conversation.
To even address the feminists means
you're getting prairie-freed up.
I disagree as a feminist I should suffer
more at the likes of your hands, honey,
your soul white as my skin, your neck red as
a Midwest turkey gobbler gettin'. (rattle)

Thank women, me you can't reach with
glass-bead words; thank women, me you can't
impact with your boxer-stance poetry;
I've become an aging lady storyteller aiming

a modern-day tale at you straight outta
The Old West:
How Foxy Outsmarted Great White Hunter

At the workplace this tall fellow worker
stud (his choice of name) who calls women
"foxes"—who I call O Great White Father—
who regards women as "beavers" and "dogs,"
requested of a woman who was visiting us
from New Mexico, (in front of a roomful of
women), "Tell us how those Southwest machos
put the make on you."

To which I interposed, "They're not macho.
They're Native American, and they're
EFFEMINATE!" The women laughed nervously.
I succeeded silencing O Great White Father
and his jollies.

The Woman who used to work in our sexist
scene inadvertently confirmed my contention
by describing New Mexico men doing a snake
dance in a formerly matrilineal society
as wearing furs, feathers, and sequins and
necklaces, and swaying, letting their feet fall
into underworld circles of hisssss. (rattle)

Female Kiva Chambers

You won't really shake the pumpkin, Hon,
until you dress up your hate, high-healin' it
in a bleached-blonde bouffant, long metallic
silverfrost nails, high-painted peacock eyebrows.
and midnightmist eyeshadow, and yes, Honey, a

dress. Fake furs, sequins, and feathers sell well.
(rattle)
You won't be liberated, Pumpkin, 'til you dress
as your old girlfriend and go out on the town
with some big man who can't/won't come through—
love you. The bride remains in her mother's house.

Yoohoo! The old girls have come back to haunt
you who make twice the money—Have Prizes Will
Travel—than most feminist writers I know, Honey.

Yah, Lynn Lonidier writes lesbian poetry.
Remember her as the girl you carried on with
one evening but just couldn't get her hot
or you under and in, while your girlfriend
waited outside for who?—you.

O dig up your One Night Stand so buried there's
more than a knee that's wounded, Honey.
O bury the poet not with epitaph: "He Knew How
To Protect Himself From Love." (rattle)

May you pass through the sweat part of
the longhouse where androgynous shamen shake
rattles at you and grasp snakes in their teeth
Without hurting them while mirroring you to
race your Coyote Life, good times and loud talk.
You have your own closet to clean and come out
of, thank you, ma'am. Like it or not, you were
born omnisexual, F.S. You're not
straight and I'm not gay. (rattle)

How ' bout a date on the town, you in your
dress and me in my bizarre. I'll ask a woman

friend to formally photograph us—you with
clover-laden hair, and I, Laughing Coyote
with your rose between my glowering,
glinty canine teeth, Honey. Smile pretty!

What a picture we make: brown as beautiful
and gay as good. I too used to be afraid of
homosexuality. Today, embracing anarcha-
feminist personhood, I come bearing Poetry,
O and Word of the Uto-Azteca, with chants
of getting back (rattle) together under a
(rattle))) DAWNING   TRUEBLUE EGALITARIAN SKY((((

THE LIVING ROOM

I. Her Story

Piano stands silent,
harp stands harsh,
harpsichord sits down,

the lamp now stands sounding
in the living room
of my lover's body—

her hair color & shape
of Movement Of Music on paper—
breath o' harp-weighted chest.

Her father gave her himself;
he turned into a coughing piano.
Her mother did not give herself,

and it turned into a wistful harp.
Her husband gave a harpsichord,
and she knew to keep it covered

with a gorgeous spread o'flowers
and not him; bed.
I gave my love a stained-glass lamp

and turned stained and glass
and silent   oracular
          (globe)
miraculous   absent.

II. Return

The father is dark, massive—
an incomplete Chopin
with slowed movement.

The mother resembles a column
at an angle on a gilded cliff
remote-tuned by sea;

the mother is Beethoven
listening to a shell.
Husband is away forever

like a wipe of keys
with cloth that attracts
sunlight and Hathor, Lady Egypt.

III. Anniversary

June 24 my love and I met
in Amazon hills in full music
'midst Celtic harp moon

orchestrated by Joanna of Crete
(a griffin in white tuxedo).
My V of legs tremoloed and pedaled.

IV. Honing

Harp, harpsichord, piano, lamp
hold concourse in the living room
of a wild field of bluest irises.

Feelings tumble on the page
of the homing poet,
tendril out her fingers;

V of her legs trundles and petals.
Daytime instruments turn
in toward one another; night

quartet crescendos: her hearing,
slivered and silvery as set glass
or whirrrled string.

V . . . .*

*Read ellipsis with horizontal extension of hand across the air.

BY THE LIGHT O' THE SWEDISH
BABOON

My stomach into not
since talking to you:
"I opened the pearl card."
Crossing the bridge,
kept saying,
"I wanted you
virgin except with me
and that famed woman
author; it's in the stars."

Dogs couldn't be wrong.
My crawl stomach
down the freeway
I glimpse
the billboard
of no message
except tacky real laundry
hung across it.

Some anarchist took
the laundry down
and painted a picture
of a baboon
looking backward,
an arrow pointing
to his aurora rear,
word "poet"
etched near him.
A distant billboard
totem:

"I was a sled
for the sled dogs."
Forget civilized dinner.

I suggest your scrimshaw
friend, her fingers
coursing through
ground-blue maize of you,
perform
a ceremony from her
wanderings of shamans,
with you me her(shawl?
bone? horse?)—give
tongue to such traversings
I can hear
miniature drawings happening
on whales' teeth,
taste the zag of ethnic zig.

"Zing to me!"
I would risk (rattle)
ritual would work, and she
would risk (bells)
it might not
ease the beast
who opened the beauty card
mindful of the labyrinth view.

SIX YEARS SORTING MOTHER'S PAPERS

O long-living wait of old pages of the parents . . . . Father's
petrified forest of poses before logs larger than cabins;
Mother's violin bow drawn by frailer arm than tenderest
Stravinsky refrain; snow maidens; Eastern Star; fame of the
political photography of the depressed son; dream poetry
of the Freedom Socialist lesbian-feminist judgmentalist
youngest cousin;—I, the oldest ageing guppy anarchist of
them all; a Northern mother canning up auroras from emersed
gardens; racist Southern father sliding Marian Anderson
alongside Caruso; savings of misspellings of the family name;
family string quartet recording for the blind; all day
socializing at peace marches; night potlucks with Bolsheviks.

(Touchknot.)

Long live children wondering over the pages of parents
remembering unearthing an Indian—reassembling the skeleton
in sitting position in Lakeview's hardware store window;
Pietry of the daughter making small-town news; lost favored
clarinet uncle-at-sea; stormy Atlantic crossing of Grandma
by Svenska liner; starry quilt of a cross-stitching mother;
relatives I love not to be looked up much. Pins, needles
of the old ways of parents, boxed, passed down to strangers
in strange stores by children of parent providers of photos,
news clippings, histories: a few sorted for keeping by
individuals awed by looks of face, dress, mannerisms;
period-piece settings, borders, frames, yearnings.

Freezings and meltings, hands of collectors touch not.

A DREAM—A HALF RESURRECTION

A former lover insisted we take a ride on a motorbike—the
putt-putt kind. I didn't want to and straddled over and didn't
rest on the seat. She positioned herself in the sidecar and
steered from there along a waterway. I wound up jogging beside
the motorbike. The path was slightly submerged in places, and my
shoes became soaked. I was also annoyed with the silent presence
of my past lover and her usual, non-communicative ways.

I was slightly ahead of her as she steered 'round a bend in
the trail. The motorbike with her in the sidecar was unbalanced.
I looked back and saw her hypnotically miss the curve. She and the
bike slipped into the water and sank. I scanned the deep water but
could only see the bike. I expected my years-ago lover to struggle
into view so I could grab her or slip in and rescue her. There
wasn't a ripple or splash. I suspected she might be pinned under
the bike, but even it soon disappeared.

Minutes passed. No one was around. I tried to realize the
drowning. Then the water turned translucent blue and white. I
discerned her curled up, naked, foetally in a cave-like formation
deep at the edge of the water. Hearing voices in the distance, I
yelled, "Help! Help!" Some boys came running. The oldest one
pulled her from the deep. I was sure she was dead. He knew
life-saving techniques and forced water into her chest and air
into her lungs I was amazed she revived. She didn't react to
what had just happened. She stood palecold and remote as ever.

anarchAMAZE

For Celeste

A BE SEE OR A B SEIZE?
Manmade Eve: an anarchAmazon
    in a box . . . Born-again in Eden,
         an anarchAfeminist would be
           Ugly and Awful and
              There for Him.

And when she told him she'd been to Tijuana
    at Christmastime, he said he'd been
        there too, Had she heard that
    border town has girlie ramps where
        they hook up women with mules
        on stage, for you'll-tied men?

        No, but she 1987 saw small women
        in grey flowered huipiles*
           with tiny children begging in
           Yuletide dust of freeway ramps
             on the Outskirts of Hell.
    Oh, the Work To Be Done O,

On Earth, Women! In the Name of the Riddled Eyes

Of Hope O, Create A CRETE On the Eve of Adamant, O Earthwomen. Men.
                      Children. Animals.
                      Plants. Inanimates.
                      Environment?
                      Life?
                      Pleasure?
IN DENUDED EDENIGHT—OUT OF NECROPHILIAC EDEN—

FROM MILTON'S TURGID REVILEMENT Of female—
EARTH'S MILTONIC "RIFLED" "BOWELS"' defilement—
appears modest anarchAfeminist Eve—O Last Wisdom-Saving
                                        Possibility!!!—
And Everything—

    snakeBREATH (WISDOM-flickering) :

    BREATHE—:

    B-RR—EEE—A——THHHH—E——SSSSSSS—— :

    Returning the snakes to Golden Gate Park,
    she sweeps up a hawk's feather Artifact . . .

*loose-fitting, embroidered dresses.

walking the olive grove

SWANSONG

Yoohoo Trotskyites

You whose history murdered masses of anarchists the pogroms of Russia
today romanticize anarchists   call yourselves that when you're really
authoritarian commandeers   living for AFTER THE REVOLUTION you'll
be IN CHARGE of change

Dear Karen,*

I figured you'd get fed up with   Marxist-Socialist rhetoric   and
decide to have a field day daily   Enjoy life not dogma   Truth is
no matter how much workers gain control: A institution is   A
institution is   A institution   The workplace   ain't no place   fitting
workers' wrists TO BE shackled FREE   O Sweet Shacklee & Company

Ultimate and most visionary

Spokeswoman for anarchy Hannah Arendt   Jew ostracized   by Jews
so anarchistic she didn't label herself   wrote WE'RE BORN FREE
Yes corny as lion cubs in Africa but when we were children weren't
beasts freeerrrr roaming

---

* Karen Brodine, Lonidier's cousin, a poet, and activist with Radical Women and the
Freedom Socialist Party. Tributes to Brodine, who died from breast cancer before
her 40th birthday are here https://www.redletterpress.org/about_karen_brodine.html
and here https://socialism.com/fs-article/karen-brodine-poet-feminist-revolution-
ary-1947-1987/ .

Let's work

Not only to not have bosses Let's create   pleasure sensual physical   joy
feeling aesthetic kiss touch music laughter eat enjoyment cooperative
endeavor   instead of closing ourselves in workplace prisons producing
consuming things   Let's close the factories and OPEN PRODUCTIVITY
Computers CAN & SHALL   RUN THEMSELVES

In later years of the cousins   431

The difference between us Karen: That Lynn   she doesn't have
consciousness of the work ethic she isn't   union-organizing or buying
economic class differences   as sole factor of humanity's earthen hell

Lynn fought not for organizing Organization   I fought by sabotaging
sense out of supposed high places   made bosses cringe in their rumpled
stilted skins   rant & stamp through institutional floorboards
That Lynn I'd like to light a fire under her   my worst & littlest boss
burst & disappeared

Yes Lynn wants to work love flesh fondling days dreaming taste fruit maze
entertain talk walk write do away with bosses workers the workplace
The Works   Out out with all institutions   Let's commune one-to-
one   or in small groups sit in circles in windowed rooms   or gather
together in grassy knolls   or see the sea   decide   what there is
in reason to be together   or not   Not Marxist   Anarchist
                              o
              K   f
        r   k
     a   e
       n   y
     A   s

"POWER TO NO ONE"*

Work enclaves attract gamey people to grasp Like magnets manipulating
the paperclip world   Kissing flesh pleasure feelings nature reading
sharing birthing poems   Tai-Chi revolutions   eight-hour sunsets
picnic absorptions in one another's realms and spheres   identities'
acceptance   as long as   composing scenarios for The Self doesn't hurt
another   You understand words' ultimate aesthetic hunger for   the body
Of caring   Burst grapes pleasure wordplay flesh taste non-hierarchical
seaSHALLS   dwelling of us in breath of exuberance   life listening
tasting learning fresh love you Karen

I'm talking trade

I'm talking moccasins   small communities   I made a vase I'll give for
your beads   a poetry book for a six month's feast   After you opened
poetry and   moved to my town   you ever yearly more turned your back
on THAT that did not agree with your beliefs   like a shut book   Judge
me TRUE in wake of your powdered remove

I was audience

I was present when those close to you responded We   a cadre of leaders
of the Freedom Socialist Party Now   Will   after The Revolution
Head up The Masses   until they're able to govern themselves   (Cattle
and sheep never come home   prodless   alone)

Total body taken

I took up the cello you were drawn   to ballet You were cinched into
Marxism   certain as you donned the skin-tight suit of THE BALLERINA

Last poetry reading

Beyond brambly fences and backyard spectrum   some unknowing neighbor's
opened window provided background music   Tchaikovsky's "Swan Lake"

---

* Coined by Jean Lyons, Seattle poet-philosopher

pummeled on soft feet   without slippers of mime's of limbs flittering
pas de deux   and   pas de trois   Last words of your poems came 'midst
dashes of cymbals   thralls of flute   emotion-ridden strings   violas
like cello-thickened violins   override of trumpets   air-riddled bows
Strident tympanies   your   every word   poised to fend distant
storm of orchestra

Once I went to see you dance

Most-astutely proportioned of all young lady dancers in form of Tradition
your limbs shaped to orb   performing visions of sugarplum men   woods
bursting sprites   the gong and dong of castled dawn

You defied the wispy an-a-wreck-sick kind   moved   more lithely than
white devas hoed to daisies all in a row   Sleeping princesses' hold on
acceptance of audience dwelling in The Abode of Choreo-Iconography

> You were more fairest,
> reflective of all
>
> leotard wavelets—
> lake itself.
>
> Hours of
> self
>
> discipline
> the practicing bar
>
> unhairless lit arms
> hair swept back in a crescendo
>
> arrowed foot
> of a point-of-toe
>
> fluted
> waterfall

cascade of
toe steppings

sliding sounds
on floorboards

creaking
totalitarianism.

DANCE
      ARISTOCRACY.

Open again to life

The anarchAfeminist and the Socialist-Feminist would occasionally meet
on San Francisco streets   exchange politenesses   In Europe Marxists
shot anarchists on streets and in their homes on GRAND SCALE It got
so   only in poetry were we open   Last time you visited you came to
sell me a subscription to the Freedom Socialist newspaper   Knowing it
would only last a year   I grimaced and bought   a subscription

Years living near San Diego

Every midnight Thursday L.A. Tarpits TV station ran Boris Karloff mummy
flicks   Soundtrack of Tchaikovsky accompanying   scientists to the tombs
of their ruin   Boarding a steamer to America the evil Egyptian curator
lets the mummy loose to bring back the paternal scientist's sole
daughter to her rightful place as Queen or the Night   The mummy
unraveling swathing holds her vapidity   evaporates her denial into
oceansplash like a backward sun   In my mind I walk you backward alive
to the time   you were seeking

I never got to tell you

Of blond blueyed Nordic Indians   The pre-Vikings weren't kings or serfs
They wore horned headgear   had teepees and round single-person canoes
made of animal skin lined with fur—were migratory   clan-like
Family drawn to discipline denial & partyline

Forgive our uncles and aunts their frozen communism   Their afterlife
lies in Russia I lately learned Aunt Juliet (born of Uncle Charles's
Romeo rib   enlarged to Ibsen's dollhouse) asked your mother a number
of times after she divorced your dad   to join the family for music
and political gatherings   Your mother always had excuse   not to   I do
it too   At least they're not as closed   off as we'd thought

Last request

You wouldn't let me show feeling   Now I will show the sunset before
first rain of a long drought   lasting   the length of last rays or
tonight's striated horizon lost to this world   O Half-Daughter of
the Mediterranean   inheritor of collective caring   Karen leapt in Time
to   women bull-jumpers   Your Grandma Harriet's magnanimous irradiating

Poetry reading

My favorite part   harp of oboe   the mummy rounding up his beloved
through All Time   the Old Boys'   violins and tin-pan-knee   we knew
what   they are

I'll never forget your years-ago reading: a young man appears afterwards
and announces he is the bearer of essential information for you about
yourself   and you saying What!   (Was he referring to his semen)

He repeats his line insisting he immediately must get together with you
to convey his message   Your replying I don't think so   He had nerve to
reiterate his again cloaked privilege   to put the make on beauty   My
two cents: Karen doesn't need information about herself   She knows her
SELF A   nd this guy backing down and out the door   two laughing women
tall beyond terror   we stood

Our mutual distain for transcendentalism

Spiritualists and psychic phenomenon folks spouting power epithets
commensurate with the degree of powerlessness   they're feeling
Your father

Named after social satirist pre-French Revolution author Voltaire
Imagine living up to being castigated by kings   and yearly cast in
Ye Olde Bastille Motel   Even with an ulcer your gardening father
was family-famous for swallowing   slices of blackberry pie whole
Competition stuck to his seldom-talking largesse blue lips   Voltaire
entered a harpist contest   got to play with the Seattle symphony for
donning   affect of Harpo Marx   curly-wigged   girl-ogling   honking
his horn   big Goodwill coat and all   A dream-staid gentleman

436

Photo

Don't believe
them.

We're just kids.
Your coveralls are falling,
and I have no confidence.

I'm holding
your hand, and
we're fording a stream.

Allie Light,* bearer

I was heading to the sun the same week Nancy Reagan's left breast set
in the cowboy sea   made me think of crater-shaped periphery of the
Persian Gulf   when   my mind on pages ⋅ I got word and   paced sand

Sun-streaked shoreline reddened   warmed memories of you   moved me
though disappearing In Time   to print one anarchAfeminist's reading
list   a bibliography for the very late world to consider   everglean:

---

* Allie Light was a close friend of Lonidier's and spoke at her memorial service.

Analytical Alternatives to Patriarchy and the Authoritarian Left

Radical thinking before Marx was essentially a complex of libertarian and egalitarian ideas advocating distributive justice. Marx fused these ideas into an authoritarian and absolutist mode. Marx's idea of history as moving inexorably to a preordained end was outdated when he conjured it into existence. But Marx demand-ed obeisance from his cadres and postulated their only purpose as being to ease history toward the magical and inevitable demise of capitalism. Leftists of all philosophical hues have been exiled from the left or murdered by the Marxist juggernaut.

In addition, radical political critiques have rarely adequate-ly indicted patriarchy as a system of privilege maintained through continuous violence toward all life and toward women in particular. Radical feminist thought most clearly depicts the devastating and brutalizing strategies of patriarchy.

This abbreviated list of readings is offered in the hope that it will provide an indictment of the Marxist left as well as introduce some current concepts of a libertarian, egalitarian, and materially just society.

—Jean Lyons

Clitoris Lost

Authoritarian Versus Libertarian Left

Animal Farm, George Orwell

The Unknown History of the Russian Revolution, Voline

Anarchism, George Woodcock

Reinventing Anarchy, Ehrlich, de Leon, and Morris

The Ecology of Freedom, Murray Bookchin

The Anarchist Movement, John Clark

Cultural Materialism, Marvin Harris

The Origins of Totalitarianism, Hannah Arendt

Feminist Analysis

Going Out of Our Minds: The Metaphysics of Liberation, Sonia Johnson

When God was a Woman, Merlin Stone

The Creation of Patriarchy, Gerda Lerner

Women in Search of Utopia: Mavericks and Mythmakers, Rohrlich and Baruch

Beyond Power: On Women, Men and Morals, Marilyn French

The Politics of Reality: Essays in Feminist Theory, Marilyn Frye

Philosophy and Feminist Thinking, Jean Grimshaw

SEVEN-HUNDRED FIFTY DOLLAR POEM

As Lesbians Fallen from Heaven Lie

My hands counting seven crisp 100 dollar bills,
then a twenty, another twenty and a ten land
in another angel's hands.

I riveted on her arrival like a lover, thought
it strange she wasn't on time to receive money,
began to believe she wouldn't show, flashed
I had wasted half the morning. I had parked
in the space of a handicapped person.
I considered leaving and letting the woman
I waited for come all the way to me next time.

Among green trees stood a telephone booth: two
stalls. I was pissed I had to waste two dimes
because this person had already used up seven
hundred fifty dollars of mine. The Telephone
Company ate the two dimes and pretended dead.
I moved to the other phone, reached the contact
person's answering service—lost two more dimes.

As I hung up, heard the coins final clink into
Ma Bell's* lower intestinal tract, I spied the
contact person nonchalantly coming down the path,
looking around as if glimpsing pigeons picking
at pennies on the ground. I wondered if she
wondered was I here? We met in the park in name
of some meddling god set down on earth to taunt

---

* The Bell Telephone companies, with monopolies on telephone service in the 1970s
and 80s, were colloquially referred to as Ma Bell.

lesbians. Metal god come back to give lesbians
a pyramid—his base home: now you see gold, now
you don't.

You start hearing things—different messages,
NC Simultaneously or from the same person,
but depending on where you are on The Pyramid—
oh, how you hope—I.

I was told if I put in 750 dollars, I would get
in matter of weeks, eight thousand dollars.
I was greeted warmly by the people at the top
and heard what success everyone was having.
Everything was "hot," meaning, happening fast,
and we were a "family." Rules were read, quote:
"This workshop does not guarantee you will receive
money for your participation, and there are no
refunds." I was told, "You'll at least get your
money back. What you earn you report to I.R.S.
as having taught an abundance healing workshop,
and you'll learn a lot about yourself. I doubted
that. I know myself sensible, I know.

Everyone chose a poetic name to protect identity,
such as "Hip Number Picker," "Radiant Rush," or
"Potato Skin," and each pyramid was distinguished
by a label unto itself, like "Trust-In-Us."
The poetics appealed to me—and because poets
tend to mess with pyramids—I must comment on
my foibles, this confessional on greed, my own.

I trusted the encouragement of a long-lost friend
who suddenly appeared out of the lesbian blue,
announced she had just made $12,000 on a $1,500

investment in three weeks' time, and let's go out
and catch up on old times. I highly respected her
artistry, regarded her as a person of integrity.
Over hamburgers she told me she'd effortlessly
made a ton of bucks boarding an invisible plane
rising to the top of a pyramid and piloting out,
only to reenter a new pyramid. SHE VERITABLY
GLEAMED. She took me to her crew. Everyone's eyes
shone like Christmas party lights on me. She said,
"Use a credit card if you have to."

I've never bought a single lottery ticket
to even find out what it's like. I have never
loaned out money or feel I have money to loan.
I know people get hurt by pyramid schemes,
but I was about to be laid off from a part-time,
ten-years' job and—as lovers fallen from heaven lay—
have no other visible means of getting up moo-lah.

Yes, Virginia, pyramids existed before Jesus Christ
came alive and Santa Claus dipped mittens in your
kitty stockings, and pyramids still take the shape
of kindly old patriarchal figures made-of-straw.
I gave my $750 over in-between meetings. Meanwhile,
back at pyramid meetings of mostly lesbians,
I was told this scheme is not illegal. The worst
that can happen: you can be cited with a misdemeanor.
Two weeks into this, I received my first phone call
from a sister-pyramider telling me Our Pyramid—
the plane I'd boarded—was about to split in half
before the person or persons at the top had received
their money-in-full. Guidelines of the Abundance
Game imperatively state this won't happen.

Poor Peer-Admitter

Can a poet sue for breach or word and violation
of "language" when she doesn't have money, to sue?
I knew full well I might lose $750 or any portion
thereof. I've never lost sleep over that.
True poets don't dwell on greenbacks' stench.

When I heard The Pyramid process was changing
midstream and I hadn't been asked what I thought
of it—let alone would I go along with it—and
I knew that the person at the end of the line
espouses feminism: next meeting when someone said
"we"—referring to this maneuver—I said,
"What do you mean 'we?'" She admitted only a few
people—those at or near the top—had agreed
to jump with the moneybags, leaving the rest of us
stranded midair.

Hey, whatever happened to "The Family"? No fun.
Lesbians insisted it was for my own good and
they were doing me a favor, and when I argued back,
they said I was making them mad. And then
one of them admitted things in the money-exchange
department were slow at the time I'd entered
The Pyramid—unlike what they'd originally claimed.

And now my trust is totally shaken, confirmed
by the comment of one of the angels above
that people there could do whatever they wanted
to those below because <u>this</u> is a pyramid and wasn't
a pyramid hierarchical?

No, no one told me the workings of the "Trust-In-Us"
Pyramid were on a hierarchical basis. According
to the handout, people at the top are supposed to

facilitate the smoothness of meetings and
money-exchange, but not make up rules as they go.
"This is what makes The Pyramid creative," they'd
retorted, like poets fallen from reason laid.

Don't spring sudden bosses on me. When I joined,
no one told me things weren't working. This
Pyramid's been slow for a month. That's why
they want out. We're not people on an airplane
going to heaven on a cloud; we're thin-aired suckers
(Trust-In-Money) jumping board.

Humans pride themselves on being the exception—
and there are examples of such sacrifice through
history—but when you have one life to give, hey,
I admit that once in my life an appeal for a quick
fix to my finances overrode my feet on the floor.
I laugh thinking back who to call to get on board
the "Spruce Goose." My close friend is unemployed,
so she can't even consider a pyramid. One friend
I called has the bucks but knows better. Another
just said no thanks. Another wanted to know how
it went. Another creative soul ventured, "Hey,
the certainty of my earnings now is such a gamble,
I wouldn't risk anything beyond daily living—
and she's well-fixed compared to women's yearly
medium income in this City of Love by the Bay.

By the bye, I received news of The Split Pyramid,
just when I figured out to invite a co-worker
friend of mine who cooks fabulous Filipino food
and has strong ties to her community and some
savings and perhaps can afford to risk money,
and maybe her fellow minority friends/relatives
would like to participate. We'll crack open
Daly City! (The Pyramid people are talking of

a picnic in a Berkeley park!)
I call my Daly City friend and tell her things
aren't working in The Pyramid so as not to enter
her into belief of what is not true. I tell her
down the road there might be fallout in the
Filipino community—it could come back to her:
"<u>Don't do it</u>!"

One lesbian's tear-welled eyes; one lesbian
suggesting we pray: another lesbian leading us
in incredulous meditation. What did one lesbian
poet do? I'm not going to feed on feminist guilt.
I quit The Pyramid and lose one hundred, two
hundred, three hundred, four hundred, five hundred,
six hundred, seven hundred—twenty, forty, fifty
smackeroos in this "sceptered angels"* land o'Fair-0.

In the Land of Feminist Pharaohs

If she had it to do over, Christa McAuliffe,
the first schoolteacher in space, whose body
took three minutes to disintegrate—and NASA's not
telling you—would call from the grave, "Don't do it."
She/I knew what we're doing. Or should I call my
soft-on-pyramids friend, see if she won't giveth
physical energy to some real fences needing
mending, let loose of "abundance" to pay for
rumored publication or a fabled book of poetry?

I know what "flight" rhymes with. I'm a retarded-
in-math kind-of-person. I have trouble picturing
pyramids in my heads. I can't visualize splitting
a pyramid in half so you get two pyramids or half

*Quote from *Paradise Lost*.

hat they told thee thou would. How does one plus
one make nothing? I am unable to picture passengers
moving one seat up at a time on an airplane that
trusty pilots have ejected from—and not crash-land.
I tell my Filipino friend to flee flight: scram.
'Tis better to have loved than to smash into
mountain's majesty. So far, from contacting
friends out of fright, I've received two dinner

engagements and an evening at a gay film fest.
Captain Lonidier, Ace Pilot at making words fly,
announces, "We have just entered ground zero.
Do not board hope, evacuate all entrances, for
stormy visions aboundeth." I found myself thinking
in dark, devious and discolored ways.

I started hearing what I'd felt all along: scam.
For me, the experience with pyramids was like
a speeded-up, low-grade infection, like being
impaled on a point and single-handedly trying to
get people to come down from dis-ease. Sleepless-
ness was justified. Out of women's mouths I heard
platitudes of sistership, and not a soul spoke
their minds. At least feminists have my money.
Consolation. Aren't facilitators not
supposed to harbor hidden agendas, give a sou?

Do you believe in ghosts? No. Do you believe
in spirits? No. Do you believe hard-worn faith
can evaporate in flash of a parachute's snap?
It did. Do you see manna fly out of the sky
to your own hands? No. Then why.did.I.do.it?

Lucky you sitting there with your money telling
numbed-me we share the uneven pain: you've lost
sleep, I haven't. The hole in my shoe is going to

grow into your soul. I've had enough of Berkley
foothills folks.

Tell you who it was who hoarded the plane: "Prism."
I, a pilot of synergetic anarchy. When I first
heard the word, I didn't know "synergetic" meant
"cooperative." I knew that people who wanted to
and small, cooperative enclaves, to farm or not,
and offer services and home goods rather than money
& drugs & institutions—similar to clans, but with
computer-ease—to counter pyramids that are
put upon us . . . were anarchistic. Anarchy: equated
with chaos—the jewel-scourge-of-the-earth—while
back at Pyramid Ranch, the United States is,
in fact, becoming a vast, empty, land-poor land.

For energy, remember the exuberance of the seven
last astronauts boarding promised air? Christa
McAuliffe calling, "Don't do it! Don't get in
the spaced ship!" Beside white lesbians, who
were other passengers on my flight into loss?
Two Blacks, an Asian, a heterosexual White couple
with partial banker-friend backing. To this day,
I'm haunted by articulation of one gambling Latina:
"I participated in the Pyramid Game in Peru.
Peruvians actually helping one another was truly
really beautiful." Spare me.

I've seen the streets of Peru in the flesh.
In Peru and in almost all third world countries,
there are two kinds of people: the poor and the rich.
Oh yes and a smattering of middle-class and a
smidgling of upper-middle class. A very few rich
owning and controlling everything that has to do
with Martian sightings and tourist landings. Peru,

where I witnessed masses of poor spend all day
selling one pack of gum to pay for enough sustenance
to stay alive. Yes the poor help each other in Peru.
The wear shows on their faces' stares of malnutrition.
Peru, where the poor piss in the dirt—no asswipe
paper—not even newspaper—blow their golden noses
in infernal air . . .

My overland pyramid friend called to offer some
remuneration. I told her, "Never mind. I'm okay.
I'm writing a $750 poem." I've never heard from her
since, nor she, me: the trade-off <u>O as Angels Fallen</u>
<u>From Gay-Heavenly Grace</u> . . . <u>"Through Eden took their</u>
<u>solitary way."*—Beaded, feathered, crystaled</u>
<u>lesbians wend their crepuscular, legion way.</u>

*Last line of *Paradise Lost*.

TEACHING THE 5 SENTENCES

To be a 1980s schoolmarm—
thirty children to a classroom—
is to feel incensed to death
countless times already only
the second month of Californians
saving cents.

They run movies in the wake
of bleached window shades.
They show green pictures
at school because the TV don't
work right. They want me
to show these pictures to kids,

but I won't run videos of people
cut off at the jugulars.
In college I was an Audio-Visual
major. Easy. They call it
irrelevant. I call it—
bringing color to the unconscious.

How, out of the mouths of suns,
slips babes? Teaching five senses
without breathing, am I—
and the kids—gonna last as long
as the looks of the latest
old Driver-Ed. film?

DOGGEREL FOR ROBERT

He was, we strive to be—pray no one tries
take tonight's* Chair. He had his Mind,
presence of a nun asking [Robert Duncan?—],
"Have you been saved?" while Capitalism
clicked by his last weeks of humored eyelids
and black humor eye, and Freedom takes place.

What's to miss? More of the doggonest
dichotomous Bobby quintuplets running for
single-sighted office In Potomac bogmined
landmire.

Jess-brought tripe soup under hospital
room's hunkering TV set, and the nurse
"What's tripe?" Jess-gentled appeals
and Robert-endearing rumblings, they
enduring describe jarred contents.
The nurse is not sure she can intercom
sustenance of the last batch of previous
tripe. How so really Robert with tubes
and bags and heating vats, so optimistically
proceed in Time?

Though he went bye-bye by car, he was
always walking in Time—contradictions
in our humanity's trips out, dogs me.
On innards or outings, I could always find
what I wanted to know and listen to him
or not. With Robert there was room
not just for writing or spirituality,
but space for dreambeings, allowings.

Fire-Rimmed Eden

I once contrasted him with a certain
feminist poet who, 'tis rumored through
Seattle grapevine, has come to Anarchy.
Welcome realizing meeting oneself—
most gradual, natural birthings every
body's born with/we here/I hear bees
in Robert's heads buzzing—realizing,
walking my dog, San Francisco's no longer
San Francisco, without 'I'm.

In shelved books' surrounds, say, "Robert,
I been reading Murray Bookchin!—(and
bedding down and up with Hannah Arendt). Or,
"What enchanted music matches female Maxfield
Parrish's woodlands figures?" More simply,
"How does one create genuine horror in
fiction?" sent 'im stacking, pulling books,
inquiring, "Lynn, what'd'<u>you</u> really fear?"
That way, Patriarchy became My Bad-Guise
prose pose.

In some dark corner to this dogma day, yet
may refrigerated stand—over in the other
unit of another ward—gleaming jar's lost,
translatable soup. Certainty supplanted
by rallying cries of bees/his words/Robert's
legacy-baby. Rosewater-confounding, Nikola
Tesla tungsten edge of L. Frank Baum's vision
alighting one of two oak filing cabinets—
this one resolutely labelled O thru Z, Baby—

<u>Dear</u> . . . <u>Baby</u> . . .

* Poets' memorial

TREE MEDIUMS & SPANISH VISITATIONS

To Gloria Anzaldúa

In aeolian light

I picture you photographing the olive grove I picture you photographing
the olive grove I walk past daily talking to my dog and breathing deep
green leaves silver on the undersides pungent as stilettoes while
meeting lotsa lesbians walking assorted dogs   and I AM IN CRETE

LISTENING to clickings of the needled necklaces of priestesses visiting
bee orchard—dream ground of powdered history . . . Moon-darkened
music o' olives—sun round leaves gentled exclaimings in the glintwind
I meant this poem to be in Spanish but I am a warp away from

a learning time   Four o'clock my dog started yapping   I headed to
the door of someone knocking heard knocking Opening the knowing door
I would've sworn 'twas you Gloria: 'twas nobody but bees in fragrant
toppings of my yard   Not a soul not even expecting evangels distributing

captions in ecclesiastic mode: "¿Qué me pasa?" "¡ESTA FUE TU VIDA!"
I couldn't catch even sight of restoration of the haunts of Eden
Pre-Eden egalitarianism hunts me walking the olive grove timewarp trees
haunted by Park & Wreck Department spray cans in a pit bull neighborhood

Branches: LET THE WILD SPANISH my learning Spanish begin! Velvet
                                                            sunlight
shadows my shoulders' realization "&"* is in shape of a lyre The handheld
harp preceded Golden Greeks by silver centuries Pocked trunks centuries-
daily assume personified woodland shapes: nymphs lizards lakes streams

Fire-Rimmed Eden

Dark-turned daze I read   the history of   Spanish anarchy   <u>dream</u>
<u>Emily Dickinson is alive "&"* plying poetry to the oil-light of</u>
<u>evening</u> On "&"* on into the harp-playing wind of pre-Dorian-Ionian-
Phrygian-Lydian night strings of an aeolian harp   tuned low

to vibrate themselves in wind create harmonic overtones offset
wired manmade night <u>TREMULOUS OLIVACEOUS FORBEARANCE</u>
<u>BY FEMALE</u>
<u>DWELLING IN THE MAZE THAT DWELLING IN THE MAZE</u>   451
<u>THAT DWELLING IN</u>
<u>THE MAZE   THAT   TENDERS HEARTS' GREENERY</u>

Clitoris Lost

*Instead of reading "&" as "and", hand-draw this figure in air.+

+ In the original printing, Lonidier hand-drew the and.

from *THE RHYME OF THE AG-ED MARINESS*

THE RHYME OF THE AG-ED MARINESS

The Last Poems of
LYNN LONIDIER

EDITED BY Janine Canan
PREFACE BY Jerome Rothenberg
PHOTOGRAPHS BY Fred Lonidier

BERNAL HILL

A tree-laced road leads to radar
screens overlying the Mission,
Morning sun timbres the bay—
Oakland— Berkeley— Mt. Tam—
in by breathtaking eye.

Two hawks cavort on Bernal Hill,
between three crows cawing
and one starling darting. The hawks
may be young peregrines,
their white breasts speckled,
large dots on the undersides of
greytan wingtips.
¿Que hacen en la ciudad?
I am with my dog.

The pair of hawks sail overhead,
dizzying me, circling us—
and disappear as soon as
we were heard along the trail.

Bluesky afternoon,
I am "la maestra," a penguin walking
school children-pilgrims.
One of the children cries, "Look up!"
*Mientras espias and hatchetmen
take breath,* the child has spied
a hawk just like the ones I'd
sited: ¡Peregrino! "Pilgrim"
Is another word for
"Peregrine" in Spanish.

From *The Rhyme Of The Ag-Ed Mariness*

"Looks like a cross,"
a second child announces.

Multicolored children of the Mission
ooh and ahh while signals against
nature drone metal membranes of
criminal radar screens overlying

distant clamor and chatter of
culturas diversidades de la Misión.
Cyanide-laced thinkers y hitmen de
milicia—take away aura
of reverencia de
sacred breath.

CINGCONG* SINGSONG GODDESS POEM

To the Guerrilla Girls on East and West
coasts, who have been protesting lack
of representation of women artists in
America's museums and galleries.

New York's got the Empire State Building,
why can't we have King Kong? I saw him
from the Bay Bridge one night on top of
a San Francisco skyscraper, blinking his
red eyes, flicking his fey wrist at the fog,
diverting cars off an ongoing, winged vision.
What're the odds of a local sculptress
persuading The National Undoingment of the Arts
to pay Her to put one up there? King Kong
Would enhance the cityscape and Up the Pyramid
Building by One. Mighty Joe Young tilting
at wind and mill-white briefs of cases winding
in & around & trashing the daily, dark downtown.

At the top o' Nordstrom's spiral staircase,
tourists could pay to enter a chrome dome where
they keyboard King Kong to do computerized
gyrations and corporate escalations to the sky.
Observe his earthquake chest pounding up cement,
read storm fronts off his fur ends, roll
his eyes at the tickering stocks, marquee
his low brow with Clairol blondes he's
programmed to ogle, blow smoke outa cigar he's
chompin' to let ashes out on the City of Love
—a true art (advertising stogies) object—
transcending New York/L.A. art scenes
by leaps, while bound.

From The Rhyme Of The Ag-Ed Marines

Urgency of alternatives 'midst 49er football
chumps and tinygiants' unbuilt new stadium
attempts to gobble up Downtown with the egos
of ants: let's make King Kong female: Goddess
Kongess— a gargantuan guerrilla stance of
towering feminist ideals spanning the Grand
Lady with the gargoyle** on her back. Largessa
bandida novices of anarchAfeminist voice
making Goddess Kongess's Caduceus of Caring
N U M E R A   U N A !!!—making me collide
with excitement, started writing this poem
on the Female Freeway, hurtling from one kind
of gorilla to another.

Fire-Rimmed Eden

*Pronounced "King Kong"

**A sculpture placed on the Bay Bridge to ward off earthquakes and other evils.

RINGING IN THE DARK

A Clearing Ritual for the Montreal Fourteen+

Attempting thinking

Attempting thinking of the complexity of the life of any human
being—joys body functions daily effort the caring or lack
the thoughts that stray through the mind *Learnings*

The house that Jack built

In a glade and wooded area in Glen Ellen California a four-story
Fortress of boulders and timbers servants quarters trophy and
game room the ultimate male domain the Colossus of the North
went up (how cum) in flames one drunken Jack London night
soon after he'd master-planned it (A gay man has stashed away
personal letters by Jack London of the paranoia of Jack London
crumbling to be touched by a man)

Callings of the Wild a wolf wouldn't touch

The satisfaction of killing a woman who first turned her back
on men because they let her know she wasn't pretty
*
The cruelty of killing a woman because boys resented her because
she did better in school than they
*
The privilege of killing a woman whose uterus was too narrow
to birth a baby and who didn't want one anyway
*

+ On December 6, 1989, fourteen female students were murdered at École Polytech-
nique in Montréal.

The flamboyance of killing a woman who at twenty-five gave up on
men because the man she gave herself to kept acting vanished
*

The arrogance of killing a woman who hears music rhyming lesbian
with separatist
*

The selfishness of killing a woman training to work with young
children who would have learned eight-year-old boys bond
in clubs while the girls pass notes on love

*

The spoiledness of killing a woman who would've witnessed
the same boys building a castle—a stronghold with an elongated
drawn-up drawbridge
*

The immaturity of killing a woman watching cardboard additions
to the castle of boys making a cardboard jail putting
themselves in cardboard bed together in jail
*

The slyness of killing a woman while the boy-hero looks on in
constant taking motion the trickster that saps and flags
the careless hard-looker alert-one who never minds the leader o'
the pack who binds the boys in rivet-action of Pacman pills
*

The impotence of killing a woman knowing girls fantasize
finding a cat or a rabbit or tiger and taking softness home
feeding it and it can live there forever
*

The uselessness of killing a woman wearing a man's suit to
ward off men covering herself with superiormaid cloths of
their deceptions
*

The defeat of killing a woman whose biggest wish is to keep
the land alive looking out upon the grave of the human race
*

The honor of killing a woman who thinks she's bonded with men
*

The fear of killing a woman in this refuge den of strength
house that Mama Bear built keeps men from it
*

Men Kind

The man returning to the Stockton schoolyard of his youth
shooting thirty-five Southeast Asian children because he claimed
foreigners were taking the jobs He left behind a motel room
littered with plastic toy soldiers

The man kind to his girlfriend 'til mind of her own he didn't
get his way donned army fatigues entered a University of
Montreal classroom in one of any Ol' Boys' departments he couldn't
measure up to and falsely brandished browns yellows & reds
of nature dead leaves heaped up in conflagration The walking
barrage separated the men from the "feminist" "I want
The women!" He lined them up and released the men He uttered
"You're all a bunch of feminists!" and shot the women then
Hunted down more before dismantling himself from his scene

Attempting imagining

Attempting imagining now a young woman who IS no longer
the efforts of parents in raising her her attributes yearnings
tears pride confusions contributions doubts struggles love hurts
laughter tone of voice presence any of us most certainly
each menstrual individual here for Solstice 1989 all that you've
been through your whole life to be here tonight yourself myself
the fourteen women of Montreal Time between each weathering
to attempt to ponder the essence fullness and loveliness of Being

****

CHRISTMAS KITTY EN BILINGUALAND, OR, WHAT I DID THIS YEAR*

Mision Satánica

I found a
kitten
In the Mission
on the Sabbath.

Gatito negrito
with buttercup
eyes like
pale yellow
saucers.
Who could refuse?

So laden
with fleas,
my milk porcelain
sink spotted with
brujas' blood.

This Halloween
I was an
airline pilot
with a kitty
in the cargo,
hungry as sin,
rescued in
flight on a
school building
doorstep.

Fire-Rimmed Eden

_____
* This poem was a broadside, though I have been unable to locate a copy of it.

I named kitty
"Hallo*ween.*"
the "wee"
Or "ween" part
pronounced
with a squeal,
"Hallo*ween!*"
to capture
the misterioso
subtleties
of his feminist-
winning ways.

Kitty Católico

I think
Halloween kitten
is Catholic, for
on Thanksgiving,
he pulled
from the bookcase
a text de religioso:
The Little Office
Of the Blessed
Virgin Mary
And Prayers of
Our Blessed Lady
of Mount Carmel
and St. Teresa
of Jesus,
teethed it.

Oven's gurgling.
Warmth overlies
blessed frosted

Mission morning
as we say oven's
gurgling warmth
overlies blessed
frosted Mission
Morning, and
we said—!Gracias!
for the turkey
Reagan's cooking,
donated by
Israelis, Iranians,
Contras, Costa Ricans,
Etcétera, watered down
to goddess stew.
¡Qué lástima!
Lasting turkey
soup for Christmas!
¡Sopa deliciosa
para anarchistas!

Me and the dog
and Christmas Kitty
and fishes tropicales
watch TV winter
proceedings, revelations,
reapings, unwindings,
of Private Wars
of eyeless, lipless,
Knows-no, wire-browed,
mouthless men.
I, as author, and
Animals of the Earth
plot BEGINNING HAPPY
ENDINGS BETTER
NEW ERAS!

I WAS A TEENAGE LESBIAN,
AGE THIRTY-FIVE

An Anarchist Response to a Marxist-Socialist "Three-Way"

I was involved in a three-way once.
The lovemaking perhaps lasted five minutes.
The preparation involved the suggestion
in which my former lover told me her new love interest
who looked a lot like Ms. Liz Taylor—dark, Italian,
and gorgeous—wanted to make love to two women
at once.

I was invited over for drinks with them
so she and I could see if we'd feel comfortable
in this love-making arrangement. Trouble was,
Ms. Liz Taylor had a girlfriend she'd lived with
for years who, because of Liz Taylor's
inclinations to wander, was always at her side
to make sure she didn't lose her.

However, on this day, Liz Taylor had managed to slip
away while her girlfriend was at work. Liz had assured
her that she was going to drop by my ex's for
a single drink and wouldn't be staying. A "single drink"
was laughable. The three of us sat with our feet up,
lounging among flounced Italian decor of my friend's
Surreal-tasteful waterfront apartment.

My ex-girlfriend was Italian also—not dark but with
the body of Venus de Milo—but freckled, the mind of
a philosophical panther and the white hair of an exotic
snow leopard. I was a burgeoning writer, intrigued with

From *The Rhyme Of The Ag-Ed Marines*

themes & variegations on womanly desires. We sat sipping
brandy & wine from our snifters, eyeing the tide and boats
slipping by the bay window, making small talk and getting
decidedly drunk. Maybe half an hour passed and
Liz Taylor indicated to my friend that she liked me;
and I, her. So, blushing, we moved to the bedroom,
growing in anticipation as we pulled off our clothes,
draping them here and there like little anarchic flags
all over baroque-modern furnishings until valances
over yellow window shades ornate with linings of pompons

bantering at previous lovemaking breezes, sounded.
Sunlight turned the room dark orange—(please explain,
scientifically). Our bodies connected in a circle
on the luxuriously wide bed with tawny lion-patterned
bedsheets. Took some doing, but possible. We
were inside each other's secret fruit, our mouths within
each other's mons veneris. Cantaloupes, tangerines—

I was tasting the bittersweet nib-hardening of Ms. Liz Taylor.
Beyond that, I don't know who did what to whom. A circle's
a simple figure, but who wants to apply themselves to math?
The smell of pomegranates growing stronger, our arousal was
heightening us out of the thaw of booze, when, at the edge
of a rush of climaxes, the phone rang. Simultaneously,
we disengaged ourselves from our clitorises, lifted our

three heads in a gorgon groan of smeared lips. Liz said,
"Oh no, I bet it's her!" My ex: "Hello?" Sure enough.
Venus de Milo handed the fake marble telephone receiver
to the dark starlet: "Hello, Honey. . . . Oh, just having a
second snifter—one for the road. You'll forgive me? . . .
You're coming here—now? You got off work early—great. . . .
You're going to join us for drinks? Sure, Sweetie.

See you in a jiff." Liz set the lighter-than-it looked
receiver back on its elegant antique hook. "She knows!"
The three-headed gorgon groaned a mighty second time.
Not only did alcohol still have a hold on our bodies,
but the throes of lovemaking had welled us inside
and made us almost immobile. "How long will it take her?"
"She'll be here in five!"

"Lordy!" We grabbed at our clothes and threw them on
and fastened ourselves into a presentable, cursing crew
with a sock or two missing. Who'd look inside our shoes?
One of Liz Taylor's cunt hairs was curled tight around
two of my teeth. I tried to pick at it nonchalantly,
put it in my pocket, a memento. My ex-girlfriend fanned
damp sheets, fluffed pillows, hurried the covers over all.

We didn't have time to comb our Medusa hair or wash
dried white juices off fingers and faces. Liz smeared
lipstick on her where it's supposed to go, without looking
in a mirror. We reseated ourselves in the front room,
our clothed bodies barely reassembled on black &white
Imitation leather, our almost empty drinks still positioned
on zebra-striped coasters on askew Chirico pillar stands.

The brass, lion-headed door-knocker resounded.
Though even this room reeked with pungency of sex, we sat
eyeing each other, nervously hoping to get away with an
afternoon's unreal real temptation. "Come in!" Ms. Liz
Taylor's girlfriend entered in a checkered tweed business
jacket with matching skirt, graciously accepted a drink and
never questioned the air fraught with unstrung shoelaces.

She made polite conversation. The afternoon passed—adieu!
The two women left together. Liz Taylor and her friend
soon moved from the Far North to Malibu, leaving my ex

467

girlfriend briefly bereft, longing for Liz Taylor.
We heard they opened a chain of gay food catering businesses
in California, naming their successful operation, "Ambrosia."
(Don't you know gays eat different food than straights?)

Maybe Liz Taylor's cunt hair wound up in some unsuspecting
gay male's stomach and lodged there as a continuous irritant. . . .
Years I've set aside that afternoon' guilty feelings
and decided dishonesty for having betrayed another woman—
though I hardly knew her. Face it: just plain bad behavior.
But, I'd so wanted orange rococo moments—we only had five—
that I did such things when I was young in lesbian love.

In love with lesbian love, I'll never forget that faraway,
shaded bedroom sun, that amber globe bedroom, glowing
midday moon burnishing our bodies with chocolate desires,
our three heads barely treading above the watermarks of passion.
When I was young, I wanted what I wanted *so bad*. And when
one gets older—one forgets so easily and yet remembers
O certain moments with total pristine recall.

As for Liz Taylor's cunt hair, I momentarily forgot it and
proceeded to wash evidence of the afternoon out of my clothes.
Even when I folded them, I forgot to look in the pocket.
But if any lesbian ever finds that eighteen-year-old hair,
it will undoubtedly bring a high price. (I'd certainly pay
a high price for it.) *Perhaps the Gods and Goddesses of Gaydom
are vying for it forever at the banquet table over my head.*

CAMILLE ON A COUCH

Wilhelmina Dopamina
That's'a me'a

People come to her, look
at her eyes, face, walk,
tell her she's in love.
She just looks at them—
the She-Stare of-a-Bear.

Her wedge-pointed shoulder pads'
hint of diamond glint
might eject a sigh.
Forgive her Her Menopause
crouching in corners,

grasping at her shadow,
cloak & dagger-style.
She forgets she's by herself,
by design. Leave her,
leave her be.

Lazarus Lonidier enters
midlife, uttering,
"Everything went right."
But the perfectionist
keeps dropping things.

Her ever-changing glasses
don't match her intentions,
and her lesbian dentist is
tender-capping vulnerabilities
of her tenderer incisors.

What good is Camille?
You can lean on her
as she faints.
A bit of a vampire—
she would love that.

She enters staged doors
from all sides,
From cracks in drafts,
she thunders in
and doesn't notice

she's lightning
contrast of white
satin & black velvet
and hasn't taken off
her red felt hat

under which is kept
Warm stream of a secret meadow.
Ah, pouty Camille on a couch—
sluggish & nauseous, close
as she'll come to pregnancy.

Will she bear a harem
or a siren? Pobre niños.
She drifts over & unfurls,
bumping into fall fashions'
stark looks, or is it

the pining season of non-stop
pinnings on the couch,
she models for?
She smiles. She's got
Top-line feminist thoughts.

Ella estudia Español
de progesterone—state of
Being eternal in the mouth
of months. Language-jumping
since you took her hand and fully

kissed her, she's forgotten English!
She too is drawn to continental
women who move montañas.
Edificio de Piramide: euphoria
keeps her afloat—

even happy—*and* she's afloat!—
Wilhelmina Dopamina—
Camille on a couch
wishing to be weakened by
a female to advantage.

She enrolls in a
finishing school for women
on How to Succumb on O
Luscious Points of Another's
Strengthening Voice of Lilies.

Multicolored changeling,
Menopausal—dropping night
veils coursing through her
glowing dreaming on the off-cycle
going nicely wet again.

Fear is: ardor will run
down her legs' replete
return to youth. She'll have
her writing to do over and
Period to live, relive.

People tiptoe up to her,
ask, "Are you in love?"—
Look at her. No answer.
Her widening, narrowing eyes
curl up into the light.

All she holds is
one photo and another's poems.
She's moist-eyed, reciting lines
on a couch past curtain time.
(Some say she's with paper and pencil.)

(None lay eyes on her
at Rilke's merry-go-round at sunset,
dolphin-endorphined and finned,
climbing onto sea spray,
ready to ride.)

GRETEL AND GRETEL

(Recorded by the gamekeeper's daughter)

El Aire Libre

Into the woodsland deep we wandered   dos niñas   lost in greygreen-
Scapes and ever-stretching cabbage patches   a baby rabbit loped
Across the road   We rose higher   Forestlight denser

Having been ejected out of your nest   your full-fledged eyes wounded
a dead leaf floated across your vision   and hung at one side of
tus dos across iris   like in O. Henry's story   You inhaled clearclean
nerve ends of evergreens   The sky turned rosey-edged blue   embossed
with start of stars   Our talk meteor-showered on every mountain turn:
confessionals proyectos dreams amorosas dificultades   Twilight
drifted down red-trunked trees' heads-towering reach

Dos picaras—"wandering female trouble-troubamaker-doures"   We don't
Trod on the living   We were Gretel & Gretel dropping feminist leaflets
on the path behind us that leads back to men   Gretel and Gretel
proceed

Women Bathing Naked in the Wilderness

In this version las mujeres   are older and therefore   more lovely
their bodies   crisscrossed with wisdom they've journeyed   to learn
Traumerei immerses their limbs in power pink sulphur moth light
filtered hues de liquid forest runes and pools   A woodsman whose
tool is cutting a path to ruin   strides forth to claim the myth
that's his   No sooner does he enter their realm than the women
turn into lesbians in updraft of swans' beating wings to   Lebenland

From *The Rhyme Of The Ag-Ed Marines*

Euro-Latin Impersonator Act*

Tú y yo assured ourselves we knew the way   *pero*   we grew less sure
Now that night shut down   except for one gas station and twenty bars
There were no 7-Elevens   or berries   *Yes?*

Crickets caressed our pelos de los oídoes under accumulating star
clusters and a cut moon   You remember su abuela demonstrandole una
secret mushroom-searching place sequestered from being taken by men

The forest murmurs I want to abscond   with you   *pero*   darker still
the path wound 'round   Hacia el sur?   *Yes?*   No.   Al norte
Towns and branches' lost feelings of musty roads and dusty views
"You are beautiful—*Yes?*"   We are anarchic Nordic dragonesses
Greta Garbos o Gretas Garbled   La nochegra Gretel y Gretel evolved
Deeper into anachronistic forest hold

*Underscored words are to be read with a lively rise of voice.

Langsam

I had to drive slow to watch for   animals   We'd never get home
You with the patience of learning languages talked to me even when we
didn't need to keep me   awake while you needed sleep

I know that you know that I love you   but I don't know you know that
I fell in love with you on first hearing tus poemas   worlds so evoked
líneas so primavera   so feeling   so caring so   mind-provoking
they pull sensitive-deep into complexida y tenderness   Altiplanos
bordering fainting

You are Your Poems are You   I couldn't help be more to you   Arquitecta
de la Heart   than a fairy godmother   ((Yo soy tu fairylover—)) No?

474

Climax and El Fin of the Fairy Elfin Lovers

¿What was a man at an egg-packing plant doing a medianoche I had to ask
(¡Que lástima!): direcciónes? We couldn't believe him ¿Trust in
Cocteau's boy motorcyclists pointing the way? The labyrinth dead-
Ended in obscuridades totales You asked the time and the way but
your inquiring of kilometers embarrassed-mathed me: How many man's-
sized shoes does it take for women to begin the trek through woods

Our eyes recoiled from dual spectre of lights Nightroad turned
into a two-car accident Committed to getting you back to the safety
of your homemade quilted bed I decided to go on because another car
had stopped to help and I already had an injured victim en route

Gretel and Gretel never did come upon a candied witch's house There
is no witch There was a woodsman— ¿their father long-gone long ago?
This is a feminist version of grim men a lesbian fairy tale without
witches and evil stepmothers with only the two Gretels Handsome &
Handsome

The witch's house is a California oasis with neon red motel signs lining
glimmering palm tree strip called the High Way En esta novela—we enter
the fabled locked door: Gretel & Gretel spinning the nights away tasting
each others' limbs in undying honeycakes swoon They drip sugar for
all that lovemaking keeps Gretel and Gretel from gaining weight
And the thrust chickenbone has been replaced with their lips tongues
fingers swimming in and out of waves' capped crests you call "orgasms"
bursting on chocolatey seacliffs undertowing into caves

Hand-in-hand all the other Gretels in the world went off the path
together hugged and were kissed by leg-shaking moonlight and
found pleasures and meaning delight in This to the belief-shattering
Moreafter Everfor/never-ending Happiness-Day

From The Rhyme Of The Ag-Ed Mariness

GRETA GARBO LEAVES CALIFORNIA FOR ARGENTINA, NOT FOREVER BUT FOR GOOD

(Ode to LavenderRose)

Crossing the invisible

Heading south   Pan Am Airlines leaves Pan Am decals on its
aeroplano   exterior   Pero   the inside of   "¿qué" (what's)
"Pasa?" (happening) at Miami Airport   is suddenly part of a
Borges plot discombobably or *disembowelingly* strung out as
a B-grade movie trailer   before "takeoff"   and *strange*

La interior of the waiting gate   la last-minute check-in desk
el ticket-taker   las attendantes   el gangplank: should the plane
be renamed "Latin-Time Airlines"?   It is 10:45 P.M. boarding time
Five hours between flights I'd caught a Miami city bus driver's
directions to a Cuban restaurant serving   Louisiana gumbo
Greta Garbo disembarked in dark glasses   ate up   and high-stepped
it back onto one of those long-awaited   live-lingual buses

Meanwhile back at L'arena del Sur

The gate's waiting room es   humongous   Masses of people are
milling about seats suddenly smaller and made of something less
than United States plastic   Pan Am's late loading passengers
It's announced: "Line up according to your seat number"   Which
seat numbers?   Almost everyone lines up   There's so many people
pushy   Stampedes turn on themselves   Have these Pan Am employees
never boarded passengers?

With two heavy carry-on bags and a small Styrofoam surfboard tied
to the bottom of one of them I sit   in one of hundreds of

diminutive seats wondering about   starcluster patterns of
Constellations overbeyond this smokey florescent-greenful aura
A few other beings appear as   isolated pinpricks   refuse to glom
with the crowdlings

Greta Garbo wants to be left   to wait

Passed boarding time and three hours beyond bedtime finalmento-
lentomente   intercom pronounces in dos lenguas: "Now accepting
passenger seat numeros 50 through 70!" *Those* people are already
squeezed in the aisle Finalmentalentamente they get to "40!"
Greta sighs   "30!"   I wiggle my toes alive   Are the masses
being run off the gangway—falling into some Dante-ish airport
netherland   never to reappear?   How they get rid of people in
Sud America?

Finalmentolente "Veinte!"   A last-minute surge of people—many
carrying four or five bags   cram onto the loading ramp   Earlier
I spied a small box at the base of an escalator and a tiny handmade
sign: "Don't carry on carry-ons larger than can fit in this box"
No one had seemed to be noticing that box except   "moi"

11:30 P.M. Nordic time

The ramp leading to Patagonia is still jammed   People steer and
shift oversized luggage precariously   Five handbags fall backwards
and almost hit my case carrying a wallet-sized broadcast quality
stereo-metered Sony tape recorder   Someone ran over my foot with
a wheel of a cart   Fortu-nuttly   Greta Garbo's wearing Her
"L.A. Gear" brand-new heavy-duty white tennies with mini-California
license plate key chain Made-in-Korea   attached   Only the tread
Her proud foot   Whoever ran over us   did not apologize
Mestizos y European Argentinians are not   small people

Next   within steps of an inviting open place door   the aisle's
jammed with Pan Am employees confiscating tons of excess baggage

out of hands arms and carts of Argentinian travelers and the few
disparate loner   A checker is eyeing my child-sized surfboard
The plane on the USA side had had long narrow cupboards and
'commodatingly received such odd-sized objects   I express concern
over a Styrofoam board being lumped in with luggage   I was feeling
smaller   The enlarged stewardess utters: "There's not one inch
of extra space aboard   Pan Am's given us too small a plane tonight
Either we leave people off   or we put suitcases where they belong
We can't have both!"

Greta Garble's guess

Every night Pan Am makes too small a plane available to people
heading south   So "Poor Surfboard—adieu!   We'll see   what shape
you're in   in the morning's wash   Will I ever see you again?"
Stewardess-checker assures me they're putting it in the Pet Area
I picture "Pobre Surfboard" in pieces: me drowned at sea   Half
Swedes Indians Argentinians gringas scattered over Amazons

11:40 P.M. a woman in a man's suit Garbo enters a plane packed with
people (Seated twelve-across)   The overhead carry-on racks looks
half as wide   as the ones in Estados Unidos   Only thing the same
is the size and surreal twilight of the toilets   Stewardesses
wrapped up in last-minute check-in stuff   One of them's   hunched
on a stool in a narrowest food-serving galley—resembles Rodin's
"Thinker"   hand-on-chin   except she's sick   Deathbed of menses
'mongst plastic breakfast faces?

Greta's got a window seat

Gar Goil goes against the tide of passenger flow   does the Lambada
overunderthrough   bodies 'til she reaches *y*   opens *Her* overhead
carrier   The carrier's big enough to house three Kleenex boxes
The other two seatmates glare at Her as if it were   *their* private

carrier   It's full of a single shaving kit and the other man's
coat   All carriers within reach are jammed full of other *theirs*

My videos camera-sized bag might fit under the seat but the larger
bag   a soft bag full of fragile taping equipment: microphone
cable   transformer   tapes   videos   books   a hundred poetry
magazines   has a rip in it and doesn't lock   Reservations
assured me I could carry on one carry-on bag and one over-the-
shoulder bag   No problema

Imagine stewardess exhausted from the crunch of bodies and bags
being nice   I clasp my surfboard claim ticket   If I get a broken
Chunk of Styrofoam back   I'm not going to wait for   the rest
I've had that "boogie board" for years   never used it   Greta's
saving it for a night swim with Argentina's greatest contemporary
woman poet (male or female)

A stewardess listens to my pleas for not checking my one suddenly
oversized carry-on bag   "I have a place for it" she whispers
and leads me to the employees' coat closet   Sure enough   there's
a spot on a rack   wide enough to squeeze it in

I'm so sleepy I stumble to my seat   push my one bag left under
the seat   find a pillow with human hairs on it from the last fight
and lean against window glass   The pilot announces: '"'We are
going to be late leaving"   (We know that) "Buenos Noches"

Over innercalm comes:

"Our flight is waiting the arrival of two late passengers"   Five
minutes pass   "The two late passengers have still not reached
the plane   Evita and Juan"   Five minutes to midnight
a pronouncement: "Bags of the two late passengers must now be
Located among the plane's cargo"   The pilot reveals annoyance:

"See what happens when someone's *this* late? We have to wait at least fifteen minutes more!" Greta utters "For Christ's sake!"

In the United States a plane would not wait for a person A person would wait for a   plane   If planes run late—once a flight's posted on a TV monitor (even if schedules change)—it's true to the latest update   USA Pan Am flights leave on time   while babies cry on board   On this plane   we wait   No one seems upset but me

Babies laugh   Not a single baby is crying—yet   Such waiting is standard procedure? Everyone sits and chats   or relaxes   Again something is said in Spanish over Intercom about the two late arrivals and their luggage   Either they've located and X-rayed them (and things)   or Pan Am's finally leaving them *them* and *that* behind: Hearthardy applause   Still   we sit   Intercom asks for this person and that to come to the front   Is this Argentine soap opera or performance art?

Many Spanish voices are talking to each other at once   One behind me   a man   is talking loudly in English with a Spanish accent about how he was years in charge of twelve people in a bank He utters an endless array of mundane information you'd know if You'd never worked in an office   I bet he doesn't know the Combination to the bank's vault   He's talking to be talking How many people aboard   are doing that right now? He's bragging to the totally silent man next to him who either has to hear every detail of nothing or know   *not* to listen

12:15 en la mañana

The take-off: one hour late   I feel the plane   start to move There's the longest take-off—or did Garbo dream it? The creaking shaking plane is real   It runs and runs and runs along the ground Is this plane is capable of entering   air   I don't care   I fall asleep (Briefly)

Fire-Rimmed Eden

Voices of Panic

In English and Spanish mixed I hear a distinct   "Is there a doctor
on board?"   Calls for a doctor up and down rows   I open my lead-
Closed eyes to peep at Pan Am employees   They're standing panicking
right at the seats behind mine   Either the man who was talking
such a streak ('cause I don't hear him now)—or the man who managed
to listen to him—is having some kind of attack

Is there a doctor aboard?   Finalmente   a doctor's found and
protests "But I'm not a medical doctor!"   *More* discussion   Perhaps
he's a doctor of education or "see-key-uh-trist"   Both useless
to the Living   or Dead   At last a stewardess suggests the sick man
may need food   Then intercom announces: "Dinner'll be served shortly"
At after dos horas en la mañana?!!!   The stewardess assures
the sick man that he'll eat first   I picture him rising up   and
with a last gasp   refusing airline food

I struggle   asleep   The man is being fed   A stewardess is
serving my row   I hear her ask loudly "What do you *want*?"   I keep
my eyes closed in disbelief   The last thing I hear her say to the
man next to me is: "Poke her—Ask her if she wants chicken or beef"

Dinner must've lasted 'til 3 a.m.

Estados Unidos airlines leave on time while babies on board cry
Latin-time airlines seem to leave-when-they-leave   and ever-arrive
Babies on board laugh   When do Latinos sleep?   After they eat
Then they sleep and sleep

During this flight I even experienced Patagonia   Now I don't need
to go there   The man next to me is holding a book   entitled that
In reasonable Pan Am morning lithe we're being pleasant   Yes he's
from that remote region of Argentina where   Indians remain
Ancient and   you can barely stand up in   wind

The Patagonian gentleman explains our flight had undergone a bomb
scare regarding late luggage arrival and ensuing disappearance
of the two long-awaited passengers   And the man with the seizure
was the son of the bank official who talked non-stop   The son
happened to be diabetic   Because of flight delay   and because
he's too quiet (with a father like that) to speak   all this
contributed to insulin shock:::   why he critically needed food

Hovering over landmasses de Ar-hen-teena

Finally touching earth   I was so distracted by the beauty of
Buenos Aires—I forgot about the surfboard I'd received back
in one piece   I abandoned it against some hotel lobby wall
or in some taxi's trunk   Anyway Greta Garbo arrived at a beach
in Argentina   smiling satisfied with a swim in a rainstorm
(sans surfboard)   humbled by magnificence   and satiated with
difference/between California drought and length and greenness
of these grasses   It is said   the most optimistic people on
Earth this year are Ar-hen-tinny-uns   Overwhelmed by different-
but-the-same Nature   and Lives—every country has its logic—
I got away   with Being Me   in Argentina   That's liberating
Despite contrary history—trials/mistrials

No wonder such big people wanted out of such little seats   as
provided by Pan Am   Not even the foreign rough dark-colored kind
of toilet paper was available at Buenos Aires International Airport
Not a roll or single sheet can be found in its restrooms Men's or
Women's   Greta Gargle checked   There's none: nada nadie nunca
Garbo was glad (and relieved) she'd brought pocketfuls of soft
tissue   white as skins of Fins   along

Female mysteries de Ar-hen-teena

Before playing the cello in honor of newly-arrived Women's Poetry
in this old New World   it's necessary and only fair to announce:

Pan Am's return flight went smoothly   had more room   and left
on time—midnight   At 2 A.M.   a diarrheic wide-awake Greta Garbo
panged with hunger   famished from being moved and touched   and
pockets emptied   ate   wild-eyed contented with the rest of the
passengers   *in awe of Patagonian tunes*   that're actually German*

**Refrains from "Familien-Gemälde" by Schumann and "Song to the Evening Star" by Wagner, or
similar cello excerpts, follow the poem.*

BECAUSE I WAS A LATE BLOOMER

Because I was a late bloomer in the realm of sewing my gay oats
I found myself arriving in Seattle in 1970   knowing no one
hankering for love   hanging out at the women's bars   appreciating
drag shows but madly searching for what at the time was
inexplicable to myself

I slowly made a few friends   and quickly glommed onto an instant
love who had a high school education—most brilliant mind of my
life and an avid reader in the arts sciences literature and
philosophical realms   and nightly wiped out her eyesight and
consciousness with alcohol

The love affair was just that   the friendship has lasted
to this day   thanks to slightly lower long-distance telephone rates
as   she is still   to this day my beaconing mentor   has remained
in Seattle   is as insightful as ever   a miracle   considering
she imbibes daily

In other words I was craving and searching for wisdom   For me it took
human form in paradox   I have never known a "brilliant" person
from Robert Duncan to Joanna Russ   who did not have some insidious
shortcomings or self-induced handicaps   The most brilliant people
—when I got to know them—are in some way   extraordinarily

Short-sighted   or creatures of some infantile debilitating habit
or constantly annoying behavior   The privilege of brilliance
by those insightful people who baffle   run-of-the-mill   mind-use
folks   which includes the realm of "professionals" college-
educated or not   has haunted my obsession with "intelligence"

"grey matter"   the "brains" that weigh the world   "the world of
Ideas" folks   Robert's half-seeing omnihead overweighted with

megalomania   Joanna's non-Hollywood shortened-tendons' beauty
(she didn't have a nose job) pouncing brilliance and flagging
Self-image   and foreshortened memory and prima donna behavior

and memory   if you believe like I believe that ALL BRAINS ARE
CREATED EQUAL—then the aberrations of intellectual and aesthetic
Reverence were brought on by enriched early circumstances and
Rigid later opportunities rejection and non-understanding in

their formative battles for acceptance as authors by society
These are my protagonists   Robin Morgan equates heroes with
demons   which is not fair   given that all monsters in mythology
are based on actual people who differed from that norm I find
so ugly

'TIL YEARS LET ME GROW WISER

I am not going to die   nor the ones I care for

I'm not going to die   just like I never get depressed
I'm not the kind that gets depressed   or Karen
But the night I went to the beach was red for Robert

also

Have you noticed the world moving in a movie

While people rare as Robert stand firm in a cyclone   or create
their own   Though I seem to be arguing I'm not going to die
Karen didn't   Robert didn't   It's an illusion   a deception
to make everyone think they're everyone else

Scaling cells' replacement

Rules out invidious comparisons   It revolves like a symphony
old-fashioned and remains I stay a child   Not a walking Eastern
Sameness-extension   Alan Watts died after all and his neighbor
Elsa Gidlow   but Karen and Robert are here   present at this minute

Cobwebs come upon us

It's a child's game simply to make the world think I'm like it
but I am the same forever alive   You'll see—or maybe you won't

History

Like the flick of a shark-cheating wrist   history is an obscene
flasher   Death is not in the cards   It's a "what-if" situation
a make-believe solution   if there's a single chance the world was made
for one child

If evangelists come looking for poets

We'll disappear into a rabbit hole   world under a heterosexual
village   I'll be an old school marm spinning   I'm not going to
die   you'll see—or maybe you won't see

Like Robert

I grew up young   Like Karen I grew up committed   When singing
evangels commit the young at middle age to institutions   they're
called crazy   Poets survive because they're crazy as queens
exclaiming upon the goings-on in Bugs Bunny Land downunder

When swinging evangels come swinging swords

We'll go underground like mall rats* where we're already there
and goodies are gooey on the trees and good children can do
anything they underworld want

It's not that the sun revolves around us it's not that the world
stands still

At age fifty   people tell me I look thirty-nine   When children
badger I tell them I'm ninety-nine and a half   At fifty I stopped
Listening to the news because of Pat Robertson and the blood-
pressure country   Pat Robertson makes Ronald Reagan look
handsome   Pat Robertson is a diminutive of Ronald Reagan and
logical heir   The poets will live through this age of
It's not that I'm going to die it's just that the world is dissolving
around me.

*teenagers who hang out at shopping centers

HAPPY DORIS ON HER 69TH

At the announcing of the closing of the zoo
and the libraries and the swimming pools,
isn't 69 one of those classic sexual positions?
I don't mean to impose or be improper to you,
but on your birthday they dared announce
they were going to close the zoo.
Where will the peacocks strut their forests?
And who will the gorillas throw doo-doo at?
That's been more fun than the bigger pen
they've been given to romp in.

I loved when you announced you are living
your second childhood. Let me introduce
you to mine: Mexican jumping bean Ritchie
who does triple flips on the floor.
Xavier with the wavy hair and the Spanish
eyelashes sifting a guilty look
for flushing a goldfish down a toilet
so he wouldn't have to feed it. His mother
in her innocence wonders where's the fish.
Chinese Cindy who thrives on straightening books.
And Alice with a growing voice that doesn't fit
her Chinese: an Alice loud as the Queen of Hearts
exclaiming over cards. Only four of thirty
children—I live with their energy every day.

The dilemma for Teacher me is how are children
going to have books with animals as characters
without animals and libraries on earth?
They'll forget what it's like to be a toad
driving a roadster down Main Street or a pig
talking wonderment to a spider in a web,

without likeness of animals, without zoos,
Without swimming pools.

You have solved such worries for me, Doris.
with your medications tied to your shift stick
so you won't forget to take 'em,
your handheld ratchet (New Year's noisemaker)
and your sausage-making machine. Who could be
more phallic than Pauline collecting all sorts
and sizes of horns with handles attached?
And your red bandana hanky cannot outdo
your honk. You dress and blow your nose
like a man. And I like how you deftly stoke
your potbelly stove with built-in window glass
called "   "* that pearls the flames
that make music sputter.

You stay awake in the quiet night
sampling gold-leaf books, taking untantalizing tastes
of Shakespeare, drinking wine, immersing
yourself in mysteries. You sleep in
in the morning, scoop up the news of the latest
closings from your seven a.m. doorstep, read it
and snooze 'til ten or noon.

At poker—you're the most, winning your share,
spelling out every hand, looking up every word:
"poke" "her"—get it? You champion beginners
to win. Ace queen heart spade take my mind
off the vanishing animals and book-stacked
libraries end and evaporating pools. I imagine
you clean winter out of your swimming pool
with classical music turned up full blast.

You are a dream cook. German Swedish Jewish
meat melts in my mouth. The asparagus

lies down with the pears. Thank you for being
so fastidious as to hand me serving spoons
wrapped in paper towels—you're infectious.

You won't kiss on the mouth, and yet you are
Walking Waves of Affection. With your
surgically oiled replacement joints you do a
jig with a dip stick planted in your RV van
with Las Vegas liner lights. You go miles
into woods sounding with lesbian laughter
spread around the camp. Many women love you.
You evade them gently, lightly, kindly.

April birthday, Ms. Fiddlesticks, you make
my pores blossom, and my veins and arteries
are outlined in spring flowers. When sirens become peacocks
in the night, I come to you. Doris, don't
worry about whether you're going to like
this poem or not. They've announced
the closing of the zoo, the libraries
and the swimming pools; I come to you.

QUEST

I with illusion
I could find a beautiful woman
by writing remarkable poetry.
I had some beautiful women
brief as a season, sometimes
brief as a flower's
singular magenta appearance.

I wanted to live with beauty.
I finally was unable to write
and complained to two women.
One of them who paints spheres
perfectly balanced in space
assured me I would write again.
The other who is long-time ill still can make
wonderous depictions with paint.
She has no lover nor is pursuing one.
One could say she's a lover of Nature.

I've always felt the universe is a
beautiful woman, and, without a muse,
I could try a different poem—a mirror image
to measure up to a handsome hillside
reflecting the wind combing a grove
of trees—one of Nature's
varied pompadours. How Her hair
tremors! How the limbs hold up
magnificent lady sighs.

I have noticed the spring this year
like never before.
With walks through neighborhood

parks and the richnesses that cover
my eyes in growth in meadows, on cliffs over-
looking the sea, I live with Nature,
and She is unbounding in Her portrayals,
sometimes man-ravaged, always changing
from the tiniest teardrop leaves
(little toes) to the pomade excrescence
of pine pitch. I could try

to attract Her heartbeat with words.
This is new to me and it's working.
It may even heighten realization
that a Van Gogh
was made for the love of the flower,
not the woman.

LESBIAN HEAVEN

All the girlfriends you ever went with
are together now, and they're all
getting along. They're lovers of each other,
and you're in the middle playing the lyre
with Greek attire in the middle of a Maxfield Parrish
forest. Doe-eyed nymphs fondling panpipes
while the pure note sounds. Purple mountains
rise over aeolian forests, and the wind
is the pianist for a women's chorus,
and the longest-fingered of all the women
plays the lute. Pluck the chord,
pour the wine. The flute chambers
Egypts of desire. And the glimmer bubble gurgles
of a brook where each stone is smoothed
to the consistency of knees and thighs,
and the sun, a gigantic pearl, livens them.
Lesbian heaven is filled with dogs and cats.
All the pets we've ever had
are tendered by the hands that kept them,
and they all behave—a beloved company
among pillars' uplift and glitter.
Where Diana sets down her hunting implements
and all the lesbians in heaven clamour
to her limbs with tambour touch,
the afternoon unfolds its leaf,
the night cadenzas its embrace,
the stars become the beaded necklace of morning
with the moon as centerpiece.
And the gold of the painting shineth
on me and thee.

From *The Rhyme Of The Ag-Ed Mariness*

Photo Credit: Mary Golden. Used with permission.

Lynn Lonidier at home in San Francisco, September 1982.

EDITOR NOTE

EDITOR NOTE

All of Lynn Lonidier's poetry collections were published by independent presses, most based in the San Francisco Bay Area. One element that characterized the independent press movement beginning in the 1960s was the attention to the material production of the book—typography, paper quality, use of graphic elements, placement of words on the page, etc. Lonidier's work is no exception. To honor this impulse of early print activists and to counter how increased computer production and new modes of printing homogenize some of these aspects of book production, I note some of the choices I made in editing this book to make them visible for interested readers to examine, interrogate, and challenge.

All of Lonidier's work published during her lifetime was typeset on a typewriter. The textuality of engaging with text in that way, where letters are all the same size, where the space between letters is always the same, where the visuality of text can be plotted on a grid, is very different from word-processors today. Today, computers automatically fix typographical errors, letters can change easily in size and appearance, and words, sentences and paragraphs automatically kern to aid the speed and efficiency of readers.

As I edited Lonidier's work, as when I edited Pat Parker's work, I imagined how both women would have delighted in the possibilities that computers and new printing technologies offer for poets and writers—and that their attentions to these new forms of textuality would be profound and exacting. I often wished that we might sit together in front of a computer and explore how their poems were presented on the page. Alas, neither was present for such an experiment. In Lonidier's absence, I have tried to remain faithful to her presentation of her work on the page. As a result, I have:

- endeavored to represent space and spacing as Lonidier did in original productions of her work.
- reproduced the interior spacing in lines with five spaces, in general, though their appearance in the original text is more capacious and not standardized.

- kept the spellings of Lonidier in the text, particular neologisms and compound words which are an important part of her poetics. On a few occasions, I deemed the misspellings inadvertent and distracting for readers, that is, lacking any element of discovery in pausing and puzzling over them. In these instances, I corrected the spelling to its usual convention. These corrections are silent, in the tradition of the *Chicago Manual of Style,* invisible to you as readers. Where I did not correct spelling that is clearly in error, it is noted with a footnote.

- utilized typographic elements when possible to reproduce the handwritten elements in the original books, or provided a footnote explanation of the original printing and what is missing in this printing.

- preserved the lineation of ostensible prose poems in all collections. There are a series of dream poems in particular in *Clitoris Lost* that seem to me prose poems, without particular lineation, just blocks of text. I considered producing them in that way for this edition, but ultimately remained faithful to the lineation produced by the original typesetting.

- retained Lonidier's notes on the poems.

I have added notes to the poems to identity people, ideas, historical events, and other reference. These editor notes are presented as footnotes beneath a line at the bottom of the page. I hope that these notes will be helpful to readers and not a distraction from the work. In particular, I focused on deepening the connections of this poetry to lesbian-feminist history in the 1970s and 1980s, my specialty. My goal is to not intrude in the reading and experience of the poems but to enhance their meaning through deeper study. I hope I have been successful in this endeavor.

Finally, while I regard this comment as somewhat intrusive to the book and to Lonidier, I must note that in many of the poems in *Clitoris Lost* where Lonidier directly addresses her cousin, Karen Brodine, particularly in "Swansong" and "Six Years Sorting Mother's Papers," I find her portrayal of Brodine unkind. This unkindness and lack of generosity to her cousin, fellow feminist and poet, may have been intentional for Lonidier at the time she composed the poems and published the book, but I hope it would not have lingered and had Lonidier had an opportunity to create her own volume of selected poems she might have softened the hammer. In the absence of that, it is my great desire that readers will not internalize Lonidier's vitriol and will take the time to explore Brodine's impressive work as a poet, writer, socialist, and activist.

Ultimately, all errors in this manuscript are my own. I appreciate the generosity of readers in overlooking them to discover Lynn Lonidier for the important poet that she is.

499

Julie R. Enszer, PhD
July 2023

Lynn Lonidier in Seattle, September 1972.

Editor Note

BIBLIOGRAPHY OF LYNN LONIDIER

BIBLIOGRAPHY OF LYNN LONIDIER

Books

Po tree & illustrations. With drawings by Betty and Shirley Wong. Berkeley: Berkeley Free Press, 1967.

The Female Freeway. San Francisco: Tenth Muse, 1970.

A Lesbian Estate: Poems, 1970-1973. South San Francisco: Manroot, 1977.

Woman Explorer. Philadelphia: Painted Bride Quarterly, 1979.

Clitoris Lost: A Woman's Version of the Creation Myth: a take-off on John Milton's ordering of a heaven, earth, and hell. Boyes Hot Spring: Manroot Press, 1989.

The Rhyme of the Ag-ed Mariness: Last Poems. Edited by Janine Canan with a preface by Jerome Rothenberg. Barrytown: Station Hill Press, 2001.

Broadsides

A Jellyfish Swim. San Francisco: Tenth Muse, 1972.

For Sale: Girl Poet Cheap. South San Francisco: ManRoot, 1977.

Christmas Kitty in Bilingualand, or What I Did This Year, 1986.

Unpublished Novels

The Banana Lady (1984, 1986)

Candy's Cane (1970)

The Hanged Man (n.d.)

The Nursery (n.d.)

Phantom of the Organ (n.d.)

Sacrificial Lambs (1976)

504   *A Very Faerie Tale* (1986)

Slideshow / Audio Production

Owed to Oakland (1973)

Scholarly Writing about Lynn Lonidier

Kathryn Flannery. ""Life's Disguise Doth Keep Flies Off": Teaching Lynn Lonidier's Poetry." *Feminist Teacher* 22, no 2 (2012): 137-157.

Line drawing of Lynn Lonidier.

Bibliography

ACKNOWLEDGEMENTS

ACKNOWLEDGEMENTS

I am enormously grateful to Fred Lonidier for agreeing to this project and for his generosity in providing materials from his archival collections of Lynn's work and photographs and other materials about Lynn's life. Fred is a tremendous advocate for Lynn's work; he responded to numerous email queries with great spirit and patience. I am grateful to him for his assistance and his generosity.

Sophia Moore, then an undergraduate student at the University of California, Berkeley, emailed me to ask about an internship with *Sinister Wisdom* and I thought, wow, do I have a project for you. I met Sophia outside the San Francisco Public Library for the first time, and we spent a day together working through the archival materials of Lynn Lonidier there. Sophia made numerous trips back to the archives and completed many of the transcriptions in this book. Thank you, Sophia, for your contribution to lesbian poetry!

Tim Wilson, the librarian and archivist at the James C. Hormel LGBTQIA Center at the San Francisco Public Library was, as always, kind and generous with his assistance in the archival work for this project. Thank you, Tim! And thank you to the Hormel Center for providing a home for our history.

Sonja Franeta, who knew Lynn Lonidier through poetry and lesbian social circles, generously shared her memories of Lynn with me.

Appreciation to my Facebook transcription crew who helped me finish up the transcriptions at the last minute: Roberta Arnold, Maureen Daniels, Chelsea Taylor Del Rio, Eric Sneathen, and Mags Oldman.

The entire Sinister Wisdom community provides light, support, and camaraderie to me in all of my work, and I am enormously grateful to them.

I completed this manuscript in the solitude and serenity of an apartment in New Orleans thanks to Gregory Gajus and the My Good Judy Residency in the French Quarter. It was an extraordinary gift to have the time and space to finish this editorial project. Thank you Gregory, thank you Judy

Grahn for the inspiration you provide across generations, and thank you to the Commonality Institute.

As always, this work is dedicated to my beloved Kim, an anarchAFeminist of her own making. Thank you, my love, for making life possible for me and our beloved brood—Samantha, Sadie, Alice, and Vita (and Tiberius of blessed memory). May we celebrate many more books and many more years of love and companionship.

Photo Credit: Lonidier Family. Used with permission from Fred Lonidier

Lynn Lonidier playing with her dog Pierre at the beach in San Francisco, October 1974.

INDEX OF TITLES

Index of Titles

Fire-Rimmed Eden

519

Fire-Rimmed Eden

Index of Titles

Fire-Rimmed Eden

BIOGRAPHIES

Lynn Lonidier was born in Lakeview, Oregon on April 22, 1937. Often describing herself as a «card-carrying anarchafeminist,» Lonidier was a teacher, author and multimedia and theater performance artist. As a West Coast writer, she was active in the San Francisco literary scene, especially within the lesbian/feminist community, during the 1970s until the time of her death in 1993. Also a musician, she studied composition and collaborated with Pauline Oliveros at the University of California at San Diego. She attended San Francisco State University where, as a cellist, she majored in performance. She also received a M. A. in Media/Education in 1975 from the University of Washington at Seattle.

Julie R. Enszer, PhD, is a scholar and a poet. She is the author of four poetry collections, *Avowed* (Sibling Rivalry Press, 2016), *Lilith's Demons* (A Midsummer Night's Press, 2015), *Sisterhood* (Sibling Rivalry Press, 2013) and *Handmade Love* (A Midsummer Night's Press, 2010). She is editor of *OutWrite: The Speeches that Shaped LGBTQ Literary Culture* (Rutgers University Press, 2022), which was a finalist for a 2023 Lambda Literary Award, *The Complete Works of Pat Parker* (Sinister Wisdom/A Midsummer Night's Press, 2016), which won the 2017 Lambda Literary Award for Lesbian Poetry and *Milk & Honey: A Celebration of Jewish Lesbian Poetry* (A Midsummer Night's Press, 2011), which was a finalist for the 2012 Lambda Literary Award in Lesbian Poetry. She has her MFA and PhD from the University of Maryland. Enszer edits and publishes *Sinister Wisdom*, a multicultural lesbian literary and art journal. You can read more of her work at www. JulieREnszer.com.

Sinister Wisdom
A Multicultural Lesbian Literary & Art Journal

Sinister Wisdom is a multicultural lesbian literary & art journal that publishes four issues each year. Publishing since 1976, *Sinister Wisdom* works to create a multicultural, multi-class lesbian space. *Sinister Wisdom* seeks to open, consider, and advance the exploration of community issues. *Sinister Wisdom* recognizes the power of language to reflect our diverse experiences and to enhance our ability to develop critical judgment, as lesbians evaluating our community and our world.

Editor and Publisher: Julie R. Enszer, PhD

Former editors and publishers:
Harriet Ellenberger (aka Desmoines)
    and Catherine Nicholson (1976–1981)
Michelle Cliff and Adrienne Rich (1981–1983)
Michaele Uccella (1983–1984)
Melanie Kaye/Kantrowitz (1983–1987)
Elana Dykewomon (1987–1994)
Caryatis Cardea (1991–1994)
Akiba Onada-Sikwoia (1995–1997)
Margo Mercedes Rivera-Weiss (1997–2000)
Fran Day (2004–2010)
Julie R. Enszer & Merry Gangemi (2010–2013)

Subscribe online: www.SinisterWisdom.org

Sinister Wisdom is a U.S. nonprofit organization; donations to support the work and distribution of *Sinister Wisdom* are welcome and appreciated.

Fire-Rimmed Eden: Selected Poems gathers poems from Lynn Lonidier's rich and varied collections. Lonidier published five poetry collections *Po Tree* (1967), *The Female Freeway* (1970), *A Lesbian Estate*(1977), *Woman Explorer* (1979), *Clitoris Lost: A Woman's Version of the Creation Myth* (1989), and a posthumous book, *The Rhyme of the Ag-ed Mariness* (2001). Her poetry links multiple poetic constellations of the 1970s and 1980s demonstrating linguistic innovations and radical reconfigurations sexuality and gender.

The poems of *Fire-Rimmed Eden* are in conversation with narrative impulses from the feminist and lesbian poetry movements of the 1970s and 1980s, including work by Judy Grahn, Audre Lorde, Adrienne Rich, and others, as well as experimental poetic impulses from the same period found in work by Robert Duncan (Duncan's partner Jess gave the cover art for *A Lesbian Estate*), Lyn Hejinian, Carla Harryman, and Etel Adnan. Some of Lonidier's work is concrete in the spirit of May Swenson's *Iconographs* while other poems are performative like Bay area poets Pat Parker and Jerome Rothenberg.

Previously completely out of print, Lonidier's poetry is ripe for a new generation of readers. *Fire-Rimmed Eden* assembles a robust selection of Lonidier's work introduced by *Sinister Wisdom* editor and publisher Julie R. Enszer. Rich and diverse, visually and aurally exciting, boldly experimental and intellectually provocative, Lonidier's poetry is imbued with wit, humor, originality, and play.

Strength, courage, humour and magical word weaving are long-time characteristics of Lynn Lonidier's poetry. This remarkable book brings together her last writings to keep the mystery of her genius with us.

—Pauline Oliveros